Explore the World

Nelles GUIDE

MUNICH

EXCURSIONS TO CASTLES, LAKES & MOUNTAINS

Authors:
Andreas Ascher, Joachim Chwaszcza, Petra Englmeier,
Brigitte Henninges, Peter Herrmann, Gert Hirner, May Hoff,
Hans und Inge Obermann, Andrea Russ, Sabine Tzschaschel,
Rainer Vestner

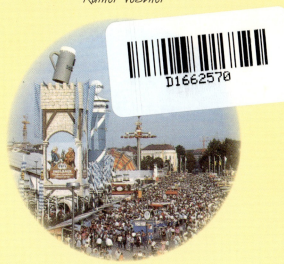

An Up-to-date travel guide with 172 color photos
and 13 maps

Third Revised Edition
1998

IMPRINT / LEGEND

Dear Reader,

Being up-to-date is the main goal of the Nelles series. To achieve it, we have a network of far-flung correspondents who keep us abreast of the latest developments in the travel scene, and our cartographers always make sure that maps and texts are adjusted to each other.

Each travel chapter ends with its own list of useful tips, accommodations, restaurants, tourist offices, sights. At the end of the book you will find practical information from A to Z. But the travel world is fast moving, and we cannot guarantee that all the contents are always valid. Should you come across a discrepancy, please write us at: Nelles Verlag GmbH, Schleissheimer Str. 371 b, D-80935 München, Germany, Tel: (089) 3571940, Fax: (089) 35719430.

LEGENDE

✱	Sehenswürdigkeit		Fußgängerzone		Autobahn
■	Öffentliches bzw. bedeutendes Gebäude	U S	U-, S-Bahn Station		Schnellstraße
		P	Parkplatz		Fernverkehrsstraße
■	Hotel	Tutzing	im Text genannter Ort		Hauptstraße
■	Einkaufszentrum		Staatsgrenze		Nebenstraße
✝	Kirche				Eisenbahn
✆	Postamt	✈	Internationaler Flughafen	E52 30	Straßennummern
⊕	Krankenhaus	Zugspitze 2968	Berggipfel (Höhe in Meter)	18	Entfernung in Kilometer
⌂	Denkmal				

MUNICH – Excursions to Castles, Lakes & Mountains
© Nelles Verlag GmbH, 80935 München
All rights reserved

Third Revised Edition 1998
ISBN 3-88618-120-0
Printed in Slovenia

Publisher:	Günter Nelles	**Cartography:**	Nelles Verlag GmbH,
Chief Editor:	Berthold Schwarz		by kind permission of:
Project Editor:	Peter Herrman		Freytag & Berndt, Vienna
Editors:	Dr. Alex Klubertanz,		City Surveyor's Office, Munich
	May Hoff	**Color Separation:**	Priegnitz
Translation:	Angus McGeoch	**Printed by:**	Gorenjski Tisk

No part of this book, not even excerpts, may be reproduced without prior permission of Nelles Verlag. - X04 -

TABLE OF CONTENTS

Imprint / Legend 2
Map List 7

HISTORY AND CULTURE

Munich's History and Culture 13
Munich Life....................... 34

MUNICH BY DAY

THE INNER CITY 45
Around the Station.................. 45
Karlsplatz (Stachus) 49
Around Lenbachplatz 50
Through the Pedestrian Zone 51
Marienplatz...................... 56
Im Tal: "The Valley" 61
Viktualienmarkt 64
Around St. Jakobsplatz 66
Hackenviertel..................... 70
The Residenz 75
Kreuzviertel 79
*GUIDEPOST: Transport System, Restaurants,
Sightseeing* 82-83

SCHWABING 87
Around Odeonsplatz................. 87
Ludwigstrasse 90
Maxvorstadt 93
*GUIDEPOST: Transport System, Restaurants,
Sightseeing* 100
Leopoldstrasse 103
Alt-Schwabing 106
Olympia Park 114
The Englischer Garten................ 116
*GUIDEPOST: Transport System, Restaurants,
Sightseeing* 119

**ROYAL SPLENDOR AND
EVERYDAY LIFE** 123
Neuhausen 123
Nymphenburg Palace 128
West End 133
Sendling....................... 138
*GUIDEPOST: Transport System, Restaurants,
Sightseeing* 140-141

TABLE OF CONTENTS

ON THE BANKS OF THE ISAR 145
Schlachthof 145
Glockenbach 146
Lehel 148
Gärtnerplatz 154
In the Au 156
Giesing 158
Haidhausen 160
Bogenhausen 165
GUIDEPOST: Transport System, Restaurants,
Sightseeing 168-169

EXPERIENCING MUNICH

The Shimmering Isar 172

Museums in Munich 175
GUIDEPOST: Museums 183

Shopping 184

All about Beer 186

The Oktoberfest 190

Munich for Kids 192

MUNICH BY NIGHT

Cultural Life in Munich 197

Munich by Night 204
GUIDEPOST: Cultural Life / Night-life 208-209

Eating Out 210
GUIDEPOST: Eating Out in Munich and Environs . . . 213

FEATURES

Munich, City of Fairs 214

Munich's "Silicon Valley" 215

On the Ski Slopes 216

The Notorious "Föhn" 217

TABLE OF CONTENTS

EXCURSIONS

Wittelsbachs and Fuggers 220

Land of the Five Lakes 222

Monasteries, Castles and Mountains 227

Mountains and Lakes 233

The Middle Ages Brought to Life 238

GUIDELINES

Practical Tips from A to Z 240
    Accommodation 240
    Arriving by Air 240
    Car Breakdown Services 241
    Car "Pilot" Service 241
    Car Rental 241
    Changing Money 241
    Cinemas 241
    City Information 241
    City Tours and Sightseeing 241
    Climate 242
    Consulates 242
    Emergency Telephone Numbers 242
    Festivals 242
    Lost and Found 243
    Media 243
    Munich in Figures 243
    Opening Times, Business Hours 243
    Parking Lots 244
    Public Transport 244
    Ride-sharing Services 245
    Sports 245
    Swimming, Indoor and Outdoor Pools and Lakes ... 246
    Taxis 248
    Telecommunications 248
    Tourist Information 248
    Trade Fairs 248
    What to Wear 248

Authors 248

Photographers 249

Index 250

MAP LIST

Greater Munich	6-7
Munich City	46-47
Schwabing and Englischer Garten	88-89
Olympia Park	115
Neuhausen	124
Nymphenburg	126-127
West End and West Park	134-135
Schlachthof and Glockenbach Districts	147
Lehel / Au / Giesing	153
Haidhausen / Bogenhausen	161
Western Upper Bavaria	224
Eastern Upper Bavaria	232
High-Speed Rail Network	246-247

HISTORY AND CULTURE

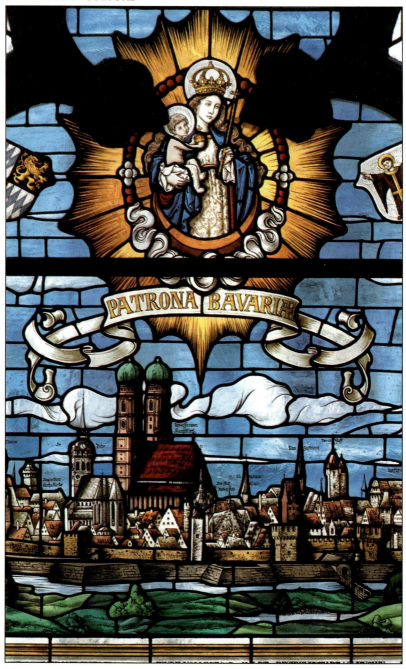

MUNICH'S HISTORY AND CULTURE

From about 530 AD, the area around what is now Munich began to be settled by Bavarian immigrants from the East. Everywhere, settlements with names ending in *-ing* sprang up, such as Sendling, Pasing and Schwabing, long before there was any mention of "Munichen."

The city's original name, *Munichen*, indicates a monastic settlement, as does its coat of arms of a later date, which depicts a monk. Were they Benedictine monks from the Tegernsee monastery founded in 746? Or were they from the Schäftlarn monastery founded in 762? No one knows.

During the Augsburg Imperial Diet of 1158, Emperor Frederick Barbarossa confirmed that the bridge over the River Isar, and the right to hold markets and strike coinage, would remain with the 200-year-old settlement of "ze den munichen" (with the monks). By doing so, he legitimized the violent action of the Guelph Duke Henry the Lion (whom he had made Duke of Bavaria two years earlier). The Duke had burned down the Isar bridge and the adjacent village of Feringa (now Oberföhring) in order to prevent Bishop Otto of Freising from collecting the bridge tolls. Henry had then built his own bridge over the Isar near the monks' settlement at Munichen, so that the salt merchants had to pay their tolls to him on their product, which was the only food preservative known at that time.

The new settlement grew fast and prospered, but a hard bargain was struck at the Imperial Diet of 1158: Henry was obliged to pay a third of his revenue from

Preceding pages: Bustling life at Marienplatz. The beer garden at the Chinese Tower. Left: View of the historic city of Munich, with the "Patrona Bavariae."

the tolls to the Bishop of Freising. Since then, the date of the Imperial Diet Charter has been accepted as the official date for the founding of the city of Munich.

After Henry the Lion had gone on a pilgrimage to the Holy Land in 1172, Adalbert, the new Bishop of Freising, appealed in 1180 against the Augsburg judgement. This came at a convenient moment for Emperor Barbarossa, because he had inherited the territories of Southern Germany and Italy from Guelph VI. Since Henry the Lion had refused to support him against the Lombard League of Northern Italy in 1176, he held courts of provincial jurisdiction in Worms, Magdeburg and Kaina in 1179, at which Henry failed to appear. These were followed by a court of feudal law, at which Saxony and Bavaria were taken away from Henry. Barbarossa then declared Imperial War on him and, at the Imperial Diet of 1180 in Regensburg, revoked the decision to transfer the market and bridge to Munich.

A sentence of destruction was passed on the city, but was never executed because Munich had already become too important. The Bishop of Freising became its new governor. Henry was outlawed and fled to England with his family. The Count Palatine Otto von Wittelinespach (Wittelsbach) was granted the Dukedom of Bavaria.

Munich as a Ducal Seat

In the years that followed, Munich continued to expand. According to the chronicles, merchants from Munich began supplying cloth to the monastery of Schäftlarn in 1190. The first hospital in Munich, the Holy Ghost Hospital, was founded in 1208, followed two years later by the first synagogue. The leper hospital, St. Nikolai, was set up on the opposite bank of the Isar in 1213. A year later we have the first mention of the word "city." This *civitas* was variously

called *Munichen*, *Muenichen* or *Muoenechen* in different documents. The first of many great fires occurred in 1221, most of the houses still being built of wood.

In 1255, Ludwig the Stern became the first Wittelsbach duke to make Munich his ducal residence. He built the *Alter Hof* (Old Court) as his fortress. He also built simple lodgings outside the city near the Talbruck Gate for the wagoners on the "salt road," which is why there are still many inns in that area today. The wagoners' quarters were quite cheap because the prevailing wind in Munich is from the west all the year round, and the foul-smelling trades (like tanneries) had all been moved away to the east outside the encircling city walls. The population grew rapidly during this period. General tax legislation was introduced, and a city council (Council of Twelve) was formed

Above: Henry the Lion gives orders for the building of Munich. Right: Medieval idyll in the Alter Hof.

from the wealthy elite. But among the poor there was much unrest, which culminated in a revolt caused by debasement of the coinage (or galloping inflation, as we would call it today). After a mob stormed the mint in the market place, it was moved to the safer neighborhood of the Alter Hof.

Jews were persecuted in Munich in the Middle Ages, as elsewhere in Europe. They were blamed for fires and outbreaks of pestilence. In reality, however, people envied the Jews their wealth and many were in debt to them, because Christians were not permitted to lend money at interest. In 1285, no less than 180 Jews were killed for allegedly carrying out a ritual murder, and the ghetto was destroyed.

Munich as an Imperial City

Duke Ludwig IV (known as "The Bavarian") was elected King by the German princes in 1314, and was crowned Emperor in Rome in 1328. During this

period, Munich became the center of the Holy Roman Empire of the German Nation. The city was given the imperial colors of black and gold, which it still bears on its coat of arms today.

Ludwig the Bavarian was Duke of Bavaria for 53 years, but he did not spend many of those years in Munich. The imperial insignia (the crown, imperial orb, holy lance, scepter, royal mantle and ceremonial, imperial and Mauritius swords) were kept in the chapel of the Alter Hof. Munich owed a great deal to Ludwig the Bavarian. He extended the city walls, repaired dilapidated areas of the city and obtained a Golden Bull giving the citizens of Munich a monopoly over the salt trade throughout Southern Germany.

The most important scholars of the time stayed in Munich during the reign of Ludwig the Bavarian, including, among others, Marsilius of Padua, William of Occam, Michael of Cesena, Bonagratia of Bergamo, Henry of Talheim and Henry of Preising. Through them, the city became a center of European intellectual activity.

However, in 1327 another great fire raged through the city: the timber houses with reed or shingle roofs burned like straw, and fully one third of the city went up in flames. Ludwig the Bavarian then issued building ordinances to the effect that the streets had to be widened, and new buildings were to be of stone with tiled roofs. Unfortunately, the citizens of Munich paid scant regard to the rules and, as a consequence, fires continued to break out.

Plague and Revolution

Munich was not spared when the Black Death swept across Europe from 1348 onwards. The epidemic was probably introduced into the city in goods brought in from the south, and the first outbreak of the plague occurred in 1349. Munich suffered a total of 25 outbreaks up to 1680, the final year of the epidemic. The city council tried desperately to introduce hy-

HISTORY AND CULTURE

giene regulations, keep the streets clean and drain sewage into the city brook. Trade was continually disrupted because of the plague and markets had to be closed. The entrances to the city were strictly guarded to keep visitors from plague-ridden cities out of Munich. Helpless in the face of death and treated by ineffective doctors, the population turned to God. Huge pilgrimages, some numbering in the thousands, were organized, usually to Andechs, to Freising or Ebersberg. The coopers performed their famous dance for the first time in 1517 and promised to repeat it every seven years, a promise kept to this day.

The religious life of the late Middle Ages was more colorful than we might think. When a monk called Jakob Dachauer found relics in Andechs (parts of Christ's crown of thorns and miraculous

Above: Since 1517 the barrel-makers have performed this dance. Right: Agnes Bernauer is drowned as a witch.

hosts), Duke Stefan III persuaded Pope Boniface IX to name 1392 as "Munich's Year of Grace." Anyone making a pilgrimage to Munich was given a plenary indulgence as if he had made a pilgrimage to Rome. This became a thriving business. On some days over 40,000 visitors came to Munich, an incredible figure for a city with a population of only 11,000. Traders and entertainers came from far and wide to get money out of the crowds of people anxious to enter the Kingdom of Heaven without sin.

The late 14th and early 15th centuries were a period of political unrest in Munich. Between 1397 and 1403, its citizens tried to free themselves from domination by the patrician families. They were led by guild artisans who wanted greater influence and persuaded ordinary people to join their cause. The city hall was occupied, Mayor Jörg Kazmair was forced to resign, and noblemen were thrown into a prison called the "Poor Sinners Tower." The revolution succeeded; the insurgents formed the "Great Council of Three Hundred" and declared a feud against the Duke. Those loyal to the Duke were beheaded, and torture was used for the first time in Munich. The artisans held power until 1403, when the Dukes Wilhelm III and Ernst besieged the city, burned down the outlying areas and literally drained away the drinking-water.

On June 1, 1403, Duke Ernst rode into the city in triumph with the banished Mayor Kazmair, and the patrician families returned. The revolution was not altogether without result, however: under the so-called "suffrage letter," the community was reorganized, and the "common man" and the guilds were given more say in public affairs.

The Heyday of the Merchants

Between 1403 and 1433, the citizens of Munich were involved in constant feuds with robber barons, but the city still managed to become one of the main trading centers, alongside Augsburg and Nuremberg. Surviving ledgers demonstrate the city's commercial wealth, as it developed into a hub of trade on the north-south route. Goods from the Orient came up from Venice (which was then the most important mercantile city in Europe): gold, silver, coral, gems, spices, exotic fruits and, of course, wine. Cloth was bought in Flanders, made up by the Munich garment industry, and sold to the East through Vienna.

Despite the cosmopolitan enterprise of the merchants and patricians, widespread belief in witchcraft and superstition still thrived. In 1432, Duke Albrecht III secretly married Agnes Bernauer, the daughter of an Augsburg barber-surgeon. Her father-in-law Duke Ernst had her hunted down as a witch, and she was drowned in the Danube near Straubing on October 12, 1435. The Jews were again driven out in 1442, following which the synagogue on Gruftstrasse was converted into a church by Johann Hartleib.

The rich lived in great style, with 819 masters employing no fewer than 1,454 servants. Munich's first horse race was run at the annual *Jakobi-Dult* fair. In 1456, the first shooting contest with firearms was held.

This was the start of a new era, for the "progressive" city fathers had bought the first muskets only eight years earlier. Their great wealth had to be displayed as well as defended, and so the vast *Frauenkirche* (Church of Our Lady) was built. Duke Siegmund laid the foundation stone in 1468, and the architect was Jörg von Halspach, also known as Ganghofer. Visitors to the monumental late-Gothic building are still regaled with the story of the supposed Devil's Footprint to be seen in the floor. Legend has it that the devil visited the new church and stamped his foot in rage because the room was light, even though from that part of the entrance no windows could be seen.

Not unusually for Munich, completion took a long time and it was only in 1524 that the cupolas – the emblem of Munich

HISTORY AND CULTURE

today – were added. These were later modified to the baroque style – giving an odd combination which looks slightly eccentric, but which saved the city considerable further expenditure.

During the solstice celebrations, dances which were rather daring for those days were performed in the market place. The figures of morris dancers, carved for the city hall by Erasmus Grasser in 1477, give an idea of their suggestive contortions. On the orders of Duke Ernst, a brothel had already been set up in 1436 on Henkergässl at the village green and had quickly become popular, although it was banned to married men, the clergy and, inevitably, to Jews.

The Dukes Change Munich

In 1505, Munich became the sole ducal residence of Upper and Lower Bavaria.

Above: Portrait of Duke Wilhelm IV (1493 to 1550). Right: A view of Munich from the year 1586.

To prevent further territorial divisions, Duke Albrecht IV, known as the Wise, enacted a law of primogeniture under which succession always passed to the eldest son. At that time, the population of the capital of the Duchy of Bavaria was still only 13,500.

Albrecht the Wise was a lover of lavish feasting. He also had the first Bavarian gold ducats minted. At his funeral in 1508, a sumptuous display of renaissance magnificence was presented in the form of a feast, the like of which had never been seen before. It consisted of 23 courses, each one representing a scene from the Bible. The first course naturally depicted Paradise, with Adam and Eve and the serpent; the last one was a huge cake out of which, to everyone's amazement, live birds fluttered.

Wilhelm IV ruled for nearly half a century, from 1508 to 1550. Initially, he was sympathetic towards the new beliefs of the Reformation. Luther's writings were printed in Munich in 1519-20, and he was supported by city artisans and nobles alike. But Wilhelm soon realized that the religious controversy was causing his own authority to be challenged, making a strict ruling by him in favor of the Catholic faith inevitable. In 1522, he had a baker's boy beheaded for blaspheming the Mother of God, and subsequently issued three harsh edicts against Lutheran doctrine. Its adherents were imprisoned, fined, banished from the country and even, in extreme cases, executed. In 1527, he had a curate burned to death and a cutler beheaded for their Lutheran faith.

During the Renaissance, the darkest happenings went hand in hand with great splendor and with the first signs of intellectual progress; Homer's *Odyssey* was translated into German for the first time in 1537, and in 1548 the Duke issued general school regulations. Despite these promising signs of greater cultural awareness, feasting and entertainment were the order of the day. When Emperor

HISTORY AND CULTURE

Charles V visited Munich in 1530, a mock battle was staged outside the city, there were fireworks in the market place and a play called *The History of King Cambyses of Persia* was put on.

Duke Wilhelm IV was succeeded by Albrecht V, who ruled from 1550 to 1579. His reign was marked by lavish celebrations and active encouragement of academic pursuits. The Jesuits founded a grammar school which became very popular, and a school for poets was opened next to the Frauenkirche. A map of Bavaria was drawn to accurate surveys in 1566 and was used as a model all over Europe.

But the end of the century was a time of darkness, fear and superstition. In 1590, Regina Lutz, Anna Aubacher, Regina Pollinger and Brigitta Anbacher were accused of witchcraft, tortured until they "confessed" and burned to death. Eleven others were put to death for witchcraft ten years later. As late as 1721, the daughter of a court stable-hand was burned to death as an alleged sorceress.

Duke Wilhelm V (1579-97) was always short of money because of his two loves, building and feasting, so he brought the Italian alchemist Bragadino to his court to make gold from lead. While attempting this task, Bragadino lived like a lord and kept 36 servants. When his efforts failed, the Duke had him charged with sorcery, then tortured and hanged.

The Period of the Electors (1597-1799)

Maximilian I became Duke in 1597 and Elector in 1623, and ruled until 1651. By then, the population of Munich was already around 20,000. There were 1,790 artisans' workshops in 58 guilds, with the guild of goldsmiths alone having 50 master goldsmiths. The medieval appearance of the city changed completely. As a symbol of his power, Maximilian built the *Residenz* (Royal Residence) and increased his household from 150 to 500 people, forcing the citizens of Munich to endure high taxation. But it was not long

HISTORY AND CULTURE

before the splendor of the court fell under the shadow of the advancing Swedish army. The Thirty Years' War (1618-1648) devastated the whole of Europe. In 1632, Munich surrendered to the Swedes without a fight and purchased its freedom for 450,000 guilders. King Gustav Adolf stayed in the city for a month.

The "Swedish Scourge" was compounded by a real outbreak of plague passed on by the Spanish soldiery. Some 7,000 people died in that year alone.

"Italomania" was rife in Munich under Elector Ferdinand Maria (1651-79) – even now Munich is still popularly known as "Italy's northernmost city." Ferdinand Maria was married to an Italian, Henrietta of Savoy. Munich's architecture became increasingly baroque in style. Italian architects changed the layout of the city and built the Theatiner Church and Nymphenburg Palace.

Baroque life at court on the French model sometimes verged on fantasy. The Elector used to hold lavish parties on *Starnberger See* (Lake Starnberg) on a palatial barge in the Venetian style called the *Bucentaurus*, rowed by 219 oarsmen. Italian merchants set up businesses all over the city.

Elector Max Emanuel reigned from 1679 to 1726. After the Thirty Years' War, great danger threatened again in 1683, when a huge Turkish army, commanded by the Grand Vizier Kara Mustapha, reached the gates of Vienna. The salvation of the Christian West was due in large measure to Bavarian soldiers under the command of the "Blue Elector," as Max Emanuel was named, after the color of the armor he wore. These brave Bavarians surprised and captured the Grand Vizier's hilltop command post and were the first to force their way into the main Turkish encampment. They fought on for another five years until they had also liberated Belgrade and finally defeated the Turks. The victors returned home in 1688 – by which time 30,000 men had been killed and 15 million guilders had been spent.

The son of Max Emanuel and the Polish princess Therese Kunigunde was the chosen heir to the Spanish throne, but he died at Nymphenburg when he was only six years old.

A dispute over the succession followed. Max Emanuel formed an alliance between Bavaria and France against England and Austria in the War of the Spanish Succession, that most devastating war of the baroque period which involved all Europe. Max Emanuel was defeated by his father-in-law, the Austrian Emperor. After the defeat, high taxes were levied, foreign troops were stationed in the city, and Bavarian soldiers had to fight for Austria in Italy and Hungary. But in 1705 even worse was to come – the event known as the "Christmastide Slaughter of Sendling" took place.

The Bavarians were tired of living under the Emperor's yoke. On December 25th, 3,000 poorly-armed peasants advanced on the occupied city of Munich to liberate it from the Austrians, but they were betrayed and surrounded; 250 men sought sanctuary in Sendling church and were brutally slaughtered. Their leaders were taken to Vienna, where they were hanged, drawn and quartered. According to legend, the bravest hero of the Sendling Peasant Massacre was the huge "Blacksmith of Kochel," who slew many of the occupying troops with his massive hammer, despite the betrayal and their hopeless situation.

There is a larger-than-life-size statue of him opposite Sendling Church, which also contains paintings of the desperate battle. The Austrian reign of terror continued for another ten unhappy years, until Bavaria was finally returned to Max Emanuel with French help under the Treaty of Rastatt. The land was at peace

Right: A relief showing a scene from the "Christmastide Slaughter of Sendling."

again, but had been plundered and impoverished. In Munich, a tax on playing cards which had only been abolished a few years earlier was reintroduced to finance the building of the Opera.

Elector Charles Albrecht (1726-45) and his period reflect both the luxury and the misery of the rococo era. In 1731, for example, Munich's first street lamps were erected. In 1742 the Elector was crowned Emperor of Germany (as Charles VII) in Frankfurt, at the instigation of Prussia. His lavish court expenditure left him so short of money that he even went to the length of selling 8,000 Bavarians, at 36 guilders each, to Austria. But the ambitious Austrian empress, Maria Theresia, would tolerate no imperial rivals, and the Austrians marched yet again into Bavaria.

After the death of Charles Albrecht, Max III Joseph became Elector of Bavaria (1745-77). His first task was to remedy the sorry plight of the State economy. In 1758, he founded the Nymphenburg State Porcelain Factory, which was a profitable enterprise. Angered by the passion of the citizens of Munich for excessive finery, he issued a well-meaning but much-ridiculed clothing decree in 1750. In 1770, the Elector went so far as to sell his jewelry to raise money for the people of Munich, who were starving after a crop failure.

Elector Karl Theodor reigned in Munich from 1777 to 1799. A year after his accession, Austria tried to annex Bavaria in the War of the Bavarian Succession. With the help of King Frederick II of Prussia, Bavaria remained independent, but lost its *Innviertel* territory.

The Elector held back the dawn of the Enlightenment as long as he could. He introduced strict censorship and banned Freemasonry and the Order of the Illuminati. Although he was unpopular in Munich, he left his mark in a positive way by commissioning an American, Benjamin Thompson, and a gardener, Friedrich Ludwig von Sckell, to design the first people's park on the continent of Europe, the *Englischer Garten* (English Garden).

HISTORY AND CULTURE

In 1793, the Chinese Tower was handed over to the people of Munich, but they did not take to it with any enthusiasm (as is often the case with innovative ideas). When Karl Theodor died in 1799, the inns were crowded with people celebrating their delight at being rid of him. Elector Max IV Joseph then reigned in Munich from 1799 to 1825, becoming King Max I in 1806.

Napoleon in Munich

In June 1800, the city was besieged by French troops under General Moreau. Max Joseph fled with his family to Amberg, where he spent several months. There was no fighting because the Elector allied himself with France, along with 16 other German princes. That effectively marked the end of the Holy Roman Empire of the German Nation.

Above: The princely splendor of Nymphenburg Palace. Right: Elector Karl Theodor. Far right: Elector Maximilian I Joseph.

On October 24, 1805, Napoleon rode in a coach drawn by six horses through the *Karlstor* gate and into the city, to the sound of bells and gun salutes. A few months later he was a guest at the marriage of his stepson Eugène de Beauharnais to Auguste Amalie of the Wittelsbach family. Two weeks earlier he had made Max Joseph, her father, King of Bavaria and turned the Bavarian Electoral city into a royal capital. The dissolution of the Holy Roman Empire was not long delayed, and was formally declared in 1806.

On New Year's Day, 1806, a herald proclaimed in the streets of Munich the creation of Bavaria as a sovereign kingdom (by the grace of Napoleon), and the elevation of Elector Max IV Joseph to King Max I Joseph, an event which he welcomed with the words: "We're still the same old chaps." No coronation took place, and the crown insignia were supplied by France.

At the end of 1813, Bavaria returned to the Austrian and Prussian side under the

HISTORY AND CULTURE

Treaty of Ried. Before it could be treated as hostile, Bavaria had its territorial independence guaranteed by Metternich and became a member of the German Confederation which was established at the Congress of Vienna.

Max I Joseph wanted to be an enlightened, popular and tolerant ruler. At his side was the Count of Montgelas, who had accompanied him to Munich as Elector from the Palatinate court in 1799. Within a few years he had set up a modern administrative system and drafted a Bavarian constitution (ratified in 1818), which granted basic human rights to the citizens. Members of the Lutheran and Reformed churches were at last treated on equal terms with Catholics, and the penal system was reformed.

Moves towards secularization included the dissolution of 18 monasteries, and the monk was removed from the Munich coat of arms in 1808, to be replaced by a classical gate and a lion. The old coat of arms with the monk was reinstated by Ludwig I in 1835.

From a Village to the "New Athens" of the North

The poet Heinrich Heine once described the capital of Bavaria as "a village full of palaces." From the later years of the reign of Karl Theodor, plans had been mooted on numerous occasions for the expansion of Munich. Almost the entire city walls were pulled down in 1805, and a broad, tree-lined avenue replaced the moat on the western side of the city (now Sonnenstrasse).

In February 1808, the first architectural competition in Germany was launched for a "general plan for development of the city at the Max Gate." Two years later, Ludwig von Sckell and Karl von Fischer won the commission to design a "general plan for new building in the environs of the city." The development project covered the area between *Karlstor* (Charles Gate) and *Schwabinger Tor* (Schwabing Gate) and between Karlstor and *Sendlinger Tor* (Sendling Gate). The two areas were known as

HISTORY AND CULTURE

Maxvorstadt and *Ludwig-Vorstadt* (*Vorstadt* is German for "suburb").

In 1815 (by which time Munich had a population of 45,000), Ludwig I, then still Crown Prince, had a meeting in Paris with the architect Leo von Klenze, with whose help he wanted to design the new Munich. They were in agreement on style – the city would display the beauty of classical Greek architecture. The Crown Prince inundated von Klenze with work: the *Glyptothek* museum, the royal palace and banqueting hall in the Residenz, the *Alte Pinakothek* (Old Art Gallery), the court church of All Saints, the Duke Max Palace, the War Ministry, the Hall of Fame and the *Propyläen* portico were all designed by him.

The Schwabinger Tor, where the *Feldherrnhalle* (Hall of the Generals) now stands, formed the northern boundary of Munich in 1816. Von Klenze designed a network of new streets through green meadows, and set his magnificent buildings beside poppies and grazing cows. People called his first Munich project, the Glyptothek at Königsplatz, the "Crown Prince's folly."

Von Klenze's masterpiece was his design for Ludwigstrasse as a street worthy of a metropolis, which he completed down to the last detail, even specifying the color of the plaster. He tried to eliminate the exaggerated architectural features of baroque and rococo from the city's buildings. The coat of arms of the Bavarian Electorate and the ornamental pediments with all their sculptures vanished from Nymphenburg Palace in 1826. Even the Residenz Theater (Cuvilliés Theater) was sacrificed to von Klenze's neo-classical obsession.

Ludwig's enthusiasm for the classical style soon faded, however. Von Klenze fell out of favor, and Friedrich von Gärtner was named as his successor. He took over the Ludwigstrasse project and softened the strict classicism of von Klenze's designs with touches of neo-romanti-

Above: Politicians came between them – King Ludwig I and Lola Montez.

cism. The stately buildings of the *via triumphalis* – *Ludwigskirche*, the *Staatsbibliothek* (State Library), the University, the Feldherrnhalle, the *Siegestor* (Victory Gate), the *Georgianum* and the Max-Joseph Foundation – are all the work of von Gärtner.

The Birth of Munich's Festivals

Munich's first Oktoberfest took place on October 17, 1810, to celebrate the marriage of Crown Prince Ludwig to Therese von Sachsen-Hildburghausen. Held in a meadow not far from the village of Sendling near Munich, later named the *Theresienwiese* (Therese Meadow) after the bride, it included horse racing and a banquet at which 2,000 portions of meat, 16,000 sausages, 50 hundredweights of cheese, 32,000 pieces of bread, 320 bucketfuls of brown ale and 16,000 pints of light ale were served. By 1811, a breeding-cattle show had been added to the annual event, and within a few years the people of Munich regularly expected a rich offering of showmen, swings, stalls and carousels.

During the second half of the 19th century, artists came to Munich from all over Europe. Great art exhibitions were held, and societies of artists were set up who believed in celebrating in style. One of the highlights of the Lenten Carnival season in Munich was the "Dürer Festival" of 1840, with a fancy-dress parade in which nearly 600 artists participated.

Lola Montez and the Revolution

When Ludwig I acceded to the throne of Bavaria in 1825 at the age of 39, no one imagined his reign would so soon signal a return to reactionary ideas. Although, earlier on, he had always stressed the importance of the constitution, he soon began substituting the word "subject" for "citizen" in all new laws. He introduced press censorship in 1832, and in 1834 instigated a wave of arrests of students, university teachers and journalists, whom he considered too rebellious with their calls for freedom and national unity.

As a practising Catholic, he supported the restoration of monasteries in Bavaria. At the university, which had been transferred from Landshut to Munich in 1826, he favored the Eos Circle led by the philosophers Görres, Baader and Schelling, who supported a renewal of Christian doctrine. Ludwig considered religion to be "the best and most essential thing for Man." But he certainly changed his mind in 1847 – and all because of a beautiful woman named Lola Montez! The people of Munich were shocked when this young dancer won the heart of their 60-year-old king. A warning from Pope Pius IX to return to "the path of virtue and honor" went unheeded, as did one from the Archbishop of Freising to which Ludwig replied: "Let him keep his *stola* (vestment) and I shall keep my Lola."

In February 1847, when Ludwig wanted to make Lola a naturalized citizen of Bavaria, four of his ministers went to him and said: " Either the dancer goes or we go." Ludwig let them go. He was tired of "pious committees of old women."

The new liberal government included a Protestant for the first time in ultra-Catholic Bavaria. The liberals hoped that Lola's influence with the king would keep the angry Catholics in their place, and therefore agreed to his giving her a title. But the Catholics did not give up. Their main focus was the university. Following unrest and rioting against the new government, Ludwig closed the university. On February 10, 1848, 2,000 people demonstrated in front of the royal residence to demand that the university be reopened and that Lola be expelled from the city. The king gave in and Lola emigrated to Mexico.

The Lola Montez affair went hand in hand with the democratic revolutions of 1848, which affected a large part of Eu-

HISTORY AND CULTURE

rope. Ten thousand of Munich's 90,000 citizens signed a petition demanding freedom of the press, and many of them stormed the Arsenal at Jakobsplatz on March 4.

The king finally brought the unrest to an end by stepping down in favor of his son Max. He abdicated on March 22, 1848, but only on condition that his building program would be allowed to continue.

Max II and the "Northern Lights"

Max II was a more liberal ruler than his father. He was interested in the arts and sciences, and invited eminent scholars (like Liebig, Giesebrecht, Sybel and Riehl), artists and poets (Kaulbach, Dingelstedt, Geibel, Schack and Heyse) to Munich. These men came mainly from Northern Germany and were soon christ-

Above: King "Max Zwo" (1848-64). Right: The death-mask of Ludwig II.

ened the "Northern Lights" by the people of Munich.

Max II also took an interest in new technology. He extended both the railway line, which had been opened from Munich to Lochhausen in 1839, and the Main Railway Station built by Bürklein, the main hall of which was, for those days, a very modern steel structure. In 1857, he built a very striking railway bridge over the Isar, one of the earliest constructions in Germany designed entirely by engineers. In the Old Botanical Gardens he built a crystal palace, like the one in London, in which the German Industrial Exhibition was held in 1854. It burned down in 1931.

While his father had favored the monumental style of antiquity, the son took his inspiration from English neo-Gothic and landscaped the grounds around his buildings with shrubs, trees and lawns. The buildings of this period, lavishly decorated with filigree carving, include the Upper Bavarian Government Building, the *Maximilianeum* and the Ethnological Museum.

Max II died in 1864, before the building work was completed. His son, King Ludwig II, had little love for his capital city, and his only addition was a wintergarden for the royal residence. The Bavarian Alps were where he chose to build his dream castles.

The "Mad King"

Ludwig II was happy to leave political decisions to his civil servants. His passions were architecture and music. He was an ardent champion of the music of Richard Wagner, many of whose operas had their first performance in Munich. To ease Wagner's financial worries, Ludwig invited him to stay in the capital, where he composed his great operas *Tristan and Isolde* (1865), *The Mastersingers of Nuremberg* (1868), *The Rhinegold* (1869) and *The Valkyrie* (1870). The king gave

HISTORY AND CULTURE

Wagner such generous support from the State coffers that people began to complain and scoff. Public pressure forced Ludwig to send him away from Munich in December 1865.

Ludwig had no better luck in politics. He let himself be talked into a war against Prussia, in which Bavaria was defeated and had to pay war reparations of 30 million guilders. Prussian power politics under Bismarck were far from welcome in Munich, because the 1871 unification of Germany signified the end of the independent State of Bavaria which had been in existence since 1806. Only the railway and the post office remained "Royal Bavarian."

The king's passion for building – which included plans for several other castles in addition to those of *Neuschwanstein*, *Herrenchiemsee* and *Linderhof* – consumed vast sums and seriously overstrained the state budget. His ministers soon decided they could no longer brook such extravagance, and had him declared mentally unfit to rule. Without even examining King Ludwig, a Munich neurologist, Professor von Gudden, reported that he was incurably insane, and Ludwig was locked away in *Schloss Berg* on Lake Starnberg.

He drowned in the lake under mysterious circumstances along with Professor von Gudden on June 13, 1886. Ludwig II was more popular among the people than any ruler had ever been. The news of his death gave rise to deep mourning and complaints against the government, and against Luitpold, the Prince Regent, who took over the reins of government in place of Ludwig's brother Otto, who really *was* insane.

Munich's "Good Old Days"

Luitpold, the third son of King Ludwig I, took over the Regency in 1886 at the age of 65. As a result of the establishment of new industries, the population of Mu-

nich increased under his rule from 230,000 to nearly 600,000. Under the supervision of the architects Von Seidl and Thiersch, Prinzregentenstrasse, the Prince Regent Theater, the National Museum, the Angel of Peace, the Palace of Justice and the German Museum were built. The New Town Hall, in the neo-Gothic style, was completed in 1908. Munich was at its heyday as the "City of the Arts." The arts scene in Munich was dominated for many years by the so-called "princes of painting," August Kaulbach and Franz von Lenbach. It was the fashion in Munich at that time to have one's portrait painted by Lenbach "à la Titian," which earned him enough money to build himself a magnificent villa.

Franz von Stuck was one of the first to initiate, and actually bring about, a split, or "secession," from the traditional exhibitors. His painting *The Sin* was the artistic shocker of the day when shown at the 1893 exhibition of the Society of Artists. The "Stuck style" became fashionable. Architects in the city began to use

HISTORY AND CULTURE

Above: High spirits in the banqueting hall of the Hofbräuhaus in the year 1911.

his witty ideas, and decorated mouldings, balustrades and all with plump centaurs, fauns or athletes. Stuck's combination of *Jugendstil* (Art Nouveau), classical elements and gloomy mysticism was a phenomenon peculiar to his age and its taste.

In 1910, August Macke and Wassily Kandinsky shocked both the press and the public with expressionist and abstract canvasses shown for the first time at the avant garde exhibition of the "New Artists Union of Munich." The break with traditional art had reached Munich, although the paintings shown in the first exhibitions by the group of artists called the *Blauer Reiter* ("Blue Rider"; founded in 1911 and including Kandinsky, Klee and Marc), had to be cleaned every evening to remove the spit deposited on them by outraged visitors.

At this time Munich, and particularly Schwabing, was also the adopted home of many *literati*, most of them having an unconventional lifestyle. Erich Mühsam called the place a "collection of eccentrics," but Munich soon grew accustomed to their foibles and happily tolerated them. Countess Franziska zu Reventlow described the legendary life of Schwabing of this period in her letters and diaries. In 1901, the first Munich artists' cabaret was set up in Schwabing, described as the "best variety theater in Germany." The shows, called "executions," were a declaration of war on petty bourgeois values, hypocrisy, dishonesty and *kitsch*.

A living expression of the cultural atmosphere of Schwabing was the satirical magazine *Simplicissimus*, with contributions from eminent cartoonists (Gulbransson, Slevogt, Kubin, Kollwitz, etc.) and writers (Thomas Mann, Ludwig Thoma, Hermann Hesse, Wedekind, Meyrink, Rilke). The intellectuals living in Munich gathered at Karl Wolfskehl's home to discuss poetry, mythology and history. A new political consciousness developed as a consequence of industrialization. The SPD (German Socialist Party) expanded rapidly in Bavaria under the leadership of Georg von Vollmar. Lenin lived for a time in Munich and began his treatise *What is to be Done?* on Kaiserstrasse in Schwabing under the pseudonym of "Meyer."

Munich's Troubled Republic

The reign of Ludwig III (1913-1918), who acceded to the throne on the death of his father, Luitpold the Prince Regent, was overshadowed by the First World War. The start of the war was celebrated in Munich with patriotic songs, as in other European cities, but disillusionment soon set in. Unemployment, black market profiteering and hunger were rife, and the people yearned for peace.

On November 7, 1918, more than 100,000 people gathered on the Theresienwiese to demonstrate for peace. Erhard Auer of the SPD and Kurt Eisner of the USPD (German Independent Socialist Party) demanded a democratic constitution. The demonstration ended in revolution. A few hundred independent socialists and Spartacists went to the barracks and won the war-weary troops over to their ranks. With their help they occupied the railway station, the telegraph office and the State Parliament. At midnight, a council of workers and soldiers elected Kurt Eisner prime minister, proclaimed a victory for the Revolution and the deposing of the Wittelsbach dynasty. Ludwig III was forced to flee but did not abdicate.

There was no resistance from the Bavarian people, royalists for so long. Eisner allowed the ruling classes to retain their official posts and was in favor of compromise, while the right wing of the Social Democrats argued with the left, and the anarchists with the communists about the way forward. Eisner was not only criticized by the Right, but also by the press of the right wing of the SPD. Nor was he supported by the population as a whole, as was demonstrated in the elections to the State Parliament which were held two months after the revolution and which resulted in his defeat. On the day that he had intended to announce his resignation, he was shot while on his way to Parliament by the young Count von Arco auf Valley.

Hoffmann, a Social Democrat who wanted to set up a democratic republic, was elected Prime Minister on March 17, 1919, but was not radical enough for some sections of the working class.

A general strike was organized. At the beginning of April, the writers Gustav Landauer, Erich Mühsam and Ernst Toller proclaimed the *Räterepublik* (Republic of Councils, based on the Soviet model), and Hoffmann's government had to flee to Bamberg. On April 14, the Communists under Eugen Leviné and Max Levien seized power, but reactionary forces were already organizing a food blockade against the city from outside. The German Army and the Volunteer Corps, led by Franz Xaver, Knight of Epp, advanced on Munich. The Army deployed artillery, flame-throwers and armored cars to recapture the city. Every armed man arrested had to face a firing squad, and some of the leaders of the Republic of Councils, including Landauer, were brutally murdered. The Republic of Munich also went to its death in the blood of mass executions. Hoffmann returned to the city as Prime Minister – but not for long.

The Hitler Putsch

On March 14, 1920, Hoffman's SPD government was replaced by a rightist regime under Gustav von Kahr. Policy moved in a conservative, nationalistic direction, and Munich became the headquarters of a large number of reactionary movements. Adolf Hitler, who had been living in Munich since 1919, joined one

HISTORY AND CULTURE

of these newly-formed splinter groups which became known for its mass meetings in the Hofbräuhaus – it was later named the National Socialist German Workers Party (NSDAP). Exploiting the themes of unemployment, inflation and antisemitism, Hitler won over the combat units of many different right-wing groupings, and in 1923 he attempted to overthrow the government by force.

On November 9th of that year, he and General Ludendorff organized a march through the city center. Near the Feldherrnhalle the demonstration was broken up by police and Ludendorff was arrested. Hitler escaped but was arrested at a friend's house two days later. He was put on trial, but was given a very lenient sentence. He was sent to Landsberg prison from which he was released at Christmas in 1924. He had made good use of his time, however, having written his book Mein Kampf there.

Above: Munich's short-lived Republic was overthrown in 1919. Right: Karlstor, 1946.

The Twenties in Munich

Between the catastrophic inflation of the early 1920s and the slump of the 1930s, following the Crash of 1929, there was a period of rapid economic expansion in Germany. Trade and technology continued to develop in Munich, too. The *Deutsches Museum* (of science and technology) was opened on May 7, 1925, a year after Bavarian Radio had begun transmissions. Munich's first airport was opened on the *Oberwiesenfeld*, now the Olympic site. Large housing estates were built in Neuhausen, Freimann and Ramersdorf. One of these, the *Borstei* on Dachauer Strasse, is still one of the most attractive places to live, with its charming courtyards and gardens, small shops and open-air cafés.

Culturally, though, Munich sank inexorably into provincialism in the Twenties, and many young artists and writers left the city. Nobel Prize winner Thomas Mann described the intellectual climate of Munich in a speech in 1926: "We have

lived to see Munich become notorious in Germany and beyond as a stronghold of reaction and a seat of obduracy and intractability to the will of our age."

The "Capital of the Movement"

Adolf Hitler became Chancellor of Germany on January 30, 1933. And the building of the first concentration-camp began in Dachau, just outside Munich, in the spring of that same year. In 1935, Hitler named Munich the "Capital of the Movement." The NSDAP retained its headquarters in the "Brown House" on Briennerstrasse. Königsplatz was paved with granite slabs – and renamed the *Plattensee* or "slab lake" by the populace. This was where the Nazis held their huge parades and demonstrations (the slabs were finally removed in 1988 and replaced with lawns). The square in front of the Feldherrnhalle, scene of Hitler's failed putsch in 1923, was declared a place of martyrdom. Two SS men were permanently on guard, and all passers-by had to raise their arms in the Hitler salute. To avoid this, many people went a different way along Viscardigasse, which soon became known as "Dodgers' Street." *Führer* buildings in the "Reich style" sprang up along Arcisstrasse, some of which now house the Institute of Classical Archaeology, and the College of Music, where the Munich Agreement was signed by Hitler and Chamberlain in 1938. The building, now called the *Haus der Kunst* (House of Art), on Prinzregentenstrasse, was opened by Goebbels in person in 1937 for the "Grand Exhibition of German Art" – on the eve of the opening of the notorious exhibition called "Degenerate Art."

The holocaust began for the Jews. Their synagogue was demolished (only 200 out of more than 10,000 Munich Jews survived the Nazi period). Anti-Nazi resistance groups were constantly set up in Munich from the beginning of the Third Reich, by communists, social democrats and monarchists. Father Alfred Delp and Father Rupert Mayer are

HISTORY AND CULTURE

examples of resistance by the Church. Father Delp was hanged for suspected implication in the July 1944 attempt on Hitler's life, and Father Mayer spent many years in Dachau concentration camp. He died just after the war.

After the crushing German defeat by the Russian army at the Battle of Stalingrad in 1944, the members of the White Rose group distributed leaflets criticizing the Nazi regime in the central lobby of the university. Hans and Sophie Scholl, Alexander Schmorell, Wilhelm Graf, Hans Leipelt and Christof Propst, all students, and a professor, Kurt Huber, paid for their courage with their lives.

Defeat and Reconstruction

The Second World War was the greatest disaster in Munich's 800-year history. 22,346 soldiers from Munich fell, 6,632 citizens were killed in air raids, 16,000 were injured and 80,000 were taken prisoner. A deadly rain of 60,000 high-explosive bombs and 500,000 incendiary bombs fell on the city; 16,000 major fires destroyed or damaged 12,500 buildings.

Almost half the city's building stock was destroyed and no district was spared. One third of all dwellings were totally destroyed, forcing the population to crowd into the remaining 182,000 homes in the final days of the war. Traffic was paralysed with the main roads buried under rubble. Drains, gas and water mains, power and telephone lines were broken. Hospitals, schools, generating-stations and water-works were destroyed.

On April 30, 1945, the city was occupied by American troops. The American Military Government reinstated Karl Scharnagl, who had been Chief Burgomaster of Munich before the War, to his former office. Under Scharnagl and his deputy, Thomas Wimmer, Munich's new slogan was *Rama dama* (freely translated: "Let's clear up this mess"). Over 10 million cubic feet/meters of debris had to be removed from streets and squares. The population of the city rose by 233,000 from 1945 to 1947, due to the return of evacuees and the arrival of large numbers of refugees who had fled from the Russian invasion of eastern Europe. The first free elections in 1946 were won by the newly-formed Christian conservative party, the CSU, which is unique to Bavaria and has governed the state more or less continuously ever since.

Modern Munich

In the years that followed, Munich's economy profited greatly from the Iron Curtain, which cut off much of Germany's former industry. The city soon became the most important industrial and commercial center in southern Germany. Many large corporations established themselves in the Greater Munich area, and the city became an important center for the publishing and film industries. By 1957, the population of Munich had reached seven figures and the "village of a million" came into being.

With the 1960s came the transformation of Munich into an "automobile-friendly" city. Huge satellite towns were built to the north, east and west of the city, which soon led to new kinds of social problems. Munich fell victim to the spirit of the times. Only when preparations began for the Summer Olympics of 1972 did the authorities start to consider the needs of the ordinary people of the city, and a traffic-free zone was created in the center.

Despite all the planning disasters, Munich is now one of the most beautiful and popular cities in Germany. It is the largest university city after Berlin and has wonderful sport and leisure opportunities, a wealth of cultural offerings and – last but not least – a superb hinterland.

Right: One of many Munich beauties on a bike-ride around the Englischer Garten.

HISTORY AND CULTURE

MUNICH LIFE

MUNICH LIFE

Mention the name Munich and hearts beat a little faster, and not just German hearts, for the capital of Bavaria has a magnetic attraction for millions of people from all over the world, mainly but not exclusively for the two weeks of the Oktoberfest. Very few cities in the world have collected as many honorary titles as Munich: Village of a Million, Secret Capital of Germany, Cosmopolitan City with a Heart, Athens on the Isar, Europe's Silicon Valley, etc. One in three Germans would apparently like to live in Munich, and thus for many years the *Zuagroasten,* as non-native incomers are known by the genuine locals, have formed the majority of the 1.3 million population of the city.

What is the fascination and the special

Above: A stall-holder at Viktualienmarkt.
Right: A typical autumnal scene in the Englischer Garten.

quality of life of this city? According to one of the most eminent outsiders who made their home in Munich: "It was an atmosphere of humanity, tolerant individualism and lack of pretence; an atmosphere of cheerful sensuality and artistic endeavor; a mood of vivacity, youthfulness and popular tradition, a tradition that provides a rough but healthy soil in which the strange, the tender and the audacious exotic plants indeed could thrive in an atmosphere of genuine benevolence." These are the words of the novelist Thomas Mann, writing about Munich before the First World War. Though born in Lübeck, in the very north of Germany, he lived for many years in his adopted city.

He was right about Munich – at least in the first decade of this century, and a good part of its later history, despite its close association with the rise of Nazism. It must be more than mere coincidence that so many famous artists and intellectuals settled in Munich (or more accurately Schwabing) at the end of the 19th century and the beginning of the 20th; figures like Thomas Mann himself, the poet Stefan George, the painter Kandinsky and even Lenin.

And today? Is Munich just a carefully preserved myth or really the only city to live in? The answer is: both. Munich's titles are all justified because each one contains a grain of truth about a metropolis which is both cosmopolitan and provincial and, above all, Bavarian.

Munich is the second-largest industrial city in Germany, which one is hardly aware of since few of the early-morning commuters are heading for big factories with front gates and smokestacks; most work in Munich's high-tech companies, like Siemens, Dornier, DASA, MTU, MAN and, of course, the famous BMW.

Munich is also now the world's second publishing and media city, after New York. More than 75,000 people are employed by the five main Munich daily

newspapers, as well as by leading book and magazine publishers. Munich is also the film capital of Germany, with its vast Bavaria Film Studio complex situated in the fashionable suburb of Geiselgasteig.

Nor should we forget the many thousands of civil servants, Munich being the seat of the Bavarian government: one of the largest Länder of federal Germany, ruled on a tight rein by the CSU (Christian Social Union), Bavaria's uniquely conservative political party. Furthermore, Munich is Germany's insurance center, and the country's second-largest banking center after Frankfurt.

All this aggravates one of the city's main problems, the cost of living, and more especially the spiralling rents which are already beyond the reach of many people. Many minor officials are now refusing to be transferred to Munich because it is too expensive for them. Some corporations pay their executives' rent in order to keep them in Munich.

The shadow of exorbitant rents hangs constantly over both the excessive number of luxury apartments and the scarce public welfare housing. For many people on social security, this cosmopolitan city with a heart has for many years offered nothing but a hard struggle for survival.

The same problem faces the students, now numbering 100,000 (not surprisingly, Munich is also the second-largest university city in Germany), who often have to pay horrendous rents for rooms. With the high cost of living, as well as high rents, Munich now has an unenviable reputation as the most expensive city in Germany – which deters many people from packing their bags and moving here. Even the fortunate city dwellers have started grumbling and complaining more and more about the high cost of public transport and the ridiculous price of a beer and a few nibbles to go with it. Not to mention the fact that a plate of traditional roast pork costs a good three or four marks more than in Nuremberg, Bavaria's other major city. These, then, are some of the less attractive aspects of daily life in Munich.

MUNICH LIFE

But every city is like a kaleidoscope, turn it and you see new and more glittering patterns. Of course, there is the overexposed Munich smart set, much like those in other places. But although you can find the same kind of glitterati in Paris, Berlin or Rome, they do not have quite the same mix of aristocrats, business tycoons, film-makers and starlets, even famous chefs, as you are likely to see in Munich.

Nowhere else are hostesses more pleased when pictures of their tediously similar original parties are spread over the tabloids for the hundredth time to the mixed envy and amusement of ordinary people, who tend to regard these Munich beauties and cool BMW drivers as a pain in the neck in love with themselves and each other but unloved by the rest. Munich can take them or leave them.

Above: Swimmers and sunbathers on the Isar. Right: Every year the angel Aloysius returns to Munich at carnival time.

So let us turn to outdoor life, whether in summer or in winter. In a word, what every German from Kiel to Oberammergau knows about Munich and its leisure activities. The summer belongs to the river Isar, to nudists and sunbathers, bicyclists and joggers, to old folk sitting in the sun and children in the playgrounds. Despite its crowded banks and a ban on swimming, the Isar is more alive than almost any other river flowing through a big city.

The Isar is Munich's umbilical cord to the Alps, where it originates. The mountains to the south of the city are a second home to Munich people, and are regarded almost as their personal property – especially in winter. They start plainning their winter outings to neighboring Austria in the fall, as soon as the leaves have turned to red and gold. And the fact that it's only two hours from here to Lake Garda or Verona is taken for granted, because Munich is in the north – of Italy!

But with all those lakes, meadows, hills and pubs in between – how fortunate

MUNICH LIFE

the Müncheners are to be able to spend all their free time in this lovely landscape! Then, when they drive back to the city on Sunday evening, they have to sit in traffic jams, just as they would in Cologne or Berlin.

They are citizens of a metropolis, and although they like to think of their city as the much-quoted village of a million, sadly the city is fast losing its old village atmosphere. The pubs are being smartened up and the shops are more showy. Whole areas are losing their character. Schwabing was the first, followed by Haidhausen, Lehel and the West End. A plague of owner-occupied apartments has eaten its way through the city like caterpillars, though they never delight its inhabitants by turning into beautiful butterflies.

It's rare nowadays to find locals in the Munich pubs like those caricatured in the *Abendzeitung* (Munich's evening newspaper) as Herr Hirnbeiss: a gruff and cynical grumbler who is convinced he is always right and complains about everything and everyone from politicians to Prussians, the weather and the short measure of beer in his liter mug.

From the break of dawn Munich, like any big city, is in danger of a heart attack. The center is jammed solid, the Middle Ring Road is at a stand-still and the air is choked with fumes. Plans to ease the situation have been discussed for years, but in spite of the good local transport system, traffic congestion is a chronic problem. So set a good example, use public transport. You will learn more about the city and its people.

Use it when you go for a meal – perhaps to the Tal, Neuhauser Strasse or Marienplatz, where you can try some very good typical Bavarian dishes, such as *Schweinsbraten* (roast pork), *Leberknödl* (liver dumplings), *Lüngerl* (lung stew) and *Züngerl* (tongue), *Semmelknödeln (*bread dumplings) and *Weisswurst* (veal sausages) with sweet mustard.

Anyone from a tradition-loving local to a cautious Italian can try the substantial food of Munich, served by waiters

37

MUNICH LIFE

and waitresses whom one should address in a respectful tone: "Excuse me, please, but might I perhaps have..."

But if you prefer food from your own or another country, it can certainly be found in Munich – Italian, Chinese, Greek, Spanish, Japanese, Thai, Indian, etc. Only English food is missing, but not many people notice. The city prefers its food very international and often very ethnic.

Munich life, of course, has a lot to do with drinking. Everyone thinks immediately of Munich beer. At the end of September, when horses, decked out in their finery, pull huge wooden barrels to the opening of the Oktoberfest on the *Wies'n* (Theresienwiese) and the world's biggest booze-up begins: any visitor can see that Munich really is the beer capital of the world. Eating and drinking goes on everywhere – in the decreasing number of large, old-fashioned restaurants, in the many beer gardens for which Munich is greatly envied, in the hundreds of inns, pubs and bars, and in the bistros which have recently sprung up everywhere. In this city, quenching thirst is not viewed simply as a necessity; it is a ritual in which everyone has to take part.

Which cannot be said of discotheques and fashionable night spots. Getting into these places usually depends on whether your appearance is right. The clientele is hand picked, so lots of people head for home earlier than they had planned, seething with rage. And this brings us to the subject of Munich's night-life: Munich's Achilles heel, in the view of people who claim to know all about cosmopolitan cities. Munich certainly looks small-time and provincial in comparison wth other major cities as far as night-life here is concerned. Of course, there are bars which stay open late into the night and which are more easily accessible and somewhat livelier since night buses,

Above: We're one mug of beer short at this table! Right: There is never a shortage of entertainment at Marienplatz.

MUNICH LIFE

streetcars and trains were introduced, but what Munich calls night-life would make a Berliner or Parisian tear their hair out.

By way of compensation, Munich points proudly to its cultural offerings, although its new productions are seldom hailed as revolutionary or exciting by newspaper critics, despite – or perhaps because of – being staged in the overpowering architectural splendor of theaters like the National, the Cuvilliés, the Residenz, the Prince Regent and the Theater am Gärtnerplatz.

The lively and varied fringe culture and theater scene is suffering from cuts in funding while Munich's theater supremo earns more than the Bavarian Prime Minister: yet another indication of how valuable culture is to the city. And how hard it is to enjoy. To get a ticket for the Munich Opera Festival, for example, you used to have to take a warm sleeping bag and wait in line for three days outside the box office. These days, it generally suffices to get to one of Munich's many ticket outlets before 10 a.m., though tickets have been known to be sold out thirty minutes later – and this a full month before the performance! For those who want tickets on short notice, their only hope is to pick up an unclaimed reserved ticket at the box office on performance night.

On no account should you miss a visit to one of Munich's typical beer oases. And not just for the beer: these *Biergärten* are the real symbols of the city and the best example of Munich life. It is here that the famous Liberalitas Bavariae – the generosity of Bavaria personified – sits under the chestnut trees gazing benevolently upon friend and foe alike.

Over there a Bavarian in creaking *Lederhosen* is on his fourth liter *Mass* of beer; behind him is a blue-haired punk in torn jeans; middle-aged women wearing beige outfits and neat hats cast disapproving glances at both, in between taking delicate sips from their beer mugs; lovers turn the eyes tenderly heavenward;

families unpack their picnic baskets, laying out fresh bread, radishes, cheese and various tidbits on the Bavarian blue-and-white tablecloths they brought along with them; chidren and dogs are searched for between chestnut trees and playgrounds; grey-haired executives loosen their ties and exchange a *Prosit* with their secretaries. And over the whole scene wafts the tantalizing scent of roast chicken, roast pork and spare ribs.

In a beer garden distinctions cease to matter; everyone can be themselves and no-one minds. The beer garden, especially the one at the Chinese Tower, is a kind of Vanity Fair, where the true personality of the city is on show. It is also a meeting place for people from every part of town. A Munich beer garden can be loud and frivolous, but also idyllic, peaceful and relaxing. It is a meeting place for family and friends, a debating club and a place for card games. When the first warm breezes of spring arrive, generations of Münchners have shouted: Hey, the beer garden season starts today!

FRAUENKIRCHE

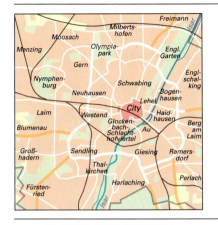

THE INNER CITY

AROUND THE STATION
KARLSPLATZ (STACHUS)
LENBACHPLATZ
THE PEDESTRIAN ZONE
MARIENPLATZ / IM TAL
VIKTUALIENMARKT
JAKOBSPLATZ
HACKENVIERTEL

AROUND THE STATION

People arrive in their thousands every day from the towns and villages of Upper Bavaria, in local trains with old-fashioned second-class carriages that have sticky plastic seats, a deafening clatter heard through their open windows, as well as in the modern white-and-turquois-colored double-decker train cars with their comfortable plush seats and panoramic windows. A colorful variety of humanity streams out of Munich's *Hauptbahnhof* (Main Station): housewives come in for their monthly shopping trip for things they can't get in small-town shops. They are accompanied by senior citizens, foreign workers, high-school students and, of course, commuters, who have chosen a quieter and more economical life outside of the city.

Businessmen with briefcases climb out of Inter-City trains; well-dressed businesswomen head confidently into the city; one sees visitors from northern Germany with piles of luggage and young people from all over the world with their backpacks and Inter-Rail passes.

Preceding pages: Panorama of Munich with the Frauenkirche and the new Rathaus; Ludwigstrasse with the Feldherrnhalle and Theatinerkirche. Left: The Mariensäule.

Many new arrivals head straight to the Tourist Information office outside the main entrance, others to the Travel Center, to the taxi stand or downstairs to the subway trains (*S-Bahn* and *U-Bahn*). Nearly every one in the throng of people coming out of Munich's Main Station has the same objective: to get from the station, through the busy shopping streets to Karlsplatz, and from there into the old inner city – an area roughly a mile (1.5 km) in diameter which lies, besieged by traffic, within the modern ring road, and whose borders correspond roughly to the medieval city walls. This is Munich's front parlor, where you will find not only shops of all kinds, but cafés and restaurants, beer gardens and street musicians, theaters, museums, cinemas and many fine churches. Here, where scarcely 9,000 people actually live, there is daily employment for 90,000, and 300,000 more come to do their shopping, sightseeing and other things.

It is difficult to believe that when the **Hauptbahnhof** was built, in the middle of the last century, it was at the edge of the city. The uncontrolled building boom of following decades had soon encircled it. During the war it was largely destroyed, and in the postwar rush to modernize, the surviving frontage of F. Bürklein's building was torn down. Further

45

THE INNER CITY

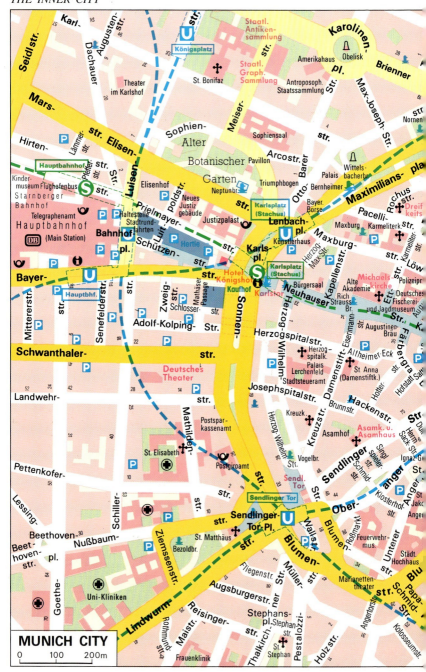

THE INNER CITY

AROUND THE STATION

modernization with an internal structure of glass and aluminium has turned the station into the hub of all rail traffic in south and south-east Germany, as well as of the S-Bahn (suburban) and U-Bahn (undergound) rail networks. The small, overpriced shops in the station and its extensive shopping-mall, below street level, are often the last resort when other shops are closed. Travelers with a long wait can pass the time pleasantly in the station: there are bookshops with foreign-language books, magazines and newspapers, as well as specialty shops for things as diverse as comics and fashion. There are snack bars and restaurants, and there is even a Burger King upstairs next to the Post Office.

Across the street from the station's main entrance is the first department store to be built in Munich at the beginning of this century: **Kaufhaus Hertie**, between Schützenstrasse and Prielmayer-

Above: Opposite the Old Palace of Justice is the Old Botanical Garden.

strasse. It faces the station and harmonized architecturally with its old façade. Of reinforced concrete construction and featuring a clear glass dome, it was considered to be the architectural masterpiece of the city in its day. The building was enlarged in the 1970s and now reaches almost as far as Karlsplatz. In the basement, gourmets in a hurry can buy choice delicatessen items in **Käfer's food hall** at very fancy prices.

The modern building with its shimmering blue glass frontage, not far from Hertie, is called the **Elisenhof** and was built in an attempt to bring the flavor of inner city shopping out as far as the station. The broad interior passages are lined with small shops, a cinema and several cafés, bars and restaurants.

Despite these ambitious projects, the station district has remained just what it was in the 1960s: the arrival point and transitional zone for the many foreigners who came to Munich seeking work, and who were met here and shown around by their fellow-countrymen; a place where one could buy the latest newspapers from every land under the sun, where shops selling the foods of all the main guest-worker countries had sprung up, right next to the numerous import-export firms and dealers offering the lowest prices on anything from a Walkman to a washing machine, no questions asked.

The adjoining area between **Schillerstrasse** and **Goethestrasse,** which both run at right angles to **Bayerstrasse**, has seen a big expansion of the computer business in recent years, with a greater concentration of shops in this neighborhood than anywhere else in the city.

The stream of itinerant consumers also supports a lot of hi-fi and electronics shops, and a great deal besides, from snack-bars to bordellos. The usual sex-cinemas, peep-shows, pin-ball arcades and seedy strip-joints complete the entertainment scene.

At least one-fifth of Munich's 350 officially-recognized hotels and guesthouses can be found in the small district which is bordered by the station, Mittererstrasse, Sonnenstrasse and Landwehrstrasse. The **Information Office** next to the main entrance of the station will help you find accommodation and provide you with a map of the city and other essential information.

A short distance from the station, adjoining Karlsplatz (Stachus), the **Old Botanical Gardens** (which was laid out by Friedrich Ludwig von Sckell between 1808 and 1814) provides a sanctuary in which to get your breath back. At Lenbachplatz, the classical (former) entrance gate can be seen. Heedless of the swirling traffic close at hand, secretaries and pensioners, tired shoppers and tourists, come to sit on the benches by the Fountain of Neptune to take in a few rays of sunshine or to eat their lunch. Across from the fountain is the **Old Palace of Justice**, a rather grandiose building in a strange mixture of baroque and renaissance, dating from 1891-97.

KARLSPLATZ (STACHUS)

Providing a link between the *Altstadt* (Old City) and the station, **Karlsplatz** has always been an important traffic intersection. The original and official name dates back to the Elector Karl Theodor, who was not greatly loved by his people. This is why the Müncheners stubbornly persist in calling the place Stachus, probably in honor of a hostelry named the Stachusgarten which was opened in 1755, and whose owner, one Eustachius Föderl, was apparently held in higher esteem than the Elector. Today, with its streetcars, U-Bahn and S-Bahn lines, to say nothing of the thundering motor traffic, it is far and away the busiest square in the city, some say in the whole of Europe.

The elegant **Königshof** hotel and restaurant, the newly-renovated **Galeria Kaufhof** department store and a number of other shops squeeze together on the side nearest the station, as well as the famous Mathäser Beer Halls, which were closed down in 1997. In their place the largest cinema complex in Germany is to be built, with a total of 14 screens.

To the right, **Sonnenstrasse** swings round in a wide curve following the line of the old fortifications down to Sendlinger Tor. On the six-lane boulevard are more big cinemas and countless shops. A few steps along **Schwanthalerstrasse**, at number 13, is the **Deutsches Theater**, which has been Munich's favorite variety theater and a major venue for *Fasching* (carnival) festivities since its opening in 1896.

Beneath Stachus is a subterranean maze of small shops, selling everything from flowers, jewelry and shoes to health foods, carpets and books and more. There are also cafés, bakeries and snack bars down here. Signs point out bus and streetcar stops, the U-Bahn and S-Bahn stations and the car-park several levels below. It was in the 1960s that they had the idea of building a high-rise down-

LENBACHPLATZ

wards instead of upwards, so to speak. It is a somewhat daunting task for the uninitiated to find their way around down here. The City Council and the Office of the Environment both have information kiosks here, handing out leaflets on the many little problems faced by Müncheners in their everyday lives: from getting rid of bulky refuse, to the measurement of pollutants in the atmosphere. It gives the visitor an insight into the complex machinery that keeps this big city running smoothly.

In your subterranean wanderings you may come across the warren of passages which serve the big department stores. There is a long tunnel linking the Hertie store with the station and with the pedestrian zone. Approaching from the pedestrian zone you are irresistably led to it by delicious smells. Here, numerous small shops offer the passer-by all sorts of delicacies that he would search for in vain in the fast-food joints at street level.

AROUND LENBACHPLATZ

When you have tired of the hectic pace of Stachus, you may want to catch your breath for awhile before stepping through the Karlstor gate and into the bustling pedestrian zone. In this case you should take a left turn and walk the short distance to **Lenbachplatz**. It is well worth looking round this impressive example of city architecture from the turn of the century. A number of neo-classical buildings face the square: Lenbachplatz 2 is shared by the Deutsche Bank and the **Bavarian Stock Exchange**; No. 3 is the **Bernheimer House**, one of the first combined residential and office buildings in Munich, built by Friedrich von Thiersch in 1887-89, in which the huge new Lenbach restaurant is located. Flaming torches illuminate the restaurant's entrance at night. Other up-market businesses have

Above: The sparkle of fountains at Lenbachplatz. Right: Karlsplatz (Stachus) is the start of the pedestrian zone.

THE PEDESTRIAN ZONE

moved into the newly-renovated building as well, including a store called Kokon, which features oriental furnishings, Persian rugs and Indian fabrics.

On the opposite side of the square stands the **Künstlerhaus am Lenbachplatz** (Artists' House), a grand ball-room in the style of a Florentine palazzo, built in 1900 by G. von Seidl and decorated inside by Lenbach. Intended as a place for Munich artists of the day to meet, it now serves as a venue for rather grand social functions and glittering carnival balls. It also has the excellent **Mövenpick** restaurant under its roof, and in summer you can eat outside on the terrace.

In the restaurant's "Venezia Room," which is decorated in the Venetian style and is illuminated by an enormous chandelier, you can enjoy a superb meal in wonderful elegance while admiring the bay windows, which are protected as a historical monument.

However, the aesthetic focus of the square is without doubt provided by the magnificent classical **Wittelsbach Fountain**, designed by Adolf von Hildebrandt (1893-95). Behind its cluster of trees, the green lawns of **Maximilianplatz** stretch across to the **Platz der Opfer des Nazionalsozialismus** (Square of the Victims of National Socialism).

THROUGH THE PEDESTRIAN ZONE

The favored meeting point at Stachus is the big round **fountain**. Located in the semi-circular group of buildings around the fountain are the Gloria-Palast cinema, the Hugendubel book store and the Obletter toy store. From among the confusion of lottery-ticket sellers and vegetable stands, the people lounging beside the fountain and the crowds heading every which way, you will get a glimpse through the Neuhauser (a.k.a. Karlstor) gate and along the slightly upward sloping Neuhauser Strasse of a teaming mass of bobbing heads. It is about half a mile (800 m) from here to Marienplatz, and in the evening when it is empty of people

51

you can walk it in less than ten minutes. But during shopping hours or on a sunny Sunday, the same distance may take you three-quarters of an hour.

The walk takes you past the city's leading stores – the cheaper chains as well as the smartest shopping addresses – in fact, all the firms which, through the 1970s and 1980s, have managed to defeat the competition by buying up old, less successful shops. Sadly, almost all the old shops have long since fallen victim to this trend and the present-day shop-fronts have mostly taken on the identical international look.

Yet even this uniformity has not succeeded in completely wiping out all traces of the city's past. The walk starts at the beginning of the pedestrian zone: **Karlstor**, a relic of the city wall which, in the 14th century when the the city became too crowded, was built outside the older 12th century wall. The broad

Above: After business hours the pedestrian zone has a southern-European feel.

swathe of the *Altstadtring* still marks the course of this wall. After it was pulled down around 1800, the symetrical semi-circular terrace either side of the Karlstor was built to symbolise the opening up of the city to the world. The area was re-modelled in 1972 after the opening of the Stachus S-Bahn station.

The gate itself, once the main tower of a larger gate complex, has been elegantly integrated into the cityscape and is decorated with attractive figures of musicians. A memorial plaque on the gate is dedicated to the city's building officer, Jensen, who in the 1960s was a driving force behind the creation of the pedestrian zone in the face of strong opposition from shop-owners, who were convinced that the wide, traffic-free street would seem boring and would stay yawningly empty.

The section of the pedestrian zone that begins at Karlstor is called **Neuhauser Strasse**. On both sides of the street the biggest shops in the city center draw in their customers. Proof that a thriving department store need not be an eyesore is provided by **Haus Oberpollinger**; built at the turn of the century, its elegantly-jointed façade, austere gables and nautical ornamentation give it an almost Hanseatic appearance.

Beyond it and scarcely noticeable among the other façades is the **Bürgersaal**, a baroque building designed by Giovanni Antonio Viscardi in 1710, and commissioned as a meeting-hall for the Marianist Congregation, a lay society inspired by the Jesuits, which played a significant role in the Counter-Reformation. This two-storey building is used as a church, the vaulted crypt of which has contained the tomb of Father Rupert Mayer since 1948. This priest is held in honor by the people of Munich for having ceaselessly spoken out against Nazism from the pulpit. He was frequently imprisoned or sent to concentration camps, and he died in 1945 as a result of his mistreatment. He was beatified by Pope John Paul II in Munich in 1987.

A little further along, the shop-fronts retreat to create one of the few quiet corners along this bustling thoroughfare: it is the **Richard Strauss fountain**. Hardly have the first pale rays of spring sunshine begun to appear before the Müncheners start pulling up chairs here on this wide, sheltered inlet and put down their heavy shopping-bags in order to relax for a while, often still in their heavy winter overcoats.

The **Alte Akademie**, which was erected at the end of the 16th century, flanks this sheltered square. In the 18th century it became the seat of the Academy of Sciences, and today it houses the Bavarian Office of Statistics.

The adjacent **Michaelskirche** is considered to be one of the finest renaissance churches north of the Alps. The gabled front faces the square and shows, beside the figure of Charles, the greats among the most important of the Wittelsbachs. The founder of the church, Duke Wilhelm V, is also portrayed; the third figure from the right in the first row. In a niche between the two doorways, above the Wittelsbach coat of arms, is a statue of the archangel Michael triumphing over the devil.

The interior, in typical high renaissance style, features slender pilasters and choir sections. Light floods in and onto the altar, which has a further depiction of the archangel Michael. The Gothic shrine to the twin brothers Cosmas and Damian, who were martyred under the Roman emperor Diocletian, is in the third chapel on the right and dates from the 14th century. It has beautiful reliefs in silver gilt. The tombs of the church's founder and of 41 other Wittelsbachs, including that of the ill-fated "Fairy-tale King" Ludwig II, are in a mausoleum beneath the choir, known as the *Fürstengruft* (Princes' Crypt).

The next important building we come to, the former **Augustinerkirche**, was converted to other uses in the secularisation of 1803; in 1911 shops were built on to its street frontage, and these are among the last remaining small shops on the street. Then, in the 1960s, the vaults of the church were turned into a museum of hunting and fishing, the **Deutsches Jagd- und Fischereimuseum**, which contains a collection of more than 500 stuffed animals, paleontological skeletons and hunting equipment. It is quite a surprise, in the middle of the stream of shoppers, to see a wild boar and a bronze fish guarding the entrance.

On the other side of the street, behind a magnificent renaissance façade, is **Augustiner-Bräu**, one of the authentic traditional brewery inns in Munich. Around the charming courtyard, with its secluded beer garden atmosphere, are grouped a series of beautiful rooms with decorations from the turn of the century, each having a particular aura of its own. Here you will find Munich hospitality at its best, though not, it must be said, at its cheapest.

FRAUENKIRCHE

Specialities from the field of international cuisine are on offer at the Mövinpick restaurant **Marché**, across from Michaelskirche. You can watch your food being prepared in the lively market hall atmosphere here.

Frauenkirche

Looking down Augustinerstrasse and Färbergraben, it is still possible to see that they both follow the curve of the old city boundary. For centuries, the *Bach der Färber* (Dyers' Brook) flowed along here. Today however, **Färbergraben** (Dyers' Ditch), with its multi-storey carpark, post office and modern office buildings, is hardly what you would call attractive.

Branching off from here and running parallel to the pedestrian zone is a small street named **Altheimer Eck**. Before the foundation of Munich, the village of Altheim stood on this spot; but the street has literally become the obverse side of Munich's Golden Mile. It is filled with an endless stream of cars making their way to the parking lots and delivery vehicles unloading goods for the shops. Recently the commercial success of the pedestrian zone has started to spread in this direction. An airy passageway containing boutiques, bistros and cafés – including a new Internet café – known as the "Arcade" has been broken through the block.

On the north side, the line of the old wall is marked by **Augustinerstrasse**. It is flanked by the rather gloomy back of the **police headquarters**, whose front entrance is on **Ettstrasse**, a name synonymous with the police headquarters to criminals and honest citizens alike: Ettstrasse has the same significance for Müncheners as Scotland Yard has for Londoners.

Augustinerstrasse leads into the former "hermits' quarter" and to **Frauenplatz,** in front of the cathedral. In the shadow of

Above: Summer visitors relax in front of Michaelskirche. Right: In the midday sun around the Frauenkirche.

the cathedral's twin 330-foot (100 m) spires, the emblem of Munich, this small square is usually cold and drafty. But on hot sunny days it is a popular refuge. The stone steps around the fountain are crowded and children refresh themselves by splashing around in the bubbling water of the fountain.

The **Frauenkirche** (Church of Our Lady) stands on a rise of land hardly noticeable today, and was originally known as the *Marienkapelle*, Munich's second parish church. In 1468 the foundation-stone was laid for the *Kirche zu Unserer Lieben Frau* – in short, Frauenkirche. The late-Gothic brick building is 119 yards (109 m) long and 44 yards (40 m) wide, with absolutely no embellishment except for the cupolas which were added to the towers in 1525 and which were the model for the baroque onion-domes to be seen all over Bavaria. The overall impression is of strength and simplicity, a single vast hall church with no transept. Inside, however, very little of Jörg von Halspach's original design has survived.

The Counter-Reformation and neo-Gothic purists who managed to obliterate much of the original detail left their marks on the interior of the cathedral. All that is left of the original are the basic architectural elements of the building: the three high narrow naves, separated by slender closely-spaced pillars, and the tall, broad windows. During the church's latest renovation, the interior was painted in a warmer shade which comes very close to the original color of 500 years ago. In addition, numerous sculptures and reliquaries were returned to their original places.

A footprint can be seen in the stone floor near the entrance: the legendary Devil's Footprint. The story goes that Halspach made a pact with the devil, who would help him with the building but demanded in return that no windows should be visible in the church. When it was completed, the architect led the Devil to the entrance and made him look up the central aisle.

Indeed, from where he stood he could

see no windows, only a contented congregation in a room that was bathed in light. So angry was the Devil at being tricked that he stamped his foot soundly onto the floor and left the print that can be seen today.

Among the other things to look at is the black marble tomb of Ludwig the Bavarian. On the high altar you can see some of the Gothic figures of apostles by Erasmus Grasser, which were recovered from the rubble after the war. Beneath the church are two crypts in which many Wittelsbach rulers and archbishops of Munich are laid to rest.

The narrow streets in the shadow of the great cathedral are all traffic-free and full of inviting little shops and inns. You can choose between Italian restaurants on **Sporerstrasse** and the cosy, old-established Nürnberger Bratwurst-Glöckl for beer and sausages.

Above: The Fish Fountain at Marienplatz.
Right: The carrillon in the tower of the new Rathaus is a big attraction.

MARIENPLATZ

Beginning at Augustinerstrasse and Färbergraben, the last section of the pedestrian zone within the old city walls is **Kaufingerstrasse**, a continuation of Neuhauser Strasse. The closer one gets to Marienplatz, the more dense the crowd of pedestrians becomes, and the more sought-after are the shops and cafés. To the right is an arcade leading to inner courtyards called the **Löwenhof Passage**, built in the 1980s. When the weather is good you can sit here in the peace and quiet of a garden restaurant. Another arcade was recently completed, opening up the narrow shopping street somewhat: **Kaufinger Tor**, with its shops and bistros, can be entered from Löwenhof Passage as well as from the pedestrian zone. The arcade's special attraction is the Disney Store, in which all kinds of articles relating to Mickey Mouse & Co. can be found.

A stroll down Kaufingerstrasse gives you an opportunity to savor briefly the multi-cultural side of Munich. It is like a free variety show. There are street musicians and performers from all over the world helping to make the town center a mit more entertaining.

At last you arrive at **Marienplatz**. Formerly known as *Schrannenplatz*, or Market Square, this has always been the heart of Munich. In the Middle Ages, overlooked by stately merchants' houses and the old *Rathaus* (Town Hall), it was the place where tournaments, festivals and guild ceremonies were held. But in the late 19th century the market was moved elsewhere and 24 fine old town-houses were demolished to make room for the *Neues Rathaus* (New Town Hall), which was built between 1876 and 1909. World War Two cleared away the houses on the south side of the square and the Kaufhof company tore down the elegant Jugendstil houses at the south-west corner and put up their huge department store.

However, for nearly a century the square has been dominated by the vast and unmistakeable **New Town Hall**, with its neo-Gothic façade and 250-foot (85 m) high tower, which can be "climbed" by stairs or by elevator. It is built around no less than six interior courtyards, and in the vaults you can find the much-frequented Ratskeller beer-parlor.

Every day at 11 a.m., 12 noon and 5 p.m., large crowds gather on Marienplatz to see the famous **Glockenspiel**, or carillon, come alive. This has been going on since 1903, and although the 43 bells which used to ring are now just a recorded tape, you can still see the 32 figures come out and enact a jousting scene. This commemorates an event that was held to celebrate the wedding of Duke Wilhelm V in 1568. Among the figures you can see coopers dancing a roundelay. The coopers first performed this dance back in 1517, to celebrate the city's survival from one of a series of plagues. At 9 p.m. the Glockenspiel rings out again: *Das Münchner Kindl wird zu*

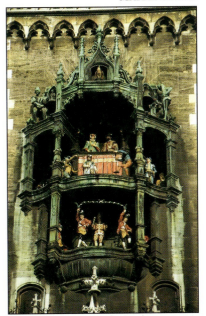

Bett gebracht ("The Munich Child is Put to Bed") is its tune, and the figures that appear this time are the nightwatchman, the Angel of Peace and the little monk from the city's coat-of-arms. There is an especially-good view of the carillon from the **Metropolitan** restaurant facing it (above the Hugendubel book store).

In the middle of square stands the gleaming golden **Mariensäule** column, with a figure of the Virgin Mary, carved in 1590. This is the point from which all distances in Bavaria are measured, and they say it is where the city's heart beats. The statue, which has become the patron saint of the city, was donated by Elector Maximilian in 1638 in gratitude for Munich's deliverance from the Swedish army. At the foot of the column is an allegorical representation of the fight against Plague, Hunger, War and Heresy.

Things are more cheerful at the nearby **Fischbrunnen** fountain, which recalls the days when the the butchers' apprentices were soaked to the skin here in a light-hearted baptism. It is said that the

THE OLD TOWN HALL

water of the fountain has the power to bring good fortune, and tradition has it that anyone who washes his purse in the water on Ash Wednesday will never see it empty. To this day, the Chief Burgomaster keeps up the custom each year by symbolically washing the City Purse.

On the east side of the square stands the **Altes Rathaus** (Old Town Hall). Built in the 15th century by Jörg von Halspach, it was almost completely destroyed in World War Two, but was later fully restored, the work being completed in 1972 with the re-erection of the old tower. Restoration has been particularly successful in the Gothic *Tanzsaal* built over the gateway. This historic banqueting hall, in which Emperor Charles V is said to have dined, now has an attractive wooden ceiling and copies of Erasmus Grasser's morris dancers (the originals can be seen in the Stadt Museum). The

Above: The Altes Rathaus forms the east side of Marienplatz. Right: The much-loved tower of "Old Peter."

rooms in the tower contain the **Spielzeug** (Toy) **Museum**, featuring the private collection of the caricaturist Ivan Steiger.

Around the rest of the square there are various department stores – the Kaufhof already mentioned and Ludwig Beck *am Rathauseck*, a clothing store – as well as smaller shops, hotels and restaurants. In the **Peterhof** restaurant, which claims to have invented *Weisswurst*, there is a good view over the whole square. **Donisl**, a restaurant that traces its history back to 1715, may not have such a good view, but it does offer zither music and an authentic Bavarian atmosphere.

Since traffic-calming measures were introduced in 1972, Marienplatz has taken on a much more civilized quality. Open-air cafés, troughs of flowers and lots of places to sit have made the square a popular rendezvous point. In the weeks before Christmas, crowds are drawn to the **Christkindlmarkt** (traditional Christmas market) with its *Glühwein* (hot mulled wine), *Lebkuchen* (ginger cakes) and variety of imaginative Christmas gifts. Traffic has been replaced by the underground and suburban railways, which have an important interchange station below the square.

Behind the Rathaus is one of the last remaining spaces that has not been built over since the war. Known as **Marienhof**, it was in medieval times a warren of little alleyways that made up the Jewish Ghetto. This small patch of green that was laid out in the 1980s offers welcome relief from the turmoil of the surrounding pedestrian zone.

Alter Peter

Leaving Marienplatz, and turning right at the corner by the Peterhof inn, you come after a few steps to the **Rindermarkt** (Cattle Market). In the middle of this square is a bucolic-looking fountain which testifies to its original purpose. At one time there were towers on both sides of the square. The only one still standing is the 15th-century **Löwenturm** (Lion Tower), which was not part of the fortifications but served both as a water tower and living accommodation. On the other side, as you go onto Sendlinger Strasse, you see the **Ruffini House**. Its tower was pulled down in 1808, but is still depicted on the wall of the house, which is built in a triangle around a central court and is well worth a look.

From here it is only a few more steps to **Alter Peter** (Old Peter). On a slight rise, called the *Petersbergl*, the monks who gave their name to Munich established a settlement in the eleventh century and created the nucleus of the future city. The parish church of St. Peter, the oldest in Munich, has a tower which can be climbed – all 297 steps – and it is well worth the effort to see the whole city spread out below you. The unusual square tower was once topped by two spires, but since being struck by lightning in 1607, it has been decorated with a single lantern-like feature, which for many a true citizen is more symbolic of Munich than the twin towers of the Frauenkirche.

St. Peter's has no less than eight clock-faces, so that, as the comedian Karl Valentin put it, eight people can see what time it is at once. The time to hear the church bells at their most resonant is 3 p.m. on a Saturday, when they ring to prepare the faithful for Sunday. In the summer months, also on Saturdays, brass-band music is played on the viewing platform of the tower. The church has been immortalized in an old Munich song, which every visitor has to join in and sing after his third mug of beer: "*Solang der alte Peter, der Petersturm noch steht, solang stirbt in der Münchnerstadt, d'Gmuatlichkeit net aus*" (As long as the tower of Old Peter stands, the cozy atmosphere of Munich will never die). And for that very reason it was obviously the duty of every Münchner to contribute to

the rebuilding of Old Peter after the war. Today the church is once more resplendent in its Gothic-turned-baroque glory. The pillared basilica is almost 100 yards/meters long, and the interior is a mixture of the two styles. The High Altar shows a life-size Adoration of St. Peter. The altar and the surrounding figures are the work of Egid Quirin Asam (1753), whereas the central figure of Peter was carved by Erasmus Grasser in 1517.

The original late-Gothic altar has side-panels by Jan Polack depicting scenes from the life of St. Peter, and the saint is also the central figure in the murals of the baroque choir. In the northern transept is the famous Schrenk altar. In the furthest side-chapel of the other transept there is an early Gothic altar-piece in sandstone, which should not be missed. It shows Christ with an almond-shaped halo, a wonderfully vivid scene of the Last Judgement, the Twelve Apostles and a Crucifixion. In the chapel facing it you will see a charming rococo group of figures by Anna Selbdritt.

IM TAL

IM TAL: "THE VALLEY"

From Marienplatz, you look through the archway of the Old Town Hall and down the **Tal** (Valley). This street owes its rather surprising name to the fact that it once ran steeply down to the river Isar. On the shore, large quantities of timber used to be stacked up, after being floated downstream from the mountains, and in the nearby streets sawyers and carpenters established their workshops, which later became the numerous furniture stores located *im Tal*. Until quite recently, it was usual for the people of Munich to go down to "the valley" to buy furniture, though now this trade is disappearing to the big marts in the suburbs. In its place large fast-food restaurants and steakhouses have sprung up almost overnight.

This broad highway, where horse-drawn wagons once used to load up with logs, in contrast to the pedestrian zone, is still open to traffic and is one of the busiest and most congested parts of the inner city. Endless tourist buses arrive to disgorge their passengers, entire school classes sit down to lunch, and taxis race through red lights. Fortunately, a few of the old inns, patronized by generations of wagoners, have managed to survive. The best known of these is the **Weisses Bräuhaus**, a few yards behind the Old Town Hall, whose *Schneiderweisse* is reckoned to be the best *Weissbier* (wheat beer) in Munich. A little further down, on the other side of the street, the much quieter **Paulaner im Tal** (formerly Bögner) inn is one of Munich's oldest.

To the left of the Tal lies a cluster of streets called the **Graggenauer-Viertel**, where hundreds of little craft workshops could once be found. The only building in this district known to the outside world is the famous **Hofbräuhaus** (Royal Brewery), which for most foreign visitors

Left: Outside the Altes Hackerhaus on Sendlinger Strasse.

ranks with the Brandenburg Gate, the Heidelberg Castle and medieval Rothenburg-ob-der-Tauber as something that must be seen in Germany.

"*In München steht ein Hofbräuhaus, eins, zwei, g'soffa...*" (In Munich stands a Hofbräuhaus, one, two, drink hearty), goes a famous old song. Duke Wilhelm V had his own brewery built in Munich in 1589. It originally stood where today a traditional shop for game is located. In 1852 the brewery was handed over to the Bavarian government. Then, in 1873, brewery activity was transferred to a riverside site in Haidhausen. Only the brewery pub remained in the Old Town.

In 1897 the building was given a neo-renaissance face-lift by Max Littmann, and its spacious rooms were equipped to handle the flood of tourists which was to come. The largest of the rooms is the *Schwemme*, where as many as 1,000 guests can sit at polished tables and drink their beer while singing to the music of Bavarian bands. There are nine other large rooms including the *Jägerstüberl*, *Fischerstüberl* and *Wappensaal*, (Hunters', Fishermen's and Coat-of-Arms rooms), all offering the kind of cosy *Gemütlichkeit* that visitors expect to find here. If the service is sometimes brusque, remember that the waitresses have to put up with this hurly-burly night after night.

The area around the Hofbräuhaus has changed a lot recently, since the little alleyways of the Graggenauer quarter were turned into a fashionable pedestrian zone. You can still find some typically Bavarian establishments, but even the famous **Platzl** variety theater, where comedians kept audiences laughing for over 30 years, had to close its doors in 1995. Today it houses a Planet Hollywood restaurant, where Arnold Schwarzenegger's famous apple strudel can be enjoyed (it's actually his mother's recipe). There is also a contrast in the shops here: along **Orlandostrasse** you will find nothing but cheap souvenirs and sex-shops, while

GRAGGENAUER VIERTEL

in other little streets, such as **Bräuhausstrasse**, there are attractive shops selling Bavarian costumes and musical instruments.

The block of 15th and 16th century town-houses between the Platzl, Pfisterstrasse and Falckenturmstrasse has been expensively restored. Its covered arcades are now called the **Platzlgassen**, and are full of elegant shops and cafés. Behind this block is the old **Pfistermühle** (flour mill) in whose 16th-century vaults there is now a good restaurant. To this day, the flawless natural sourdough bread from the Hofpfisterei bakery, which has branches all over the city, is the best you can buy in Munich. Weekdays after 5:30 p.m., and Saturdays after noon, the tasty *Öko-Laib* loaves are reduced in price. At Ledererstrasse 10, there is another beautifully-restored old town-house.

The little area between **Kosttor**, the Hofbräuhaus and the Altstadtring road is the least-known part of the Old Town. **Neuturmsrasse, Hildegardstrasse, Marienstrasse, Herrnstrasse** and **Stolbergstrasse** are all genuine residential streets with well-renovated late-19th century town-houses. The occasional shops, bistros and quiet hotels that you come across look thoroughly inviting. The last building you come to before reaching the ring road is the modern **Stadtsparkasse** (City Savings Bank). Its inner courtyard has been built around the exposed foundations of the old city wall and the **Lueg-ins-Land** watch-tower (1374). The little alley leading to the Isar Gate bears the same name, which means "survey the country." On the wall of the **Vindeliker House** you can see a picture of the old tower and a plaque with the words: *Hier stund der Wachthurm Lueg ins Land, ob seiner Fernsicht so genannt.* (Here stood the Lueg-ins-Land watch-tower, so named for the view it could command.) At the end of the Tal, the **Isartor** was once where the Salt Road left the city to

Above: Authentic Bavarian ambience in the Hofbräuhaus. Right: The Isartor has now been completely restored.

cross the Isar. Both the octagonal defense tower and the taller lookout tower on the city side have survived. On the outer façade of the gate is a fresco depicting Ludwig the Bavarian's victory at the Battle of Ampfing in 1322.

Since 1959, the north tower has housed the **Karl Valentin Museum** (described on page 179), dedicated to the Munich comedian and satirist, as well as the archive of the Munich *Volkssänger* (folk singers). In the café located in the tower you can take in the view while sampling their excellent Weisswurst or *Schmalznudel* (a kind of pastry; a Munich speciality). Mind you, the view is nothing special since at this point the Old Town ring-road broadens out into a huge intersection before disappearing into Isarvorstadt. The ten traffic lanes seem enough to deter anyone from trying to reach the river beyond, and you may prefer to head back towards Marienplatz and Viktualienmarkt.

At the beginning of **Westenriederstrasse** one cannot help noticing the handsome glass pavilion of **Pelzhaus Rieger**, with its MAXX cinema center. Continue down the street and you pass 15th and 16th-century houses, interspersed with snack bars, a specialist cheese-shop called *Kasladl*, and shops selling traditional costumes and crafts. In the side streets numerous antique-shops are clustered together. Anyone looking for old jewelry should make for *Radlsteg*.

In the passageway leading from No. 26 you will find a very strange establishment: the **Center for Unusual Museums** (ZAM), which contains several peculiar exhibits: pedal-car, chamberpot, Easter bunny and cork-screw collections can be seen, along with a "Sissi" Museum containing memorabilia of the last Austrian empress. A traditional inn, *Beim Sedlmayer* (Westenriedstr. 6), is a great favorite, even though the well-known entertainer for whom it is named has since passed away.

Where Westenriederstrasse bends sharply to the left, one comes upon **Dreifaltigkeitsplatz** (Trinity Square) and the entrance to Heiliggeiststrasse. **Heiliggeist-Kirche** (Church of the Holy Ghost) was original built in the 13th century to serve a hospital, and after the great fire of 1327 was rebuilt as a typical Bavarian hall church, with no transept. However, almost nothing has remained of its Gothic form. In the early 18th century it was given the baroque treatment, and in the 19th century the church was lengthened by three "spans." Inside, the frescos in the central nave, by C.D. Asam, were fully restored after the war. Near the entrance stands a bronze memorial to Duke Ferdinand of Bavaria from 1608.

A number of small shops, built up against the church, lead you onto **Heiliggeiststrasse** – a little lane which can easily be missed. Old-fashioned shops here sell the genuine Bavarian *Lederhosen* (leather shorts) and hand-made brushes; the **Marktcafé** has a pretty courtyard, and at the **Weinschänke** you can grab a glass of wine to warm yourself with. The lane leads back to Dreifaltigkeitsplatz with its pubs and cafés, where it is pleasant to sit in the shade of the trees.

VIKTUALIENMARKT

From here you look out over a large square which was once a village green. Here coaches once parked, and fields, warehouses and bleacheries ranged across the square. In the little houses located round about lived craftsmen and launderers, wagon-menders and woodworkers; in other words, the common people of the city.

Since 1807 the area has been occupied by Munich's largest and most popular market square: **Viktualienmarkt**. The word *Viktualien*, like its English equivalent "victuals," is simply an old-fashioned term for "food." And food of every conceivable kind and variety is on offer here.

Right: View from Viktualienmarkt towards St. Peter and the Altes Rathaus.

At one time the hundreds of little stalls were crowded together in a small space, bounded and criss-crossed by streets. Since those days, Viktualienmarkt has become a Mecca for gourmets who can assemble the ingredients for a great meal here; a piece of aged cheese, a bottle of vintage wine, a joint of hare, perhaps, or a couple of lobsters, a mango or some lychees for dessert. During the lunch-hour, office workers wander in to grab a quick sandwich or to sit under the blue-and-white maypole in the beer-garden, along with the old folk who make one mug of beer last all morning while they happily soak up the autumn sunshine.

In the market stalls you can find everything from Chinese tofu to Greek goat's cheese, as well as every kind of fresh, seasonal local produce. But you may be baffled by some of the dialect. Parsley, for example, is sold in two languages: as High German *Petersilie* for the "bloody Prussians" and as *Bädasui* for native Bavarian customers. The transition from traditional to kitsch, from native authenticity to imitation rip-off, is observable all around Viktualienmarkt.

Thanks to the extension of the pedestrian zone in 1975, the market is free of traffic and the present stalls were designed to give the market a uniform appearance. They were also made wind- and weatherproof. Permanent stalls have also been provided at one end of the square for the agricultural market, to which local farmers bring their produce twice a week. All this has been given the Upper Bavarian look, and consequently the prices have, alas, increased rather steeply. Finally, in 1991, the through-traffic route from the Rosental was closed off, whereby, thankfully, motorists were deprived of their last secret "rat-run" through the Old Town.

Unfortunately, one's enjoyment of the market is somewhat diminished by the horn honking and exhaust-fumes of the traffic that still passes along Blumen-

strasse and Frauenstrasse, at its southern end. The hordes of reckless, bell-ringing cyclists also give the market-women something to grumble about. These splendid ladies are famous for their loud and colorful invective, but it should not be taken too seriously. Many an innocent stranger shrinks back in terror when greeted with the Bavarian equivalent of: "Hey, you! Geddouta there! That stuff's only for buyin', not fingerin'!"

The market-women are as important to the atmosphere of the market as the goods they sell, and they also play a key role in the *Fasching* celebrations, the German equivalent of carnival.

Unlike the Rhineland, Munich does not have a very long carnival tradition. Official ceremonies are limited to choosing a Carnival Prince and Princess, and bestowing the Order of Karl Valentin (for comic achievement). Around the turn of the century, artists and students began to hold carnival parties, which the market-women became involved in. In the grey dawn of Shrove Tuesday, when the market stalls were just opening, they celebrated their own Fasching, drinking and dancing with the last of the revellers who were weaving their unsteady way home. Word got around, and more and more Münchners joined in. Nowadays, on Fasching Sunday and Tuesday (the week of Ash Wednesday), the whole pedestrian zone and the Viktualienmarkt turn into a huge open-air party.

The market-women dance just as they used to, and are now joined by early risers, by children who have waited weeks to try on their costumes, nightclubbers in rumpled tuxedos, and heavily-made-up transvestites. There is no particular special offering: music blares from loudspeakers; someone sprinkles confetti down your neck; you have to stop every hundred yards and buy a *Schnaps* to ward off the cold; and the whole market bubbles with irrepressible high spirits.

As you stroll through the market there are no less than six attractive fountains to serve as landmarks. One has a statue of

ST. JAKOBSPLATZ

the eternal **Marktfrau** (market-woman) and others are dedicated to various popular Munich actors and folk singers. Firstly, and perhaps most notably, there is the statue of the immortal **Karl Valentin**, and another of his partner, **Liesl Karlstadt**. These little memorial fountains are seldom to be seen without a small boquet of flowers on them, placed there by some nostalgic admirer.

Due honor is also given to **Weiss Ferdl** (surname and first name reversed, in the old Bavarian way), who sang so movingly about the long-gone streetcars on Route No. 8. It is no accident that the statues have been put here – these were entertainers of and for the people. In the 1920s, when cosmopolites and intellectuals filled the cabarets and revues of Berlin, Munich was, in spite of its satirical magazine, *Simplicissimus*, still a very provincial town.

Above: Enough to make your mouth water – market stalls at Viktualienmarkt. Right: The Karl Valentin Fountain.

These Bavarian entertainers trod the boards in the Bierkellers of Munich's many breweries, as well as on the stage of the Platzl Theater and the *Blumensäle* at Viktualienmarkt, long since closed. People from the city and from all over surrounding countryside came to applaud simple and crude performances based on a repertoire of favorite Bavarian jokes and local idiosyncracies; but they laughed just as loudly at the sharper and more scurrilous sketches put on by Karl Valentin.

AROUND ST. JAKOBSPLATZ

At the south side of Viktualienmarkt there is a large open space bordering **Blumenstrasse**, which is used as a parking lot. Formerly it was the site of the 1,300-foot-long (400 m) market hall, built in the reign of Maximilian II. Only a small part of the building remains, now used as a *Freibank*, a market where low-priced food is sold to the needy. This green corridor today separates one of the sleepiest corners of the Old Town from the traffic-laden *Altstadtring* (Old Town ring road).

On nearby **Sebastiansplatz,** between Prälat-Zistl-Strasse and Nieserstrasse, the city has set up a center for senior citizens, which enables them to go on living in the neighborhood where they have their roots. Opposite is a group of medieval buildings; the last to have survived in the city. Nos. 8 and 9 have fine old gables, and the staircase of No. 8 runs in a single flight from the ground floor to the loft, in the traditional Gothic manner. Known as **Sebastiansblock**, they are part of a city-run renovation scheme whereby the buildings' owners, many of whom are not especially well off, are given the financial and administrative assistance necessary to refurbish these valuable houses. In this way it is hoped that the population of the Old Town will not drop below its present figure of 9,000, having already declined from 40,000 since the turn of the century.

Around Sebastiansblock, with its old-world atmosphere, the footsore tourist will find plenty of small pubs and cafés of the kind one looks in for in vain in the pedestrian zone. **Café Frischhut**, decorated with a Madonna and morris dancers, is a well-known Munich institution; open from 5 a.m., it is as popular with the early shift of street-sweepers as with people in need of solid sustenance after a night's heavy drinking. A cup of steaming coffee and a freshly-baked *Schmalznudel* will put them back on their feet again.

A little further on we come to **St. Jakobsplatz**. Since through-traffic was largely banned, plans for the square's future have been widely discussed. It is hoped that the square will again one day become a "citizen-friendly" area, in the meantime, it still serves mainly as a popular parking lot for cars and tour buses. Beyond the Angerbach stream with its *RossSchwemme*, where horses

came to drink, stood, in the 16th century, the city's grain-storage depot and later the arsenal. Next door, the royal stables were grouped round a courtyard.

In 1888, all these buildings were converted into a historical museum. Now called the **Stadt Museum** (City Museum), it has been steadily enlarged and is one of the most interesting museums in Munich. Its café, where you can eat outside in the courtyard in summer, has become a fashionable meeting place. Whether you have visited the museum, or are just strolling past in the evening, you can treat yourself to delicious cakes and Italian snacks.

Stadt Museum

The section of the museum devoted to the city of Munich (first floor) displays various plans and engravings of the city in all its stages of development. Models show that Munich sits on a sloping plain of glacial deposits brought down from the Alps. You can also look at coats-of-

STADT MUSEUM

arms and documents from the city's history. In pride of place is Sandtner's model of the city, a replica twice the size of the original (in the Bavarian National Museum), which was commissioned by Duke Albrecht V in 1570. For the next hundred years the model was always referred to whenever any urban alterations were proposed, and it shows very clearly how Munich looked in the Middle Ages. Every house is represented, though the width of the lanes is deliberately out of scale so that you can see the house fronts clearly. You can even see the streams, which have long since disappeared, running north of the Alter Hof, and along the present-day Färbergraben, Oberanger and Viktualienmarkt.

The museum is known far beyond the borders of Munich for its **Film Museum**, which has several showings daily of films, some strips of which are not to be found anywhere else. A further delight for camera buffs is the **Photography Museum**, which vividly documents the history of photography; from the *camera obscura* to flick-books, every stage of the technical evolution of photography is shown, and there is a complete reconstruction of a precision optics workshop. Something not to be missed is the 19th-century *Kaiserpanorama*, a circular wooden structure which, by a clever method, projects lantern-slides three-dimensionally. The viewers sit on stools on the outside and look in at the pictures through peep-holes.

On the fourth floor there is a real treat for music-lovers: the **Musical Instrument Collection**. This is one of the most important collections of its kind in Europe. Instruments from every culture are rather soberly displayed. However, if you are expecting to hear them played you will be disappointed, the instruments here remain sadly silent.

Most visitors will find more to interest them in the suite of rooms which are fully

Above: How much is a Schmalznudel in the Café Frischhut? Right: The famous Morris Dancers by Erasmus Grasser.

furnished in various historical styles so as to create an exhibition of **middle-class domestic life from 1650 to the present** (second floor). Most of the rooms make you wish you could move in straight away. No less than seven of them are devoted to the elegant but unaffected Biedermeier period of the early to mid-19th century. There is also a complete wine bar and a typical artist's studio.

The **Puppet-Theater Museum** on the third floor is charmingly presented and, since there are live performances, it makes a perfect outing on a wet afternoon for adults as well as children. There are about 50,000 puppets of all sizes and from all periods from Europe, Africa and Asia, showing the enduring magic that puppet-theater exerts on children and adults alike. You can also see exhibits relating to the showmen and clowns, which recreate vividly the way they used to enthral audiences at markets and seasonal fairs.

On the ground floor, Erasmus Grasser's famous 15th-century figures of **morris dancers** are on display. It is generally accepted that these are the most important non-religious carvings of the Gothic period. They were commissioned for the inauguration of the Old Town Hall in 1480. Sixteen of the figures stood on corbels beneath the ceiling, of which only ten, unfortunately, have survived.

In the late Middle Ages morris dances were performed all over Europe by travelling players. Originally called *Danzas Moriscas*, they were derived from the dances of the Christianized Moors in medieval Spain. The dances were characterized by exaggerated movements and foppish costumes, and were intended to ridicule typical social figures of the day. The figures, carved from linden wood, are from two to two and a half feet (60-80 cm) tall. Each one is painted in bright colors and is a work of art in itself.

Likewise on the ground floor, you will find the **Waffenhalle** (Weapons Hall), a collections of historical weapons, helmets and more from the former armory, as well as a small **brewery museum**.

SENDLINGER STRASSE

In the little street behind the museum, called **Nieserstrasse**, there is a very unusual institution. Known as the **Artothek**, it is a public lending-library of art, where for a nominal sum you can borrow a new original work of art every two months and hang it in your own living-room.

The Stadt Museum's adminstrative offices are housed in an attractive rococo building, **Ignaz Günther House**, which is where the noted sculptor had his studio in the years 1761-65. It was only after a public outcry that the house was saved from demolition, and the ground-floor rooms are now used for a variety of exhibitions.

HACKENVIERTEL

Leaving the Stadtmuseum, take **Dultstrasse**, or if you are at Marienplatz follow **Rosenstrasse** either way, and you are soon on **Sendlinger Strasse**, the southerly street of the four which quarter the Old Town. It was once a highway leaving Munich at the Sendlinger Gate, but since the construction of the rail terminus in the 19th century, the east-west axis of the city has become much more important than the one running north-south, and Sendlinger Strasse has remained relatively under-developed. It has also been spared rocketing real estate prices and the attentions of the demolition-men; and the many shop-keepers on the street have been wise in promoting its small-town atmosphere. Though traffic has not yet been banned on this one-way street, expensive parking costs are beginning to take their toll.

The top end of the street is dominated by clothing stores, large sports-outfitters, and by the publishing offices of the *Abendzeitung* and the *Süddeutsche Zeitung* newspapers. But the closer you get to Sendlinger Tor, the smaller and more manifold the shops become. While it is true that rising rents have led to long-established businesses being pushed aside by more prosperous firms, some family companies have survived, such as the rope-makers at No. 60. Above a jeweller's on the corner of Hermann-Sack-Strasse you can see a pretty glockenspiel on which a morris dancer turns to the jingling of dozens of little bells on the hour. A few bars, and an ice-cream parlor at No. 54, which serves up a wonderful tropical Copacabana sundae, round out the local offering.

Some of the buildings on Sendlinger Strasse deserve at least a look up from the shop-windows. You will notice that the house-numbers here, as in many Altstadt streets, run consecutively – 1, 2, 3... – up on one side of the street and down on the other, as was the custom centuries ago; and over the doorways of some houses you will still see a carved Madonna.

On the wall of No. 89, at the corner of Färbergraben, where Munich's best-known sports-outfitters is now housed, there is a picture reminding us that the Himmelsschäffler-Haus once stood here, from which the *Schäffler* (coopers) set out on their dance of thanksgiving at the end of the plague.

The **Singlspieler House** (No. 29), with the larger-than-life-sized murals on its exterior walls, has been painstakingly restored. This building once housed a brewery, as did the **Altes Hackerhaus** (No. 75), which has seen a lot of changes in its time. The brewery's famous beer was being made here as early as the 15th century, and Hacker merged later with the Pschorr brewery.

After having burnt down and then been rebuilt several times, only a fraction of the original brewing house now makes up a part of an attractive inn. During renovation, workers re-discovered a neo-rococo reception room, the **Silver Salon**, which the brewery-owner of that time, Mathias

Right: The entrance to the "Hundskugel," the oldest inn in Munich.

Pschorr, had decorated in the 19th century. It is open to the public at certain times.

Near the Altes Hackerhaus, Sendlingerstrasse is crossed by **Hackenstrasse**, the heart of this district of old Munich, typified by handicraft shops, house Madonnas and cozy pubs. There is a particularly well-carved Madonna over the entrance of No. 10, the house occupied by the official sculptors to the ducal court, where in the 18th century a number of important artists, such as Straub and Boos, worked.

At the corner of **Hotterstrasse** is a medieval house, with welcoming windowboxes full of geraniums. But it seems to be only half a house: its gable-end, with the typical projecting beam for winching up goods, appears to be sliced down the middle. Beneath it is a picture of a dog chasing a ball, to illustrate the name of the **Hundskugel** (Dog's Ball) inn, which is the oldest in Munich, dating back to 1440. Its wood-paneled, low-ceilinged rooms have a snug atmosphere though, unfortunately, they were over-restored in a rather folksy Bavarian style. Opposite stands the neo-classical **Radspielerhaus.** Formerly the Rechberg Palace, it retains a fine courtyard and a massive, castellated balcony.

The Heritage of the Asam Brothers

In the first half of the 18th century, the architects and fresco-painters Egid Quirin and Cosmas Damian Asam were Munich's most respected artists, whose fame spread far beyond the borders of Bavaria. In 1733, Egid Quirin bought a plot of land on Sendlinger Strasse and built himself a house here, the **Asam House**, with its splendid stucco façade and one of the most impressive rococo churches in southern Germany, **Asamkirche**, and adjoining it, a presbytery. Together they form a harmonious ensemble.

The frontage of the church, which is dedicated to St. John Nepomuk, is all but swallowed up by the other buildings on

ASAMKIRCHE

Sendlinger Strasse. Nowhere can you stand far enough away to get a view which does it justice. The narrow façade rises elegantly upward from a stone plinth representing natural rock and is divided into three wings, like an altarpiece. However, the moment one steps from the noise of the street into the quiet, dark interior, one is completely overwhelmed by the variety of shapes, the countless figures, putti and murals found inside.

An oval-shaped vestibule adjoins the body of this attractive church; a single long nave with a balconied gallery and a projecting cornice beneath the ceiling. The nave ends in another oval before the chancel.

The ceiling frescos by Cosmas Damian Asam depict scenes from the life of St. Nepomuk and the pilgrimage to his tomb in Prague's St. Vitus' cathedral. The altar

Above: The Asamkirche's rococo splendor.
Right: The Sendlinger Gate marks the end of Sendlinger Strasse.

is adorned with a radiant halo. A glass shrine contains a wax figure of St. Nepomuk with holy relics embedded in it. On a ledge above, God the Father is depicted presenting his crucified son to humanity: this is the so-called *Gnadenstuhl* (Seat of Mercy).

On the entrance doors, further scenes from the life of St. Nepomuk are superbly carved in wood. You should also look above the confessionals at the strange – almost expressionist – carvings of Death, The Last Judgement, Salvation and Damnation. The Asam brothers themselves are modestly portrayed in the inconspicuous paintings above the doors to the sacristy.

A little way down the street you will come to another church on which the genius of the Asams has left its unmistakable imprint: the **St.-Anna-Damenstiftkirche** (Nunnery Church). Except for its exterior walls, the church was destroyed in the Second World War; though it was later reconstructed true to detail.

Behind the Asamkirche, a passageway leads into a courtyard called the **Asamhof**. A post-modernist complex was built here in the 1980s, which attempted to integrate expensive, privately-owned apartments into the fabric of the old quarter. Opinions vary about its success, but it is true that there have been occasional reported sightings of children playing here!

The specialy shops which are located in the complex are only the kind that can afford the high rents, and they include such curiosities as a shop for left-handed people – which stocks everything this under-represented minority might need, from scissors to fountain-pens – as well as a do-it-yourself cosmetics shop. Scattered among the shops are multi-titled café-bistro-bars, which aim to attract passing customers with their pleasant, secluded atmosphere. A couple of modern sculptures, including the cowering plaster figure of a hobo, attempt to lend the

SENDLINGER TOR

complex the impression of being a combined work of art.

Leaving from the rear of the Asamhof you can reach **Kreuzstrasse** which, in contrast, provides a good idea of what an idyllic corner of the Old Town must once really have been like. It is especially recommended to stop in at *Bodo's Backstube*, a bakery offering a different delicious speciality each weekday. Nearby is the **Allerheiligen-Kirche am Kreuz** (All Saints' Church), a single-naved brick church built by Jörg von Halspach between 1480 and 1485.

There is a truly small-town feel about the little lanes around here, and the corner where Kreuzstrasse meets Brunnstrasse and Josephspitalstrasse, where the **City Tax Office** is located, is particularly attractive. The houses hereabouts are generally decorated in the traditional manner, with figures of Madonnas and saints on the façades, including St. Sebastian and the much-loved "Madonna in the Pear Tree." The streets of the Hackenviertel end at **Sendlinger-Tor-Platz**, one of Munich's busiest intersections; with streetcars, buses and a U-Bahn station, in addition to a steady stream of traffic flowing from the main arteries of **Sonnenstrasse** and **Lindwurmstrasse**, making this one of the most hectic corners of the city.

On the opposite side of the street, the curved ground plan and swooping roofline of the evangelical **Matthäus-Kirche** (1953-1955) have earned it the local nickname of "The Good Lord's Bathtub." Beyond the **Fontänenbrunnen** (fountains) along **Pettenkoferstrasse** stretch the buildings of the University Clinic.

The old **Sendlinger Tor** (originally constructed in 1318) consists today only of two octagonal towers joined by a brick archway. The passageway through the original gateway was widened in the 19th century to accomodate the increased traffic of the time. Around the cinema here there are some inexpensive restaurants which, oblivious to the roar of traffic, put tables outside on sunny days.

PRINCELY MUNICH

Princely Munich

The previous walk took us from Marienplatz through the Tal which has always been the preserve of small traders and craftsmen. You are now going to visit a part of the Old Town that is totally different in character.

Starting again from Marienplatz, **Burgstrasse** leads into the Wilbrechtsviertel where, in the 13th century, the Wittelsbach dukes established their court in the **Alter Hof** (Old Courtyard). This group of buildings, completed in the reign of Emperor Ludwig the Bavarian, was known in those days as the *Ludwigsburg*. Sadly, no trace of its Gothic splendor remains except for an equestrian statue of Ludwig on the *Hofgraben*.

While it is true that the castle gate was reconstructed, of the block that was rebuilt on the old foundations the only original element is an oriel. This is popularly known as the Monkey's Tower, because in the time of King Ludwig a baby monkey escaped from the royal menagerie, perched on the spire of the oriel and only climbed down after a great deal of persuasion. Today the building is occupied by the Bavarian Income Tax Office, but pedestrians may stroll through the courtyard and enjoy the welcome silence.

Close by is a building which was once the royal stables. Built in 1465, it was converted in the 16th century and has a fine renaissance courtyard with three-storied arcades. From the early 19th century until 1983 it housed the **State Mint**; it is now the headquarters of the Bavarian Office of Heritage Conservation. Across the Hofgraben from the Mint is the rear façade of the former Törring Palace (the front façade looks onto Residenzstrasse, with its elegant and expensive shops) which, since its conversion by von Klenze in 1835-38, has served as Munich's **Main Post Office.**

The Hofgraben itself runs into Maximilianstrasse, close to **Max-Joseph-Platz**, where the statue of Max I Joseph sits on his throne in a fatherly pose, his hands raised in eternal benediction over his people. At Burgstrasse 5 is a building which dates from the same period as the Mint; once the *Stadtschreiberei*, where documents were drawn up and copied, it is now the **Weinstadl** restaurant and has a charming leafy courtyard. Another popular restaurant is the **Jodlerwirt** (Altenhofstrasse 4). Under an earlier name, the Wolf's Gorge, it was frequented by employees of the royal household.

THE RESIDENZ

Four centuries before this country became a kingdom, the dukes of Bavaria abandoned the narrow confines of their medieval castle and began constructing a new residence on what was then the edge of the city. This *Neu Veste* (New Fortress) was in the north-east corner of the palace complex we see today, but it burned down in the 18th century. However, the grand gateways flanked by four bronze lions are enough to give an idea of the huge scale of the medieval palace in its heyday.

Today the Residenz extends over the whole area which is bounded by Maximilianstrasse, Residenzstrasse, Hofgartenstrasse and Marstallplatz. The complex of buildings evolved organically from the 16th to the 19th centuries, presenting a harmonious blend of late renaissance, baroque, rococo and neo-classical styles, both externally and within. It is without doubt the prized treasure of all Munich – and, indeed, of all Bavaria.

A large part of the palace is taken up today by the **Residenz Museum**, various parts of which contain the royal treasury, the coin collection and the small-but-

Left: Max I Joseph still greets his subjects outside the National Theater.

impressive **State Collection of Egyptian Art**, as well as theaters and concert-halls. The conducted tours, arranged by the museum, take you through the most important phases in the building of the palace; this can be split into a morning and an afternoon tour. However, much of what you see today was reconstructed following the devastation of the Second World War, which left the Residenz, too, nothing but a heap of rubble.

The oldest remaining part is the **Antiquarium**, a long, narrow renaissance hall with a barrel-vaulted ceiling, which was built by Albrecht V in 1571 to display ancient works of art. However, at the end of that century it was turned into a banqueting-hall and decorated with grotesques, panoramas and allegorical frescos. Since its restoration it is again being used for glittering state receptions. The immediate successors of Albrecht V had a wing built between the *Antiquarium* and Residenzstrasse; most of its rooms were converted in the 18th century to form the **Princes' Appartments**, some of which contain an interesting collection of porcelain. A small wing facing Residenzstrasse is the so-called **Witwenstock** (Widows' House), built for the duchess Anna. The rooms are grouped around numerous courtyards, of which the most unusual is the **Grottenhof**, the walls of which are elaborately decorated with sea-shells.

In a further phase of construction, in the 17th century, Maximilian I added his own residence to the north, the stately **Kaiserhof**. Beyond it, the second large courtyard, the **Apothekenhof,** was linked in the 19th century to the Hofgarten by a wing containing a ball-room and throne-room designed by von Klenze. After the Second World War the throne-room was rebuilt as a concert-hall and named the **Neuer Herkulessaal**.

The **Brunnenhof** (Fountain Court), behind the Antiquarium, also received its

Above: The façade of the Residenz at Max-Joseph-Platz. Right: In the Fountain Court of the Residenz, before a concert.

present look in the 17th century. The magnificent **Wittelsbach Fountain** comprises a statue of Otto, first Duke of Bavaria, and allegorical figures representing the four chief rivers of Bavaria: the Isar, the Inn, the Lech and the Danube. The little **Hofkapelle** (Court Chapel) was intended exclusively for the princes to worship in, and resembles an oversized reliquary chamber.

In the 18th century, a wing facing Max-Joseph-Platz and a theater, the Altes Residenz Theater, were added. François Cuvilliés the Elder, the Director of Works to the electors and rococo architect *par excellence*, created this intimate theater in 1753. The glorious interior decoration was, thank heaven, nearly all removed to a safe place before the building was destroyed in World War Two, making it possible to later recreate the **Cuvilliés Theater** in its full artistic perfection on another site.

Since 1958 the theater has once again provided a magnificent setting for selected drama and opera productions. On its original site, between the Residenz and the National Theater, the **Neues Residenz Theater** was built after the war.

The last Wittelsbach ruler to leave his mark on the Residenz was Ludwig I, who enlarged it as a royal palace in the neoclassical style. In particular, the north and south façades were remodelled on Italian lines by Leo von Klenze.

On the north side, a suite of state reception-rooms, the **Festsaalbau**, was built and today is occupied by the Bavarian Academy of Sciences. On the south side, the three-sectioned façade of the **Königsbau** (King's Building) is unmistakably inspired by the Pitti Palace in Florence. Inside, the rooms are decorated with murals whose themes are classical or literary; partcularly impressive are the **Nibelungen rooms**.

Situated in the King's Building is the **Schatzkammer**, or Treasure Chamber; although the word "chamber" only inadequately characterizes this large and important collection. Alongside the crown jewels there are many fine examples of

the goldsmith's art, both religious and secular, as well as jewels from the Byzantine to the classical periods. The rulers of Bavaria began assembling their **State Coin Collection** during the Middle Ages, but the general public is only allowed to see a small, albeit interesting, portion of it.

Fitting in well among the group of buildings around Max-Joseph-Platz, the **National Theater** was built on the site of a Franciscan monastery that had been demolished during secularization. The building, designed by Karl von Fischer, is distinguished by a simple colonnaded front, with a pediment containing two triangular tympana, or gables, in echelon. In 1823, only a few years after its completion, it burned down but was rebuilt by von Klenze according to the original plans. After World War II it was restored for a third time to its former glory.

Above: De luxe display on Maximilianstrasse. Right: The "Max Two" monument.

In 1447, when the Franciscan monastery stood on that site, the monks, in time-honored tradition, built their own brewery with a simple inn attached. That same inn, the **Franziskaner Poststüberl**, still exists today, though it is no longer quite so simple, since it now has a series of extremely welcoming rooms to eat and drink in.

Maximilianstrasse

From Max-Joseph-Platz there is an impressive view along **Maximilianstrasse**, across the Isar to the *Maximilianeum*, perched high on the far bank of the river. King Maximilan II, or "Max Two" as the Bavarians informally refer to him, ruled from 1848 to 1864, and added a neo-Gothic avenue to the neo-classical buidings of the Residenz. And, although the traffic-planners of the 1960s sliced ruthlessly through it with the *Altsdtadtring* (Inner Ring Road), it still preserves a homogeneous character. With its monuments, theaters, museums and other fine

buildings, Maximilianstrasse has become the showpiece of Munich. In addition to the National and Residenz theaters, you will find six other theatrical venues here: the **Kammerspiele** and, on side-streets, the **Marstall Theater** and the **Werkraum**; and further down, beyond the ring-road, the **Kleine Komödie** near the **Max II monument**.

Architecturally, the finest theater is the **Schauspielhaus**, designed by Max Littmann and Richard Riemerschmid and built in 1900. It is a superb example of Jugendstil, Germany's version of Art Nouveau, right down to the door handles and faucets in the washrooms.

A good dozen galleries and art and antique shops, as well as high-class clothing stores, have established themselves in sterling luxury on Maximillianstrasse. Designers whose fashions can be found here include Moshammer, Yves Saint Laurent, Gucci, Kenzo and Hermes.

Prominent guests – from heads of state to rock stars – usually stay at the exclusive **Hotel Kempinski Vier Jahreszeiten** (Four Seasons), a hotel rich in tradition founded in the mid-19th century. (Maximilianstrasse beyond the Altstadtring is described on p. 151.)

KREUZVIERTEL

A great many town houses were sacrificed to make way for the construction of the Residenz, since the huge complex extended far into the surrounding area known as the **Kreuzviertel**. The nobility naturally wanted to be within easy reach of the court, and so built houses of their own in this quarter. Later on, the houses became palaces, some of which have survived to this day.

However, **Residenzstrasse** remained the province of the solid, well-to-do citizenry, as did the street parallel to it, **Theatinerstrasse**, which used to provide a direct route to the northern gate of the city, **Schwabinger Tor**.

The reshaping of this district to create the impressive group of buildings around Odeonsplatz added a further cachet to the

streets between Marienplatz and Odeonsplatz. Since the war they have become elegant and expensive shopping streets. Because street frontage was not sufficient to meet commercial demand, passages and arcades were built through the blocks, linking the streets.

In 1975, **Theatinerstrasse** and the entire area down to Marienplatz was turned into a pedestrian zone. Here there are such exclusive shops as Etienne Aigner, Burberry and Escada. In the **Kunsthalle der Hypo-Kulturstiftung** art gallery, exhibitions of world-class contemporary art are on display. There are also a few attractive cafés in and around this street, among them **Café Arzmiller**, in the midst of the elegant atmosphere of the **Theatinerhof**.

At the northern end of the street, between Theatinerstrasse and Residenzstrasse and just behind the Feldherrnhalle, stands **Preysing Palace**. Built by Effner in 1728, this fine rococo building was largely destroyed in the war, but has since been restored in every detail.

Other former palaces of the nobility can be seen on Prannerstrasse, Kardinal-Faulhaber-Strasse and Promenadeplatz. Miraculously, this corner of the city was spared the destruction of war, which was especially fortunate for the rococo buildings on Kardinal-Faulhaber-Strasse. Here, at No. 6, stands **Graf Spreti Palace** (1720), at No. 7 **Holnstein Palace** and at No. 12 **Porcia Palace**. In between them, the frontages of some Jugendstil houses blend harmoniously.

On Prannerstrasse you can see **Seinsheim Palace** (1764) and **Gise Palace** (1760). Opposite these, it comes as something of a surprise to find the **Siemens Museum** extending over several houses. The prestigious headquarters of the Siemens corporation is on nearby Wittelsbacher Platz, and the museum contains an impressive record of technical achievement. With loving attention to detail, the progress of Siemens is shown – from the first prototype automobile, through early telegraph equipment, to the advanced micro-electronics of today.

Confronted by all this aristocratic splendor, the Gothic **Salvator Church** on Salvatorplatz seems rather modest. The simple brick building, dating from 1494-99 in the reign of Albrecht IV, was deconsecrated in the 18th century. However, in 1828 Ludwig I had it restored to its proper purpose and handed it over to Munich's recently established Greek Orthodox community. The interior, with its carpets, icons and candle sticks, seems remarkably cozy, despite its curious blend of Gothic, Bavarian mural-painting and eastern mysticism.

The former Salvator School, directly beside the church, became the home of the **Literaturhaus München** in 1997. On the ground floor, which was used as a market hall in the 19th century, there are

Above: In Munich, if you've got it, flaunt it!
Right: Palatial façade on Kardinal-Faulhaber-Strasse.

exhibits relating to books and authors, and readings are also held here. There is a large coffee house with a terrace in the building (on the Kardinal-Faulhaber-Strasse side). In addition to an international library, various institutions dealing with books and media are now located here as well.

If you carry on past the church and onto **Jungfernturmstrasse**, you come to the only surviving section of the old city wall, built in 1337 under Ludwig the Bavarian. Going the other way, you see the large **Ministry of Education** building in the former Theatiner monastery.

On Kardinal-Faulhaber-Strasse and on Promenadeplatz, the leading banks are housed in palaces once owned by the aristocracy. The old Kreuzstrasse was widened into the broad Promenadeplatz to accomodate the salt trade, Munich's most important source of revenue until the 18th century. When the salt-market was moved to Arnulfstrasse in 1780, the storehouses were demolished and grand new buildings put up in their place.

Today the square is dominated by the **Hotel Bayrischer Hof**, which incorporates the former **Preysing-Neuhaus Palace** (built by Cuvilliés the Elder) and the neo-classical **Montgelas Palace** (1811). This has long been one of Munich's top hotel choices. Opposite you can see the charming rococo façade of the **Gunetzrainer House**, named after the Court Architect who built it for himself in 1730.

At the western end of Promenadeplatz is the striking façade of the **Dreifaltigkeitskirche** (Trinity Church). It was built because of a vision in which someone foresaw divine retribution that could only be averted by the construction of a church. It has a central dome, designed by Viscardi in 1718, every inch of the interior of which is covered with stucco and frescos by C. D. Asam. Diagonally across from the church stands the only remaining tower of the **Maxburg**, built in the late 16th century as a residence for electors in their old age. Crossing its courtyard and following **Maxburgstrasse**, you come back to Lenbachplatz.

CITY CENTER / TAL
MAIN STATION / MARIENPLATZ

Transport Connections

S-BAHN: S1-S8 to Hauptbahnhof, Karlsplatz (Stachus), Marienplatz, Isartorplatz.

U-BAHN: U1 to Sendlinger Tor, Hauptbahnhof, Stiglmaierplatz. U2 to Königsplatz, Hauptbahnhof, Sendlinger Tor. U3/6 to Sendlinger Tor, Marienplatz, Odeonsplatz. U4/5 to Hauptbahnhof, Karlsplatz (Stachus), Odeonsplatz.

BUS: No. 52 from Marienplatz to Blumenstraße. No. 53 to Odeonsplatz. No. 56 from Sendlinger Tor to Blumenstrasse. No. 58 from Hauptbahnhof to Georg Hirth Platz.

STREETCAR: Nos. 17 and 18 to Isartor, Reichenbachplatz, Müllerstrasse, Sendlinger Tor, Karlsplatz (Stachus), Ottostrasse. No. 19 to Hauptbahnhof, Karlsplatz (Stachus), Lenbachplatz.

Nos. 18, 20 and 25 to Hauptbahnhof, Karlsplatz (Stachus), Sendlinger Tor, Müllerstrasse.

Restaurants / Cafés / Night-life

TRADITIONAL BAVARIAN FOOD with Beergarden: **Augustiner-Bräu**, Neuhauser Str. 27, Tel. 55199257, reservation advisable; **Augustiner-Keller**, Arnulfstr. 52, tel. 594393, with large beer garden; **Franziskaner-Fuchsenstuben**, Residenzstr. 9, tel. 2318120, popular for weisswurst.

BAVARIAN: **Altes Hackerhaus**, Sendlinger Str. 14, tel. 2605026, service in summer in the small, romantic courtyard; **Andechser am Dom**, Weinstr. 7a, tel. 298481, Andech's beer with classic Bavarian food; **Biergarten am Viktualienmarkt**, Viktualienmarkt 9, tel. 297545, cozy seating in the shade of chestnut trees; **Donisl**, Weinstr. 1, tel. 2296264, traditional restaurant on Marienplatz; **Haxnbauer**, Sparkassenstr., tel. 221922, reservation advisable, speciality: pork shank roasted on open fire, expensive; **Hofbräuhaus**, Am Platzl 9, tel. 221676, very popular with tourists from all over the world; **Hundskugel**, Hotterstr. 18, tel. 264272, oldest Munich inn, good but expensive; **Nürnberger Bratwurstglöckl am Dom**, Frauenplatz 9, tel. 220385; **Pauliner im Tal** (formerly Bogner), Tal 12, tel. 2199400. **Spöckmeier**, Rosenstr. 9, tel: 268088, hearty Bavarian food with dumplings, high prices, always full; **Straubinger Hof**, Blumenstr. 5, tel. 2608444, open Sat until 3 am, closed Sun, average prices; **Weisses Bräuhaus**, Tal 7, tel. 299875, weissbier specialities; **Zum Dürnbräu**, Dürnbräugasse 2, tel. 222195, hot meals until 11:30 am.

GOURMET CUISINE: **Boettner**, Theatinerstr. 8, tel. 221210, open 11 am to 11 pm (hot meals until 8:30), Sat 11 am to 3 pm, closed Sun. Finest oysters, lobster, salmon and caviar, expensive.

SPECIALITY CUISINE: **Bouillabaisse**, Falkenturmstr. 10, tel. 297909, Tue-Sat noon to 2:30 pm, 6 pm to 1 am, Mon from 7 pm, closed Sun. French fish specialities, good but expensive; **Buxs**, Frauenstr. 9, at Viktualienmarkt, tel. 293684, Mon-Fri 11 am to 8:30 pm, Sat 11 am-3:30 pm, vegetarian, self-service, large choice of salads, organic wine; **Geisel's Vinothek**, Schützenstr. 11, tel. 55137140, Mon-Sat 10 am to 1 am (kitchen open noon to 11:30 pm), at main station, inside tip for wine fans; **Goldene Stadt**, Oberanger 44, tel. 264382, Czech cuisine, closed Mon; **Hammadan**, Augustenstr. 1 (corner of Karlstr.), tel. 554210 or 596058, 11:30 am to 3 pm, 6 pm to midnight, Iranian cuisine; **Palais Keller**, in Hotel Bayerischer Hof, Promenadenplatz 2, Tel. 221255, international specialities; **Lenbach**, Ottostr. 6, tel. 5491300, new gourmet temple of Käfer delicatessen, meeting place of the rich and beautiful; **Planet Hollywood**, Am Platzl 1, tel. 29030500, Hollywood in Munich, tasty food, great cocktails; **Restaurant Alois Dallmayr**, Dienerstr. 14-15, tel. 2135100, Mon-Fri 9:30 am to 8 pm, Sat 9 am to 4 pm, reservation advisable; **Mövenpick**, Lenbachplatz 8, tel. 5459490, speciality weeks (e.g., game, asparagus), Sun brunch 10 am to 2:30 pm, "Happy Afternoon" with cake buffet; **Vitamin-Buffet**, Herzog-Wilhelm-Str. 25, Tel: 2607418, Mon-Sat 11 am to 10 pm, vegetarian, average prices.

TRENDY CAFÉS with good food: **Kaffeehaus Dukatz**, Salvatorplatz 1 (in Literaturhaus), tel. 2919600, popular with the well-off older crowd, reservations evenings; **Internet Café**, Arkade-Passage, Altheimer-Eck 12, tel. 2607815, inexpensive food; **Iwan**, Josephspitalstr. 15, Tel: 554933, 11 am to 3 am, Italian food, Thai food Tuesdays, medium price range, outdoor seating in summer; **Metropolitan**, Marienplatz 22, tel. 2309770, romantic restaurant with a view; **Stadtcafé im Stadtmuseum**, St. Jakobsplatz 1, tel. 266949, 11 am to midnight, Mon 5 pm to midnight, Fri-Sat until 1 am, snacks, salads, popular brunch place, full evenings, cozy garden.

OTHER CAFÉS: **Bodo's**, coffe, ice-cream and pastries. Herzog-Wilhelm-Str. 29, tel. 263673, Mon-Fri 7 am to 9 pm, Sat 8 am to 8 pm, Sun 10 am to 8 pm, sun-terrace open in summer, breakfast served into the afternoon, medium price-range; **Café Glockenspiel**, Marienplatz 28 (entrance Rosenstr.) tel. 264256, 10 am to 1 am, lovely view of Marienplatz; **Café im Valentin-Musäum**, Isartor, tel. 223266, Sat, Mon, Tue 11:01 am to 5:29 pm, Sun from 10:01 am, pastries served upstairs in the tower.

BARS: **Master's Home**, Frauenstr. 11, tel. 229909, 6 pm to 1 am, imaginative decor, good cocktails, fancy prices; **Nachtcafé**, Maximilianstr. 5, tel. 595900, 7 pm to 5 am, popular with night people, live music; **Park Café**, Sophienstr. 7, tel. 598313, Tue-Thu 10 pm to 4 am, Fri-Sat 10 pm to 7 am,

GUIDEPOST INNER CITY

trendy rendez-vous with hand-picked clientele, with disco; **Pfälzer Weinprobierstube**, Residenzstr. 1, tel. 225628, excellent selection of wines and delightful atmosphere in a romantic vault of the Residenz.

DISCOS: **Atomic café**, Neuturmstr. 5, tel. 2283054, "In" club with original decor from the 70s, music from beat to acid-jazz, live bands regularly; **Far Out**, Neuturmstr. 5, tel. 226661, Wed-Sun 10 pm to 4 am, young crowd, dancefloor music; **Maximilian's Nightclub**, Maximiliansplatz 16, tel. 223252, 10 pm to 4 am; **Soul City**, Maximiliansplatz 553301, Wed-Sun 10 pm to 4 am, sould and blues for good-looking guys, easy-listening; **Wunderbar**, Hochbrückenstr. 3, tel. 295118, Tue, Thu, Sun 8 pm to 3 am, Fri-Sat 8 pm to 4 am, Tue table telephone party, Wed gay party.

Sightseeing

CHURCHES: **Alter Peter**, Rindermarkt 1, climb to the top of the tower for a spectacular all-round view. Take S1-8, or U3/6 to Marienplatz; **Asamkirche**, Sendlinger Str. 61, take U1/2 and U3/6 to Sendlinger Tor; **Damenstiftkirche St. Anna**, Damenstiftstr. 1, take S1-8, U 3/4 or U5/6 to Karlsplatz (Stachus) or Marienplatz; **Dreifaltigkeitskirche**, Pacellistr. 6, take S1-8, U4/5 or streetcar No. 19 to Karlsplatz (Stachus); **Frauenkirche**, Frauenplatz 1, Munich's trade-mark, take S1-7, U3/6 to Marienplatz or U4/5 to Karlsplatz, rococo church. **Heilig-Geist-Kirche**, Tal 77, take S1-8, U3/6 to Marienplatz. Renaissance church of **St. Michael**, Neuhauser Str. 52, take S1-8, U3/6 to Marienplatz; Sankt Michael, Neuheuser Str. 52, take S1-8, U3/6 or U4/5 to Marienplatz or Karlsplatz (Stachus); **Salvatorkirche**, Promenadeplatz, take streetcar No. 19 to Lenbachplatz.

SQUARES / PALACES: **Isartorplatz**, take S1-8 to Isartor; **Karlsplatz** and Karlstor gate, take S1-8, U4/5 to Karlsplatz (Stachus); **Lenbachplatz** and Künstlerhaus am Lenbachplatz, S1-8 to Karlsplatz (Stachus) or streetcar No. 19 to Lenbachplatz;. **Marienplatz**, Neues and Altes Rathaus and Mariensäule, take S1-8 or U3/6 to Marienplatz; **Promenadeplatz** and **Holnstein Palace** (No. 7) the rococo **Porcia Palace** (No. 12) and the neo-classical **Montgelas Palace; Residenz**, Max-Joseph-Platz 3, including Alter Residenz, Königsbau, Festsaalbau. Tue-Sat 10 am to 4:30 pm, Sun until 1 pm, entry charge. Take U3/4 or U5/6 or bus No. 53 to Odeonsplatz, streetcar No. 19 to Nationaltheater; **Residenzmuseum** and **Schatzkammer der Residenz** (Treasure Chamber), Tue-Sun 10 am to 4:30 pm, entry charge.

Free Time

Alter Botanischer Garten, Elisenstr./Sophienstr., near the Hauptbahnhof, take S1-8, U1/2 or U4/5 to Hauptbahnhof or Karlsplatz (Stachus); **Viktualienmarkt**, Munich's liveliest and most famous food-market, should definitely not be missed. Reached by S1-8, U3/6 to Marienplatz.

Hospital

Polyklinik, Nussbaumstr. 2, tel. 51600.

Pharmacies

International pharmacies: Bahnhofs-Apotheke, Bahnhofsplatz 2, tel. 594119; Ludwigs-Apotheke, Neuhauser Str. 11, Tel: 2603021 (in the pedestrian zone); Schützen-Apotheke, Schützenstr. 5, tel. 557661-63 (at Hauptbahnhof).

Police

Polizeipräsidium München, (City police HQ) Ettstr. 2, tel. 2141.

Post Offices

Postamt 1: Residenzstr. 2, Main Post Office (Hauptpostamt), Mon-Fri 8 am to 6 pm, Sat 8 am to 1 pm; **Postamt 2**: Arnulfstr. 21 (corner Seidlstr.), Mon-Fri 8 am to 8 pm, Sat 8 am to noon; **Postamt 3** (in the Hauptbahnhof), Mon-Fri 7 am to 8 pm, Sat 8 am to 4 pm, Sun and holidays 9 am to 3 pm.

Currency Exchange

At the Hauptbahnhof: Wechselstuben der DVKB, 6 am to 11 pm, tel. 5510837;

At the airport: Wechselstube der DVKB, 6:15 am to 10 pm, tel. 9701721.

Banks: Dresdner Bank, Bayerstr. 4, (in the Hauptbahnhof) tel. 593794; Promenadeplatz 7, tel. 29190; Sonnenstr. 3, tel. 592261. Deutsche Bank, Marienplatz 21, tel. 2604039. Commerzbank, Maximiliansplatz 21, tel. 21961; Sendlinger Str. 65, tel. 2608020; Schwanthalerstr. 39, tel. 554261. Kreissparkasse München, main branch, Sendlinger-Tor-Platz 1, tel. 238010. Stadtsparkasse München, Sparkassenstr. 2, tel. 21670; Bayerstr. 69, tel. 530037; Sendlinger Tor, an EC cash-dispenser (all EC currencies) can be found in the concourse of the U-Bahn station.

Tourist Information

Fremdenverkehrsamt München (Munich Tourist Office: for finding rooms, hiring guides and buses, help with arranging your program) Sendlinger Str. 1, tel. 2330300, Mon-Thu 9 am to 3 pm. Fri 9 am to 12:30 pm. At the Hauptbahnhof: beside main entrance (Bahnhofplatz), tel. 23330256, Mon-Sat 9 am to 8 pm, Sun 9 am to 6 pm. At the airport: Central Area, tel. 2330300, Mon-Fri 10 am to 8 pm, Sat-Sun 10 am to 6 pm (see also Travel Information, p. 245). Tourismusverband Oberbayern, (Upper Bavarian Tourist Association) Bodenseestr. 113, tel. 8292180.

Taxi Stands

Karlsplatz (Stachus), tel. 2161334; Maximiliansplatz, tel. 2161334; Isartorplatz, tel. 216124. Reichenbachplatz, tel. 2161331; Stiglmaierplatz, tel. 594341 or 216129; Schillerstr., tel. 216128.

ODEONSPLATZ

SCHWABING

ODEONSPLATZ
LUDWIGSTRASSE
MAXVORSTADT
KÖNIGSPLATZ
LEOPOLDSTRASSE
ALT-SCHWABING
OLYMPIA PARK
ENGLISCHER GARTEN

AROUND ODEONSPLATZ

From 1319 until 1791, the northern gate of the city, Schwabinger Tor, stood on the site where the *Feldherrnhalle* (Hall of the Generals) now stands. Ludwigstrasse was once called Schwabinger Landstrasse. The streets on either side of Schwabinger Tor (Theatinerstrasse and Residenzstrasse), were formerly called *Vordere* and *Hintere Schwabinger Gasse* (Front Lane and Back Lane). Back then, as you were leaving the city from Schwabinger Tor, you could see the old village of Schwabing.

Odeonsplatz was given its present neoclassical appearance in the years 1816-28, when Leo von Klenze used the square as a starting point for two broad streets, Ludwigstrasse and Brienner Strasse. He managed to harmonically integrate the existing Theatiner church, built much earlier in the Italian high-baroque style.

However, the most eye-catching building on Odeonsplatz is the **Feldherrnhalle**, with its three massive arches and steps flanked by the two lions of Bavaria. This monument was erected by Ludwig I in honor of two commanders of the Ba-

Preceding pages: Pageantry at the Feldherrnhalle. Left: Looking from the Hofgarten Café across to theTheatiner church.

varian army, Tilly and Wrede. Designed by Friedrich von Gärtner on the lines of the Loggia dei Lanzi in Florence, it was completed in 1844. The bronze statues of the two generals are by Ludwig Schwanthaler, and on the back wall is a later memorial, by Ferdinand von Miller, to the Bavarian soldiers who fell in the Franco-Prussian War (1870-71). A ground plaque was placed into the pavement before the monument in 1995, recalling Hitler's failed putsch of 1923 and the many citizens and policemen who laid down their lives at the end of this infamous demonstration.

One of the most beautiful churches in Munich, the ochre-colored **Theatinerkirche**, is on Theatinerstrasse just beside the Feldherrnhalle. It was modeled on the church of San Andrea del Valle in Rome, and designed by Agostino Barelli, who oversaw the first phase of construction in 1663-75. In the second phase, ending in 1690, his successor Enrico Zuccalli completed the 230-foot (71 m) dome and added the two towers which were not part of the original plans. The present-day façade, in late rococo style, was not completed until 1765-68 under Max III Joseph, who commissioned it from François Cuvilliés and his son. The exterior of the church is particularly notable for the arrangement of its façade, as well as the

HOFGARTEN

snail-like decorations on its towers which, together with those of Frauenkirche and Peterskirche, are the most characteristic features of the Munich skyline. The interior is dominated by high rounded arches and the dome. Beneath the high altar lies one of the burial vaults of the Wittelsbachs.

Situated roughly between Theatiner Church and the beginning of Brienner Strasse nearby, stands **Moy Palace**. It was built by von Klenze in 1819, and its neo-classical architecture blends surprisingly well with the baroque style of the neighboring Theatiner Church. Nowadays, the ground floor provides showrooms for the glamorous coachwork of Mercedes-Benz.

Hofgarten

The Hofgarten complex stretches away to the east of the Feldherrnhalle, starting with a gateway, the **Hofgartentor**, with the **Hofgarten Arkaden** (arcades) on either side of it. These gardens were laid out according to the principles of Italian garden design as early as 1613-17 under Maximilian I, and have remained more or less unaltered to the present day.

The centerpiece of the garden is the **Temple**, a twelve-sided pavilion from 1615, with eight large rounded arches. The southern boundary of the Hofgarten is formed by **Hofgarten Strasse** and the Residenz buildings. The main entrances of both **Herkulessaal** (Hercules Hall) in the Residenz, and the **Staatliche Sammlung Ägyptischer Kunst** (State Collection of Egyptian Art) are situated on Hofgartenstrasse.

The *Basargebäude* (Bazaar Building) by von Klenze is near the arcades, at the western end of the Hofgarten. It has several shops and other attractions, including the **Film Casino** and the bistro-restaurant **Käfer's am Hofgarten**. Facing Odeonsplatz is a "classic" Munich coffee house, **Café Tambosi**; in summer you

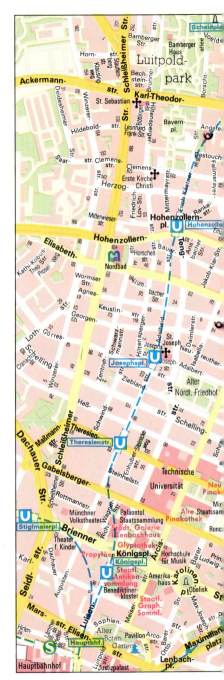

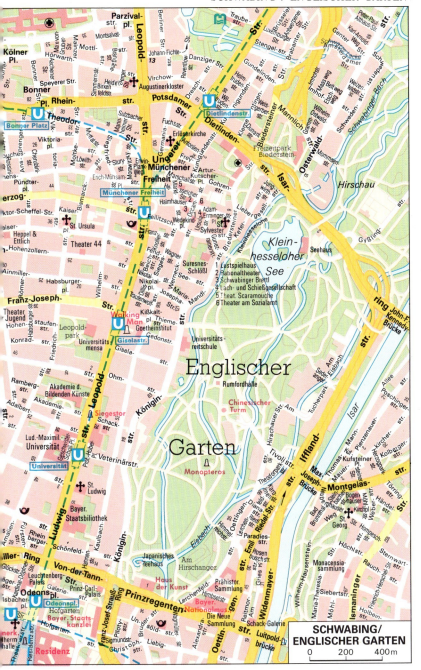

can enjoy a drink in their beer garden, which looks out onto the Hofgarten.

At the northern edge of the garden you will find the **Galeriegebäude** (Galeriestrasse 4), built by Elector Karl Theodor in 1780-81 as his personal art gallery above the Hofgarten arcades. After the opening of the Alte Pinakothek, the gallery was handed over to the **Münchner Kunstverein** (Munich Arts Association), founded in 1824. The building suffered considerable damage during the Second World War, was restored, and is once again the home of the *Kunstverein* with its regularly changing exhibitions. It also houses several other galleries and the **German Theater Museum**.

The east side of the gardens are dominated by the modern building of the **Bavarian State Chancellery**, into which the dome of the former Bavarian Army Museum is incorporated.

Above: The Hofgarten in winter. Right: The spring sunshine brings people outside at Café Tambosi in the Hofgarten.

Leo von Klenze modelled **Leuchtenberg Palace** (on the west side of Odeonsplatz) on the *Palazzo Farnese* in Rome, and built it between 1816 and 1821. Count von Leuchtenberg was the exiled viceroy of Italy and son-in-law of Max I Joseph. The former **Odeon** which gave the square its name was built by von Klenze in 1826-28 as a permanent venue for balls and concerts. It now complements the architectural style of Leuchtenberg Palace in a pleasing and harmonious way. During the 19th and early 20th centuries, it played an important part in the music scene of Munich. Though almost completely destroyed in the Second World War, it has been partially rebuilt and today houses the Bavarian Ministry of the Interior.

LUDWIGSTRASSE

Ludwigstrasse, which forms a link between Odeonsplatz and the Feldherrnhalle at one end, and the *Siegestor* (Victory Gate) over half a mile (1 km) away,

impresses with its austere simplicity. It is one of the most architecturally convincing boulevards in Europe and has echoes of Florence or Rome. This is no coincidence: when Ludwig I commissioned the avenue in 1816, it was part of his plan to make Munich an Athens of the modern age. Two architects in particular were instrumental in shaping the character of Ludwigstrasse in the years 1816-52; Court Architect Leo von Klenze, who designed the southern part (modeled on his Leuchtenberg Palace), and his successor, Friedrich von Gärtner, who in building the northern section continued to employ Italian stylistic elements, thus binding the *Staatsbibliothek* (State Library), Ludwigskirche and the University into one elegantly integrated ensemble.

The succession of rather impersonal state office and administrative buildings which line Ludwigstrasse today were not originally planned for the street; the elegantly-appointed palaces, decorated with frescoes, were originally to contain apartments for the wealthy and well-born.

Another building worth mentioning is the former **Kriegsministerium** (Bavarian Ministry of War) at No. 14. The ornamentation on the façade gives more than a hint of its military purpose; it is typical of von Klenze's work and was linked to the **Kommandaturgebäude** (Army High Command Building) which von Klenze had built in 1826 in **Schönfeldstrasse**, just off of Ludwigstrasse. The wings flanking the building and the set-back façade emphasize the grandeur of its broad ceremonial courtyard.

The **Staatsbibliothek** (Bavarian State Library), at No. 16, was designed by von Gärtner, who recieved the commission in 1827, in the style of an Italian renaissance palace, but work on the building was only undertaken in the years 1832-1843 due to lack of funds. The four sculptures in contemplative poses beside the flight of steps leading up to the entrance are the work of Ludwig Schwanthaler and represent Thucydides, Homer, Aristotle and Hippocrates. However, the present figures are only replicas of the

LUDWIGSTRASSE / UNIVERSITY

originals which were badly damaged during the war.

Today, the library has the most extensive scientific collection in Germany, containing more than six million books and over 32,600 current periodicals. In addition, there is a collection of hand-printed manuscripts and over 80,000 rare editions, as well as a musical collection, a Middle East, Oriental and eastern European collection, and a vast cartographic collection, with 250,000 maps and 800 atlases.

Next to the library, **Ludwigskirche** (built by von Gärtner 1829-44) affords some vertical relief to the austere classical façades of Ludwigstrasse. The church was conceived at the same time as an impressive conclusion to Schellingstrasse, which ends here. The church's towers, which resemble Italian campaniles, are rather eye-catching. In the interior of the church one of the largest frescos in the world can be found: the enormous *Last Judgment* by Peter Cornelius. Other frescos in the church are also by Cornelius. Directly beside the church is a popular café where students and people just strolling through town like to meet: **Café an der Uni**.

Further on, the sidewalks along Ludwigstrasse become increasingly lively, as it is only a little way from here to **Geschwister-Scholl-Platz** and the Ludwig-Maximilian University. In 1945, the square in front of the university was named in memory of a brother and sister, Hans and Sophie Scholl, who formed the *Weisse Rose* (White Rose) resistance group in active opposition to Hitler's dictatorship. After distributing anti-Hitler leaflets in the main assembly hall of the university they were arrested. Four days later they were tried by the president of the People's Court of Justice, Roland Freisler, who was specially flown in for the trial, following which they were both executed.

The broad forum of the square, with its two large dish-shaped fountains to the left and right of Ludwigstrasse, and the three-winged buildings of **Ludwig-Maximilian University**, provide a welcome relief in the otherwise severe and uninterrupted frontage of buildings along Ludwigstrasse. Munich's university has the second-largest student population in Germany (65,000) after the Free University of Berlin, and is gradually bursting at the seams under the annual influx of ever more students; during the university strike in the winter 1997/98 semester, for example, classes were even held in moving U-Bahn trains.

The university was founded in 1472 in Ingolstadt by Duke Ludwig the Rich, then transferred to Landshut in 1800 by the Elector Max IV Joseph. This is why two patrons are commemorated in its name. Finally, in 1826, Ludwig I moved it to Munich. Its handsome building was

Above: View of Ludwigskirche from Schellingstrasse. Right: The university seen from Professor-Huber-Platz.

constructed by von Gärtner (1835-40). The *Aula* (assembly hall; from 1909) is worth seeing, as is the *Lichthof* (atrium).

At the northern end of Ludwigstrasse, just beyond the university, stands the **Siegestor** (Victory Gate), one of the emblems of Munich, beyond which Leopoldstrasse begins. Ludwig I had the Siegestor built in gratitude to the Bavarian Army. It was built by Friedrich von Gärtner in 1843-52, and modelled on the Arch of Constantine in Rome. The Second World War left it extensively damaged, and during restoration the upper section was left unfinished, adding instead the inscription: *Dem Sieg geweiht, vom Kriege zerstört, zum Frieden mahnend.* (Dedicated to victory, destroyed by war, urging us to peace). The gate is crowned by a bronze statue of Bavaria in a lion-drawn chariot.

MAXVORSTADT

After passing through the Siegestor, most visitors to Munich will now be keen to stroll down Leopoldstrasse, which begins here, and experience the legend of Schwabing. Alas, not much remains of it beyond a few clichés. But why go any further, if what you are looking for is here at hand, as the Siegestor is already in Schwabing or, to be exact, in the part of Schwabing which is known as **Maxvorstadt**; an area which extends to the west of Ludwigstrasse as far as Schleissheimer Strasse.

The name of this district dates from the first planned extension of the city by Elector Max IV Joseph, who in 1807 launched Germany's first competition for urban design. The grid-like street pattern of Maxvorstadt, between Briennerstrasse and Georgenstrasse, was based on plans by von Sckell and von Fischer. This first-ever German "new housing development" is still characterized by houses and buildings in the relatively recent styles of late neo-classicism, neo-renaissance, and Jugendstil.

Nowadays, Maxvorstadt is dominated by Ludwig-Maximilian University, and

the nearby **Technische Universität** (University of Technology), with a huge complex of buildings bounded by Theresienstrasse, Barerstrasse, Luisenstrasse and Gabelsbergerstrasse. Generations of students have left their mark on life in Maxvorstadt. Probably no other part of Munich has so many cafés, pubs, new and secondhand bookshops, copy shops, travel agencies and other small businesses, as the area round the university.

The best place to begin your stroll around Maxvorstadt is probably the Universität underground station. During the opening hours of the university you can use the main entrance and its atrium, which is worth seeing, as a short cut to **Amalienstrasse**. Then, turning right towards Adelbertstrasse, the building of the **Akademie der Bildenden Künste** (Academy of Fine Arts) catches your eye. The three-story main building with two-story wings and a wide approach ramp

Above: The Siegestor – "Dedicated to victory... urging us to peace."

was built between 1874 and 1884 by Gottfried von Neureuther, who drew heavily on stylistic elements of the Italian High Renaissance. The impressive south façade attracts the eye with its closely spaced rows of arched windows and strikingly beautiful friezes.

If you double back along Amalienstrasse, you will find the **Amalienpassage** at No. 91. This passage through to Türkenstrasse is a successful example of renovating old properties and making more creative use of their inner courtyards. The complex, built from 1975 to 1977, includes 200 apartments, many small boutiques, cafés and bistros, a natural food store and copy shop, tea specialities and a gallery. You can enjoy French cuisine in the bistro, **Petit France**, dine on Italian fare in **Lunis** (where one can sit comfortably outside, too) and, if you want to rub shoulders with stars of the film and pop worlds, you will be in good company at **Rosario**. A favorite spot for meeting up is the **Oase** café, at the center of the Amalienpassage, surrounded by small shops selling crafts from Mexico, India and the Far East.

Back on Amalienstrasse you pass by various bookshops until, just before Schellingstrasse, you come upon **Café Schneller** at No. 59. From the outside it is rather inconspicuous, yet it is popular with students and local residents alike. Despite its unpretentious decor, the café is considered to be unique by Schwabing's insiders. On the other side of the street, at the corner of Schellingstrasse, is **Atzinger**, a restaurant which has been an institution for generations of students. Those who want to share a table with people from the press will fit in well at the chic **News Bar**, directly opposite.

Otherwise, the area around the university belongs, of course, to the numerous book dealers hereabouts, such as, for example, **Hueber** (Amalienstr. 77-79) and **Basis Buchhandlung** (modern used books; Adelbertstr. 41b-43). Schellingstrasse is recommended to those looking for older used books or rare editions – **Hauser** (No. 17) and **Kitzinger** (No. 25) bookshops – as well as those who are in the market for English-language books, with both **Word's Worth** (No. 21a) and the somewhat chaotic **Anglia English Bookshop** (No. 3) providing a good selection of reading matter.

The artist Paul Klee lived in the late-classical house at Amalienstrasse 39 from 1898 to 1999. No. 25 on the same street was *the* address for Munich artists at the beginning of the century, as it was here that the legendary Café Stefanie – usually known as Café Grössenwahn (Megalomania Café) – was once located. A few steps further on, at No. 45, **S. M. Vegetarisch** offers Asian tidbits and snacks. Across the street, at No. 38, the **Munix** café is popular with the in-crowd and has light meals on offer.

Another very lively street runs parallel to Amalienstrasse: **Türkenstrasse**, which offers visitors the Munich way of life in all its nuances, with its cafés, pubs, boutiques, antique-dealers and other shops. One of the best-known of all Munich's pubs is located here, **Alter Simpl**, which has long since become a Munich institution and certainly helped create the "myth of Schwabing." Alter Simpl is the oldest bohemian café in Schwabing. Way back in 1903, Kathi Kobus opened her artists' pub, *Simplicissimus*, named after the satirical magazine whose contributors were amongst her regular customers. The sign, a red bull dog, was created by Thomas Theodor Heine. From 1902 on the Norwegian Olaf Gulbransson, who "got stuck" living at Lake Tegernsee, also belonged to the ranks of the magazines artists. The poet Joachim Ringelnatz and playwright Frank Wedekind were often seen in the Alter Simpl, as well as the painter Franz Marc and the cabaret comedian Karl Valentin. The Alter Simpl managed to retain something of its aura even after the Second World War, but by then there was very little left of the fine old satirical spirit of *Simplicissimus*; instead of the house poet, Joachim Ringelnatz, one was more likely to meet German stars or members of Munich's glitterati here.

At Türkenstrasse 74 there is one of the most unusual cinemas in Munich. It is called the **Türkendolch** (The Turk's Dagger), on account of the long, narrow shape of the seating area. The modern **Arri-Kino** (at No. 91), with its espresso bar in the foyer where you can also get a bite to eat, is one of the most pleasant of all Munich's cinemas. It is situated in a building complex belonging to Arnold & Richter, makers of the world-famous Arriflex cameras and film projectors.

If you want a bite to eat before seeing a film, you will be well provided for on Türkenstrasse. Among the many inexpensive restaurants are **Türkenhof** (No. 78) and **Engelsburg** (No. 51). Then there are a number of pleasant cafés, for example the **Café Puck** (across the street from Sausalito, a Mexican restaurant at

No. 50), **Café u.s.w.** (No. 54), **Eiscafé Adria** (No. 59) or **Vorstadtcafé** (on the corner of Adalbertstrasse). For night owls there is always **Charivari**, open until 3 a.m. (Fri-Sat until 4 a.m.).

Not far away, at Adalbertstrasse 33, you will find a pub-restaurant in the great Maxvorstadt tradition: the **Max-Emanuel-Brauerei** (Brewery). Its shady beer garden is a magnet for the colorful Schwabing crowd on any fine day. Inside, there is a room sometimes used for performances by the *Münchner Volkssängerbühne*, a company of folk entertainers. Every year the rollicking *Weisse Feste* (White Festivities) are held here. They belong to a long tradition of artists' carnival celebrations among Munich's bohemian world.

Another traditional pub in Maxvorstadt is the **Schelling-Salon** (Schellingstr. 54). It is named after the philosopher

Above: In the Schelling-Salon pool is played until all hours. Right: Outside the Alte Pinakothek.

Schelling who lived in Munich from 1806 to 1841, and is a mixture of genuine Bavarian inn, Schwabing artists' pub and gaming saloon. There are about a dozen pool and billiard tables surrounded by old paintings and prints, junk and collages made of postcards. One of the oddest and funniest of these decorations is a picture from around 1890 of two voluptuous, nude beauties playing billiards.

Not far away, along crowded, noisy **Schellingstrasse, Kaffeehaus Alt-Schwabing** (No. 56) tempts you with its special Viennese coffee-house atmosphere. **Papa's Kebap Haus** (No. 24) offers a splendid selection of Turkish appetizers.

During the day, it is well worth taking a trip to the **Alter Nördlicher Friedhof** (Old North Cemetery; Arcisstr. 46). This historic graveyard, which was in use until 1939, is the final resting place of many artists, scholars and high-ranking statesmen of the 19th century, and includes a number of interesting tombstones. Nowadays, it is like an oasis amid the sur-

rounding apartment buildings; a place to rest and meditate. In the summertime it is a favorite spot for locals to indulge in a little uninhibited sunbathing among the graves.

From here, you can walk along Arcisstrasse towards the center of town, and on your way you will pass two of Munich's most famous art galleries, the **Neue Pinakothek** (entrance on Theresienstr.), with its collection of about 550 paintings from the years between rococo and Jugenstil and, right opposite, the **Alte Pinakothek** (entrance on Barerstr.), which houses works by Italian, Dutch and German masters of the Middle Ages to the 18th century. After a four-year-long renovation project, the building, completed in 1836, is once again open to the public.

Opposite the Alte Pinakothek, the right-hand side of Arcisstrasse is dominated by the straight-lined complex of the **Technische Universität** (Technical University), which opened its gates in 1868 and is now one of the largest and most important technical colleges in Germany. At nearby **Roncalliplatz,** between Barer-, Gabelsberger- and Türkenstrasse, construction was begun in 1996 on another museum complex, the *Pinakothek der Moderne*, which will house the State Gallery of Modern Art, as well as the Architecture Museum.

At the corner of Barerstrasse and Theresienstrasse you will find the **Mineralogische Staatssammlung** (State Mineralogical Collection) whose 20,000 exhibits have fascinated both young and old since the 18th century.

Arcisstrasse 12 is the address of the present-day **Hochschule für Musik** (College of Music), which was built in the 1930s as a *Führergebäude* (Führer's Building) for Hitler, in the typical national-socialist style. In 1938, it was the scene of the signing of the Munich Accord. Another building with unpleasant associations is not far away at Meiserstrasse 10 (the continuation of Arcisstrasse), where until 1945 the Nazi Party had their national headquarters. Fortunately, art has taken the place of power, and today you will find the **Staatliche Graphische Sammlung** (State Graphic Arts Collection) here; with over 300,000 drawings and graphics, it is the most important German collection of its kind after the one in Berlin.

Königsplatz

Just a few steps from here, looking westward along Briennerstrasse, you reach a group of neo-classical "temples" around **Königsplatz.** This spacious square was, up until a few years ago, covered by grey stone slabs dating from the Nazi era which were replaced by broad expanses of lawn; which Ludwig I would surely have approved of. Indeed, he never intended the area to be a military parade-ground, such as the Nazis made it, but rather, conceived it as a "Place of Classical Culture"; an integral element in his scheme for an Athens-on-the-Isar, which he commissioned from his favorite architect, von Klenze, in 1808.

Another building by von Klenze is the **Glyptothek**, on the north side of the square; one of the most famous neo-classical buildings in Germany. It has four wings and a huge pillared portico supported by Ionic columns, and houses one of the most important collections of sculpture in Europe, including the famous *Aeginetae*, figures from the Temple of Aphaia on the island of Aegina. A café has been integrated into the building, and in summer coffe, cake and sunshine can be enjoyed in the interior courtyard.

Directly opposite is the **Staatliche Antikensammlung** (State Collection of Antiquities), a classical building with a Corinthian portico, built by Ziebland (1838-48). Inside is a vast collection of antique vases, classical bronzes, terracotta sculptures, ceramics, and small sculptures.

Right: The Propyläen at Königsplatz, seen from the Glyptothek.

The most striking building on Königsplatz, however, is the **Propyläen**, which was designed by von Klenze on the model of the Propylaeum on the Acropolis and built from 1846 to 1862. Once described as a magnificent gateway leading nowhere, its Doric portico was intended to complement the Ionic of the Glyptothek and the Corinthian of the *Staatliche Antikensammlung*. The sculptures on the pediment of the central part of the building were carved by Ludwig von Schwanthaler and glorify the Greeks' struggle for independence from the Turks (1821-30).

The **Städtische Galerie im Lenbachhaus** (City Gallery in Lehnbach House; Luisenstrasse 33-35) is only a stone's throw away. The building, in the style of an Italian country villa, was built by Gabriel von Seidl in collaboration with Franz von Lenbach in the years 1887-91, to serve as the former's luxurious home and studio. After his death, Lenbach House became municipal property and was converted into an art gallery. It has gained international fame for its unique collection of paintings by the Blauer Reiter group. The museum's café is a popular meeting place. The **Kunstbau** hall, which is attached to Lenbachhaus in the mezzanine of the Königsplatz U-Bahn station, provides an unusual backdrop for special exhibitions.

More or less behind Lenbachhaus runs quietly-idyllic Richard-Wagner-Strasse, with its fine Jugendstil façades. At No. 10, you will find a museum that is known to few Münchners, let alone tourists; the **Staatssammlung für Paläontologie und Historische Geologie** (Palaeontology and Geological History Museum), with exhibits of dinosaurs and fossils.

Returning a short distance across Königsplatz, you soon come to the circular **Karolinenplatz**. Its center is dominated by a 95-foot-high (29 m) obelisk, made from melted-down canons captured from the Turkish fleet in the sea-battle of Na-

varino. It is a monument to the 30,000 Bavarian soldiers who died taking part in Napoleon's invasion of Russia in 1812.

From here, **Brienner Strasse** leads further to Odeonsplatz. This splendid street was built at the beginning of the 19th century, at a time when Maxvorstadt was being planned. The buildings either side of this street were designed in the styles of neo-renaissance, neo-classicism and Empire, and were occupied by aristocrats, prominent citizens and important artists. The homogenous townscape of Brienner Strasse has, however, been almost destroyed as a result of war damage, new buildings and the Altstadtring that now slices across it.

Landesbank-Arkaden (between Türkenstrasse, Gabelsbergerstrasse and Oskar-von-Miller-Ring), contains shops, galleries, cafés and restaurants. On the other side of noisy Oskar-von-Miller-Ring, on the **Platz der Opfer des Nationalsozialismus** (Square of the Victims of National Socialism), a number of expensive shops such as Cartier, Chanel, Hermès and *Die Einrichtung* dominate the scene. During the first half of this century, Brienner Strasse 11 was the address of tradition-rich **Café Luitpold**. The café had its heyday as a music palace during the 1920s and 30s, when the great orchestras of the day appeared there. The newly-built Café Luitpold is a good place to take a breather from shopping, with its "Palm Garden" under a glass dome.

Left of Odeonsplatz is what is probably the most beautiful of Munich's classical squares: **Wittelsbacherplatz**, another of von Klenze's designs. In the middle of the square stands an equestrian statue of Maximilian I by Thorwaldsen. Beyond it is Ludwig Ferdinand Palace, where von Klenze himself lived for 25 years before it passed into the possession of the Wittelsbach princes, after which time its name was changed to **Wittelsbacher Palace**. It is now the administrative headquarters of the Siemens corporation. To the left of it, you will see **Arco-Zinneberg Palace**, also designed by von Klenze and built in 1820.

SCHWABING / MAXVORSTADT

Transport Connections
U-BAHN: U2 to Königsplatz. U3/U6 to Odeonsplatz, Universität.
BUS: No. 53 to Odeonsplatz, from Universität along Schellingstrasse, Türkenstrasse and Arcisstrasse.
STREETCAR: No. 27 to Karolinenplatz, Pinakothek, Schellingstrasse.

Restaurants / Cafés / Night-life
BAVARIAN: **Max-Emanuel-Brauerei**, Adalbertstr. 33, tel. 2715158, shady beer-garden in the courtyard, good food, good value; **Atzinger**, Schellingstr. 9, tel. 282880, open Mon-Tue 10 am to 1 am, Wed-Thu 10 am to 2 am, Fri-Sat 10 am to 3 am, Sun 5 pm to 1 am, good home cooking, extremely popular with students; **Schellingsalon**, Schellingstr. 54, tel. 2720788, open 6:30 am to 1 am, closed Tue-Wed and the month of August, substantial food, popular pool and billiard hall.
CAFÉS: **Café an der Uni**, Ludwigstr. 24, tel. 283905, open Mon-Fri 8 am to 10 pm, Sat-Sun 9 am to 10 pm, student café, breakfast until noon, salads and light dishes, including vegetarian, average prices, in summer you can sit outside; **Café Jasmin**, Steinheilstr. 20 (corner of Augustenstr.), tel. 525160, open daily 10 am to 7 pm, a trip into the past with 50s decor and atmosphere, lovingly run by two older women, tasty cakes and pastries; **Café Puck**, Türkenstr. 33, tel. 2802280, open daily 9 am to 1 am, popular, trendy, often very full; **Café Schneller**, Amalienstr. 59, tel. 281124, open Mon-Fri 7:30 am, Sat 9 am to 2 am, closed Sundays, popular traditional student café, delicious cakes and pastries, good value; **Café Tambosi**, Odeonsplatz 18, tel. 298322, open daily 8 am to 1 am, more than 15 tea and 20 coffee varieties, fine cakes, terrasse; **Kaffeehaus Alt-Schwabing**, Schellingstr. 56, tel. 2720179, open Mon-Fri 8 am to 1 am, Sat-Sun, holidays 9 am-1 am, Viennese coffee-house atmosphere, good breakfast, snacks and salads, average prices; **Munix**, Amalienstr. 38, tel. 282845, open Mon-Fri 8 am to 1 am, Sat-Sun 10 am to 1 am, good cocktails, parking in indoor garage; **Oase**, Amalienpassage, tel. 281380, open 9 am to 1 am, excellent salads and snacks, in summer the tables out in the courtyard are a popular meeting place for a richly-assorted crowd; **Vorstadt Café**, Türkenstr. 83, tel. 2720699, open 9 am to midnight, Fri-Sat till 2 am, laid-back atmosphere.
BARS AND PUBS: **Alter Simpl**, Türkenstr. 57, tel. 2723083, open 11 am to 3 am, Fri-Sat till 4 am, tradition-rich Schwabing bohemian bar, a Munich institution; **Bar Tapas**, Amalienstr. 97, tel. 390919, open Mon-Sat 11 am to 1 am, Sun 4 pm to 1 am, Spanish tidbits; **Charivari**, Türkenstr. 92, tel. 282832, open Mon-Fri 7 pm to 3 am (Fri till 4 am), Sat 9 pm to 4 am, Sun 9 pm to 3 am, comfortable old pub, solid meals, good value; **Goldfisch Ess-Bar**, Theresienstr. 54, tel. 284233, open Mon-Wed 5 pm to 1 am, Thu-Sat 5 pm to 3 am, high-quality bar with good food; **News Bar**, Amalienstr. 55, tel. 281787, trendy meeting place for journalists and students; **Orient Imbiss**, Amalienstr. 91, tel. 282827, open Mon-Fri 10 am to 8 pm, Sat 10 am to 2 pm, Greek specialities; **Zest**, Adalbertstr. 23, tel. 2800666, open 4:30 pm to 1 am, sophisticated French and Italian dishes, medium price-range; **Zum Weintrödler**, Brienner Str. 10, tel. 283193, all-night restaurant, open 5 pm-6 am, Sun and holidays 9 pm-6 am, pleasant Munich early-hours bar, reservation advised; **Virus**, Augustenstr. 7, tel. 595917, open Mon-Fri 9:30 am to 8 pm, Sat 9:30 am to 4 pm, cool trendy pub with a small selection of tasty inexpensive meals.
SPECALITY CUISINE: **Bei Mario**, Adalbertstr. 15, tel. 2800460, pizzas from the wood-burning oven, rather expensive, reservation advised; **La Bohème**, Türkenstr. 79, tel. 2720833, open 11 am to 2 am, Italian cuisine by candle-light in an amusing jumble of comfortable old furniture, mirrors and bric-a-brac; **Garuda**, Theresienstr. 87 (corner of Schleissheimer Str.), tel. 525936, open Tue-Sun 11:30 am to 2:30 pm and 6 pm to 11 pm, excellent affordable Indonesian food; **Il Mulino** im Görresgarten, Görresstr. 1, tel. 5233335, open 11:30 am to midnight, very good Italian food at very good prices, comfortable beer garden with chestnut trees, reservation advised; **Käfer's am Hofgarten**, Odeonsplatz 7, tel. 2967530, open Mon-Thu 11 am to 1 am, Fri 11 am to 3 am, Sat 9:30 am to 3 am, Sun 9:30 am to 1 am, bistro-restaurant with French cuisine, good wine list, piano music evenings, reservation advised; **Osteria Italiana**, Schellingstr. 62, tel. 2720717, open noon to 2:30 pm and 6:30 pm to 11:45 pm, oldest Italian restaurant in Germany, very good food, tasteful decor, expensive; **Vinotheca Novecento**, Amalienstr. 42, tel. 285049, open 11 am to 10 pm, light Italian meals and excellent selected wines at exclusive prices.
ICE CREAM PARLOR: **Adria**, Türkenstr. 59, tel. 2724190, open Mon-Sun 10 am to midnight, excellent speciality ice creams at reasonable prices in a pleasantly cool interior or at crowded tables outside on the pavement.

Post Offices
Post Offices: Theresienstrasse 22, tel. 53882783; Agnesstrasse 3, tel. 30628433.

Taxi Stands
Siegestor, tel. 216141; Amalienstrasse/Theresienstrasse, tel. 216120; Barerstrasse/Schellingstrasse, tel. 2723874; Karolinenplatz, tel. 283443.

ALTE PINAKOTHEK

The Myth of Schwabing

Ever since the turn of the century, Schwabing has been a name with a magical sound – a legendary, almost mythical place. This part of Munich attracted to it countless poets, artists, bohemians and revolutionaries. Stefan George and Thomas Mann, Kandinsky and Klee, Lenin and Erich Mühsam, all agreed on one thing: Schwabing – like Montmartre in Paris – was more than just a city quarter, it was a "state of being," as Countess Reventlow wrote in her memoirs before the First World War.

The Schwabing of those days has long since disappeared. Too many changes have taken place since the Second World War, and the "village of artists" has now become the haunt of students and tourists. The area has been intensively colonized by the fashion industry, film and television, advertising agencies, newspaper publishers and other lucrative, high-profile business activities, with the unfortunate result that rents have soared astronomically. Such typically Schwabing institutions as the "Nest," where artists and other bohemian types once met to politicize, became the victim of a wave of speculation. At the start, however, things were quite different.

Long before the founding of Munich by Heinrich der Löwe (Henry the Lion) in 1158, but some time after the Romans had been forced by the restless tribes of Germanic invaders to abandon the land of the "barbarians" (around 500 AD), a certain Swabian chieftain named Swapo and his kin, one clan among the migrating hordes of Alemans and Bajuwars, took possession of the land around present-day Munich, and called this new settlement *Swapinga*.

Previous page: The main staircase of the Alte Pinakothek. Right: The "Walking Man" sets standards on Leopoldstrasse.

Schwabing was mentioned for the first time in a document dated 782 AD. Over 1,000 years later, in 1820, there were still only 703 people living in Schwabing's 91 houses. Then, when the Maffei company built a locomotive factory in nearby Hirschau in 1873, large numbers of laborers moved into Schwabing, and from then on a growing influx of factory workers led to a gradual disintegration of Schwabing's rustic way of life. By 1880, the number of inhabitants had increased to 6,350 and, on January 1, 1890, when Schwabing was incorporated into the city of Munich, that population had doubled.

It was this incorporation, resulting in a blend of old village customs with a modern big-city lifestyle, that gave rise to the "myth of Schwabing." True, it is little more than a legend now, but that does not mean that Schwabing no longer has anything to offer today. It is just very different; it is bigger, more diversified, more commercialized – and much more hectic! Today, living in Schwabing means strolling along Leopoldstrasse with its silhouette artists and kitschy paintings, seeing and being seen in street cafés, and drinking with the beer garden crowd; there are the countless students bringing life to the university quarter around Türkenstrasse and Amalienstrasse, Schellingstrasse and Adalbertstrasse; there are the many restaurants, pubs and cafés in Maxvorstadt and Old Schwabing; there is the Englischer Garten with its Chinese Tower and nude sunbathers beside the Eisbach stream; there are the Jugendstil façades, the spaciously planned streets and so much more.

Schwabing – in spite of everything – still has its *Münchner Freiheit* ("Munich's Freedom") square and the feeling of being in "Italy's northernmost city." The origins of Schwabing can be found in the narrow streets behind Münchener Freiheit. Since then, however, "Munich City" has expanded beyond the Siegestor; when you say "Schwabing"

today you mean Leopoldstrasse, "royal" Ludwigstrasse and Maxvorstadt. Just where today's Schwabing begins and ends is difficult to say; probably the only people who know are in the cartography department of Munich's University.

LEOPOLDSTRASSE

So, when you have covered Ludwigstrasse and Maxvorstadt, where should you begin your stroll through Schwabing? It has to be on **Leopoldstrasse**. Think of it as the city's only boulevard worthy of the name; Munich's *Champs Elysées*. Beyond the avenue's royally towering poplar trees, there are countless open-air cafés and ice-cream parlors, and in the summer, when sidewalk artists sell their "works of art" on the street, Leopoldstrasse has more than just a faint whiff of Montmartre about it. Here people stroll lazily about, eat ice-cream, drink cappuccino, watch other people and spend their evenings just hanging out in discos or cafés.

Munich's premiere boulevard begins behind the Siegestor, which was commissioned by Ludwig I and built by Friedrich von Gärtner (1843-52). To your right, on the eastern side of Leopoldstrasse, stand some impressive neo-classical buildings, nearly all of which are owned by major insurance companies. At the turn of the century, the Christian-humanitarian writer and interior architect Rudolf Alexander Schröder resided at No. 4. He was one of the founders, in 1899, of the magazine *Die Insel* (The Island), from which the publishing company Insel Verlag emerged in 1902. In front of the glass building of Munich Reinsurance at No. 36, a gigantic white statue called the *Walking Man* by American artist Jonathan Borofsky, has stood since 1995. The enormous figure towers tenfold above the pedestrians passing by.

On summer evenings, the **Schwabinger Kunstmarkt** (art market) is held on the wide pavement outside the elegant office buildings set back from the road between Schackstrasse and Martius-

LEOPOLDSTRASSE

strasse. Here Munich artists display their work, and portrait painters, silhouette-cutters, jewelry makers, potters and other artists and craftspeople bring to Leopoldstrasse a genuinely bohemian quality.

At the corner of **Martiusstrasse**, the display windows of the Wittenborg porcelain shop catch your eye (Martiusstr. 2). **Kunst und Spiel** is an anthroposophical store, where valuable educational toys can be found. In addition, you can browse through a virtual Aladdin's Cave of materials for crafts, weaving, spinning and painting. One department of this establishment contains exquisite clothes made of natural materials (Leopoldstr. 48, rear building section).

The popular and trendy **Roxy** is located in the building next door; the cocktail bar is owned by actress Iris Berben. A few yards beyond it, on the same side of the street, there is a sidewalk café called **Rialto** which is rather more established on Leopoldstrasse. It is a bit more tastefully furnished, has a street balcony, and waiters wear evening attire – and it is still as busy as ever. Between these two cafés, you will find the very traditional **Gaststätte Leopold**, where you can stop for a breather over a home-cooked meal. Cabaretist Karl Valentin once came here to celebrate his first successes, and later the author Erich Kästner made this one of his regular haunts. It has been altered somewhat, however, following renovation.

Not far away is the inn **Zur Brezn**, a kind of Bavarian version of the Sixties, serving traditional Bavarian dishes much like those in the Leopold. A few yards further on, the **Eiscafé Central** is ready to serve its cool delicacies. Just before the Hertie department store the oldest cinema in Munich, **Leopold-Kino**, still attracts film fans. And this brings us to Münchener Freiheit, and for the moment to the end of our stroll along one side of Leopoldstrasse – though the road continues northward, purely to carry traffic out of the city.

Above: Seeing and being seen on Leopoldstrasse. Right: At Münchner Freiheit.

Münchener Freiheit

Even beyond the boundaries of Munich, people have heard of **Münchener Freiheit** (Munich's Freedom). Up until 1946 it was called Feilitzsch-Platz, but its present name was chosen as a homage to all those citizens of Munich who, to quote the words on the memorial plaque, "in the last days of the Second World War... rose up against the tyranny of Nazism... thereby preventing senseless bloodshed."

The Münchener Freiheit that we see today, however, is quite a recent creation. Basically, where the large, secluded beer garden of the *Alter Wirt* once stretched, there is now a wide sunken **forum** of concrete which leads from the U-Bahn station and broadens out to meet the square. From Münchener Freiheit, the forum itself is reached by climbing the many stone steps here.

The original square fell victim to the expansion of Munich's streetcar and underground lines in the 1960s and 70s – until the people of Schwabing themselves fought to regain their "Freedom" and created a kind of post-modernist oasis in the concrete desert. Here you can meet your friends for a game of table-tennis or street-chess, or sit drinking and talking far into the night; for example, at **Café Münchener Freiheit** (which has a large terrace). Nearby, a sculpture to the late folk-play actor Helmut Fischer (known as "Monaco Franz"), who died in 1997, has been put up. In December, the Schwabing Christmas Market takes place on the square and at the U-Bahn exit. Whatever you might think about the appearance of Münchener Freiheit, it is still the gateway to Old Schwabing, and therefore the starting point for most visitors heading to the nearby bars and clubs, or starting out on a stroll down Leopoldstrasse.

The best time of day to take a stroll through Old Schwabing is in the evening, when the bars and cafés come to life, and locals as well as tourists from all over the world come together here.

ALT-SCHWABING

ALT-SCHWABING

So, what is on offer in present-day *Alt-Schwabing* (Old Schwabing)? Well, there are a few political and satirical cabarets, the best known of them probably being the *Münchner Lach- und Schiessgesellschaft*; there are a handful of small theaters and, of course, there are many nightspots around Occamstrasse and Feilitzschstrasse, which nearly all dutifully close at 1 a.m., as do most in Munich. Unfortunately, the most famous among them are being slowly strangled by high rents, so that many legendary landmarks of the Schwabing scene, like *Gisela*, for example, have been consigned to history.

The well-known Munich columnist Siggi Sommer, who died in 1995, long ago lovingly and ironically described Schwabing through his character "Strolling Blasius" as *"Neon, Nylon, Nepp"* (*Nepp*: rip-off).

Above: In the heart of Alt-Schwabing. Right: Tranquillity on Wedekind-Platz.

Nevertheless, every evening streams of tourists make their way undeterred from Leopoldstrasse to Occamstrasse, and wander past dreary pizza parlors, hamburger joints and pubs blaring out sterile disco music. You will no longer find many residents of Munich here, and with good reason. At most, a few locals in search of a bargain might sometimes be found hunting through a dozen or so second-hand clothing shops and the few boutiques in the area.

If you want to form your own impressions of Alt-Schwabing, start in **Feilitzschstrasse.** Until 1890 the street was called Maffeistrasse and led to the main gates of the Maffei locomotive works in Hirschau. The house at No. 3 still bears a plaque in memory of the artist Paul Klee, who had his studio here from 1908 to 1919. Thomas Mann lived at various addresses in Alt-Schwabing from 1894 until his marriage in 1905. The house at Feilitzschstrasse 8, where he worked on his greatest novel, *Buddenbrooks*, has disappeared to make way for an unattractive modern building.

A self-service snack bar on Feilitzstrasse, **Mama's Kebap**, is *the* in-spot for Turkish food in Alt-Schwabing. The food here is not only delicious, it is also inexpensive; from various appetizers and excellent *döner kebap* to oval-shaped *lahmaçun* (Turkish pizza), *börek* (filled pastries) and desserts. You eat here at small bistro tables, and in summer the large glass front is opened.

The *Museumsbrunnen* (Museum Fountain) on **Wedekind-Platz** still serves to remind visitors of the playwright Frank Wedekind. This was once the market square of the village of Schwabing, and is now a busy traffic intersection. Here you can take a break in the hectic, post-modernist **Drugstore**.

Continue along Feilitzschstrasse and you will see, on your right, hidden behind a high wall, the **Suresnes-Schlössl** (*Schlössl*: little castle; Werneckstrasse

24), built by J. B. Gunetzrainer in the years 1717-18. From here you pass by Paddy's Irish Pub and on to a traditional restaurant, **Seerose**. The name, which means "Waterlily," is still above the door, but inside a recommendable Spanish restaurant has established itself. The old name has probably been retained for marketing purposes: the Seerose was, for many years, the regular meeting place of a group of artists who called themselves the "Seerose Circle" and who held literary readings here.

If you turn left onto **Biedersteinerstrasse** at the end of Feilitzschstrasse – it is right on the edge of the Englischer Garten – you will find the oldest church in Schwabing, the baroque village church of **St. Sylvester,** built in the 17th century, though documents show there was a church here as early as 1315. From 1811 onwards, under the name St. Ursula, this was the parish church of Alt-Schwabing, remaining so until its function was transferred to the new St. Ursula church on Kaiserplatz (see p. 112).

From here you can turn onto **Haimhauser Strasse.** The building, which today houses the social security offices (No. 13), was once the first schoolhouse in Schwabing (1843). At the corner of Haimhauser Strasse and Occamstrasse is the spot where once the stables of Schwabing Castle stood. The building on the corner of Ursulastrasse is the home of the *Münchner Lach- und Schiessgesellschaft*, a cabaret theater founded by Sammy Drechsel and Dieter Hildebrandt in 1956, which became famous all over Germany through television broadcasts.

In the rear courtyard of Haimhauser Strasse 13a, there are nightly performances by the **Theater am Sozialamt** (usually abbreviated TamS). Its auditorium is unusual since it occupies the former public shower-rooms, and you can still see the huge water-pipes and boilers.

A new alternative culture has developed around Haimhauser Strasse and Hesseloher Strasse, and there are a number of original and attractive shops to be discovered hereabouts, on Haimhauser

Strasse, for example, there is the **Psychologische Fachbuchhandlung** (specialty book shop for psychology), with a large esoteric section and communications center, antique shops and a natural food store, and a person can find clothes here of all natural materials or get ahold of second hand clothes as well as the newest fashions. **Mephisto Hair Design**, at Hesselhoher Strasse 12, offers devilishly-good haircuts. The **Rational Theater** cabaret, founded by Rainer Uthoff, might be worth a visit in the evening.

Occamstrasse, lined by a succession of drinking establishmentshas, has been called the "longest bar in Munich." The Brazilian *Boteco Brasil* is the newest in-spot on the strip. The **Münchner Lustspielhaus** (Comedy House), is here. At Wedekindplatz, turn at the "Drugstore" onto **Siegesstrasse**. For anyone interested in fashion, the second-hand clothes

Above: Not quite Eric Burdon – but never mind! Right: In summer, Leopoldstrasse turns into an art market.

shops on this street are a treasure-trove, since they only stock designer models. There are also a few nice pubs here, such as **Tomate** and **Black & White**. Good live music can be heard at the **Schwabinger Podium**, one of the best music bars in Munich.

On **Fendstrasse** is the **Weinbauer** restaurant which has, unfortunately, lost its old atmosphere since being renovated. At the junction of this street with **Nikolaiplatz** you will find one of the most expensive shops in Munich, the exclusive name for leather goods: MCM. Here, turn onto Nikolaistrasse, then left onto **Werneckstrasse**, and you will arrive on **Seestrasse**, notable for its small, village-like houses which have survived from the second half of the 19th century.

To the left is the former **Crailsheim Palace**, on the site where Schwabing's first hospital was built in 1861. The pioneer sociologist, Max Weber, spent the final year of his life at Seestrasse 16, and died there on June 14, 1920. Continuing along Seestrasse, you will come to a path

leading straight to the *Kleinhesseloher See*, a lake in the Englischer Garten.

But for the moment we will carry on onto **Mandlstrasse**. At No. 14 is a neo-classical porticoed villa which houses Munich's favorite marriage registry. Continuing southwards down Mandelstrasse to Königinstrasse, at the level of Thiemestrass, you come upon the huge office complex of the insurance company **Münchner Rückversicherung**, which was built in 1912-13.

Diagonally opposite, backing on to the Englischer Garten, is a riding-school, the **Universitäts-Reitschule**. From inside the café belonging to it, popular with a younger crowd, you can see into the riding hall. On warm summer evenings the **Königsgarten** (King's Garden), just beside the riding school, becomes a rather exclusive alternative to the smokey pubs of Schwabing. There, under huge old trees, French, Greek and Italian specialities are served.

After that, you can return to Leopoldstrasse by way of Thiemestrasse and Martiusstrasse. You can take this opportunity to stroll down the other side of Munich's favorite "boulevard."

Leopoldstrasse's West Side

Opposite the bus terminal at **Münchener Freiheit**, you can admire one of Munich's most beautiful Jugendstil façades (Leopoldstrasse 77). Taking the underpass to the opposite side of the street, you come out at **Herzogstrasse**. Hidden away here, just a few steps along the street, is the popular little **ABC** arthouse cinema. Continuing along towards the city center you pass No. 59, now a bank. From 1914 to 1928 this was the home of author Heinrich Mann, whose novel *The Blue Angel* was made into a classic film, starring Marlene Dietrich. Schwabing's Rathaus once stood on the site of the present-day post office.

A row of houses on **Kaiserstrasse** (Nos. 4 through 12), a street that leads off to your right, are really worth seeing. They are beautifully designed, single-

LEOPOLDSTRASSE, WEST SIDE

story brick houses in the Nordic Renaissance style, built around 1884. Lenin himself once lived quite modestly as "Herr Meyer" in this street at No. 46.

Further along Leopoldstrasse is the bookshop, **Buchhandlung Lehmkuhl**, at No. 45. It was opened in 1903 and became a favorite meeting place for the Munich literati, where later readings were also given by leading authors such as Ingeborg Bachmann, Uwe Johnson, Siegfried Lenz and Ernesto Cardenal.

Beyond the **Marmorhaus**, one of Munich's largest multi-screen cinemas, the sidewalk is taken up once again with tables and chairs, and reduced to a narrow footway. **Eiscafé Venezia** at No. 31, where Munich's beautiful people like to gather, is well established on this side of the street, and is just as popular in winter as it is in summer.

Above: A street party on Herzogstrasse.
Right: Jugendstil façade at Ainmillerstrasse 22.

At the beginning of the century, **Ainmillerstrasse** was beloved by many artists. Kandinsky and Gabriele Münter lived in the rear building behind No. 36 from 1909 to 1914, and at No. 34 a plaque recalls that the poet Rainer Maria Rilke lived here in 1918-19.

Back on Leopoldstrasse you will find yourself passing a number of trendy shops. A **Hallhuber** outlet is located at No. 25, next to which a branch of **Body Shop** offers cosmetics produced without using animal experiments. In the basement of the building next door is one of the oldest discos in Schwabing; it was formerly called "Big Apple," and is now trading as **Singles**.

After crossing **Franz-Joseph-Strasse** you come to the Italian sidewalk restaurant **Adria**, where food is served until 3 o'clock in the morning. In the cellar rooms of the legendary *Domizil* jazz club, which was temporarily used as a disco, a live music club called **Pipifax** has settled in.

You then come to the **Studentenwerk building** (Students' Union) with the Mensa (university canteen) behind it. A few aging hippies are usually to be seen in front of the building selling secondhand clothes, old books and magazines, CDs and records, Indian shawls and home-made jewellery. Behind the rose-colored building of the Faculty for Psychology and Pedagogy, between Leopoldstrasse and Friedrichstrasse, is **Leopold Park**, a small but relaxing patch of green with the low huts of the university kindergarten.

Located on the corner of Georgenstrasse, **Café Extrablatt** has a style all of its own. This popular spot was conceived by one-time Munich gossip-columnist Michael Graeter. You can relax here between stars and starlets – but sit somewhat uncomfortably, perhaps, on the toilets with their barbed-wire seats. From here it is only a few more yards to the Siegestor.

Perhaps now you would now like to get to know a bit of the "normal" Schwabing; leisurely, plain and simple, with tranquil squares. It would be best to begin this excursion on Hohenzollernstrasse.

The Other Schwabing

Over the past few years, **Hohenzollernstrasse** has steadily evolved into a mecca of avant-garde fashion. Boutiques for ladies' and men's clothing, shoe shops, and shops selling gifts and accessories have gradually driven out the more traditional businesses. But even trendy new shops often close down after only a short time because they, too, can no longer afford – or simply no longer want to pay – the high rents that are extracted here. Whereas fashionable ladies of a certain age prefer shopping in the grander shops of the town center, the trendy teenagers and twenty-somethings can find what they are looking for in the boutiques on Hohenzollerstrasse.

Starting your walk at the corner of Leopoldstrasse, you will pass approximately 40 fashion boutiques and shoeshops, standing toe to toe, so to speak. In addition to numerous shops with a mixture of labels, braches of specific companies are also found here, such as Marc O'Polo, Diesel, Bartu, Buffalo, and More&More.

Right at the beginning you come across the **Schwabinger Party Shop**, which sells gift articles; crazy and funny articles from all over the world. In the rear building at No. 12, **Ane Kenssen** sells exclusive leather fashions.

At the corner of **Wilhelmstrasse** is the well-filled **Caffe Florian**, which serves guests outside, too, when the weather is good. If you walk a little way onto **Wilhelmstrasse** you will find, at No. 19, the preserved buildings of the former Schwabing streetcar depot, which are classified as monuments and which are now used as the rehearsal studios of the Munich Ballet Academy. Back on Hohenzollernstrasse, at No. 20, you go

HOHENZOLLERNSTRASSE

down some steps to **Theater 44**. The name dates from its former premises in Schleissheimerstrasse, where the auditorium seated exactly 44 people. In the studios of the house at the rear of No. 21, artists such as Paul Klee, Wassily Kandinsky and Gabriele Münter got together in the years 1904-14.

The next stop is **Friedrichstrasse**, on the corner of which is the trendy bar **.egger** (formerly Scheidegger), featuring elegant international cuisine, good sounds, and a small, shady beer garden. To your left, take a look at the fine Jugendstil façade of the building at No. 26. To the north, Friedrichstrasse is entirely dominated by **St. Ursula-Kirche**. This church was built by A. Thiersch in 1894-97 as the new parish church of Schwabing, taking over from St. Sylvester in Old Schwabing. Its architecture is an interesting adaptation of Florentine quattrocento and northern Italian cross-domed church.

Back on Hohenzollernstrasse again, a shop on the right side of the street catches your eye, **Africa & House e.V.**, a center for African art and culture with a gallery. In the courtyard of No. 58, a steep stairway leads down to a former beer cellar, where Schwabing artist Manfred Wamsgans has created his **Kunstoase** (Art Oasis) with a floor area of 3,250 square feet (300 sq m). Even if you are not in a buying mood, it is fun to browse among the works of art and assorted antiques.

Those interested in architecture should walk down **Römerstrasse** to see some of Munich's finest surviving **Jugendstil houses**; for example, Römerstrasse 15, built in 1900, has rich stucco decorations, and No. 11, built in 1899, has a polychrome façade. A plaque at No. 16 recalls an earlier resident, Karl Wolfskehl. The house at Ainmillerstrasse 22 also has a beautifully-colored façade, and No. 20 is conspicuous for its stucco figure decorations.

Going a little further towards the city, there are two examples of Max Langheinrich's work to stop and admire on **Franz-Joseph-Strasse**: the building on the corner of Friedrichstrasse (Franz-Joseph-Strasse 21/23), dates from 1904 and has delightfully extravagant bay-windows and balconies; No. 38 was built in 1903 as part of a group of Jugendstil apartment buildings, and displays a lively, sculpted façade. From here, by way of Kurfürstenstrasse, you come to **Kurfürstenplatz.**

The main café at this intersection is **Café Schwabing**, where you can sit behind the large windows and watch the ebb and flow of people and traffic on Kurfürstenplatz. In summer it is nice to sit outside here, though it is a bit loud. Diagonally opposite is a branch of **Eiscafé Venezia** where, at 7:30 p.m., news vendors stand outside in all kinds of weather to hawk copies of the evening

Above: On busy Hohenzollernstrasse. Right: The colorful market stalls at Elisabethplatz.

edition of the local newspaper. Another popular place is **Wolf's Bistro**, at Nordendstrasse 62.

If you walk for about 100 yards/meters onto Belgradstrasse from Kurfürstenplatz, you will find, to your left, **Kurfürstenhof**, an architecturally effective complex of buildings completed in the 1970s with a modern variation on the traditional courtyard theme. The unconventional treatment of the façades, windows and roof slopes is of special interest. 171 apartments and a good dozen shops are housed here, making optimal use of the building area.

Further along Belgradstrasse, the vegetarian delicatessen **Gourmet's Garden** has tasty cold and warm snacks on offer, and in the pink-and-grey decor of the **Nuova Italia** you can eat as cheaply and as well as hardly anywhere else in Munich. The restaurant also opens onto the courtyard, where you can sit outside in summer. A passage leads to **Fallmerayerstrasse** where, within the same complex of buildings, you will find an in-spot called **Finest** and a funny little shop selling 1950s memorabilia.

From the southern end of Kurfürstenplatz, walk along Nordendstrasse to Elisabethplatz. Though not as important as Viktualienmarkt (see p. 64), this is one of the most attractive local markets in Munich, with fruit and vegetable stalls and small shops selling cheese, fish, cooked meats and wine. A pleasant place to sit is the glass conservatory of the **Café Wintergarten,** which also has a beer garden open in the summer. You can sit on a bench here and watch the quieter side of Schwabing life, away from the crowds on Leopoldstrasse and Hohenzollernstrasse. The square is framed by the **Theater der Jugend** (Youth Theater), the buildings of the Gisela-Gymnasium (a high-school dating from the turn of the century), and by the city trades school.

A two-minute walk from here takes you to a curious sort of place: Munich's first erotic shop for women, **Ladies First** (Kurfurstenstr. 23), which opened up in the mid-1990s.

OLYMPIA PARK

Among the many green spaces and parks which have earned Munich a reputation as the "greenest city in Germany," is the small **Luitpold Park**. It nestles between Petuelring to the north and Karl-Theodor-Strasse to the south, and is only a stone's throw away from Olympia Park. **Bamberger House**, located in the park, is worth a visit. This attractive park palace houses an extremely popular café-restaurant. When the weather is good, there is seating available for 100 on the restaurant's large terrace.

OLYMPIA PARK

The Bavarian Motor Works (BMW), is the largest industrial corporation in north Munich. The company was founded in 1916 and to start with only built aircraft engines. In 1923 they went into motor-cycle production, then moved on to automobiles in 1928. An eye-catching attrac-

Above: A bird's eye view of the Olympic complex in the afternoon light.

tion for more than 300,000 visitors each year is the silvery, windowless, concrete envelope of the **BMW Museum** and the four cylinders of the nearby **BMW building**. The museum not only displays BMW's history, through its power-units, motor-cycles and automobiles, but also enables the visitor to follow the history of transportation technology from its earliest beginnings on to the present and into the 21st century.

From the BMW complex you can look out over the intriguing skyline of **Olympia Park**. This is a sport and recreation area, covering more than one square mile (3 sq km) which was laid out for the 20th Olympic Games in 1972. At the time, it earned worldwide acclaim for its architects, Günther Behnisch, Frei Otto and Partners, designers of the immense tent-like roofs, suspended from giant pylons, which cover the entire area like gigantic spiders' webs. The best view of this futuristic looking structure is from the 950-foot-high (290 m) **Fernsehturm** (television tower), from which there is a splen-

OLYMPIA PARK

did view of the whole city – especially when the *Föhn* weather seems to bring the Alps close enough to touch. If you find this airy lookout platform too windy for your liking, you can enjoy the view from inside the revolving restaurant.

Originally, the Olympic area was a training ground for the Royal Bavarian Army. In 1909, the first airship landed here, and from 1925 until 1939 it was the site of Munich's airport. After the war, in which the city suffered heavy bomb damage, all the resulting rubble was dumped here, and in the late 1960s work began on the creation of an artificial landscape which now represents a successful combination of nature and man's ingenuity.

When you leave the *Olympiazentrum* underground station, the first thing you see are the terraced buildings of the former **Olympisches Dorf** (Olympic village), which were later converted into owner-occupied apartments. A small settlement of colorfully-painted low houses is next to these apartments; the so called "bungalows" are rented out to students.

The most impressive of the former Olympic sports venues is still the **Olympia Stadium**, which can seat 75,000 spectators. Today, it is a venue for National League soccer, athletics meetings and pop concerts. Crossing the Hanns Braun bridge, you come to a monument on the north side to the members of the Israeli Olympic team who were killed here by terrorists in 1972.

The neighboring **Olympiahalle,** a multi-purpose hall with seating for 14,000, is more frequently used for pop concerts or large-scale cultural events, as well as carnival balls and sporting events as, for instance, the popular six-day bicycle race. Diagonally opposite is the **Olympia-Schwimmhalle** (Olympic Pool), a swimming paradise with a 160-foot (50 m) pool, a diving pool, heated whirlpool, sauna, solarium, table tennis and billiard area, and a 42,000-square-foot (13,000 sq m) sunbathing lawn with a playground.

The Olympic sports areas are roofed over with over 245,000 square feet

ENGLISCHER GARTEN

(74,800 sq m) of transparent acrylic tiles, suspended from twelve steel masts, up to 266 ft (81m) in height, and costing a staggering DM 168 million. The theoretical design of the project was based on calculations derived from the surface-tension of soap bubbles.

Just below the Olympic Pool is the **Theatron**, where for two weeks every August free concerts of folk and pop music are held. At the same time there is a *Sommerfest* (Summer Festival) on the open ground in front of the Olympiahalle, with carousels, shooting booths, raffles, beer gardens, and a firework display every night.

South-west of the **Olympiaberg** (Munich's former rubble mountain), set in a small garden, is a little architectural gem, the **Russian Orthodox Chapel**, which a Russian hermit named Timofei built here after the Second World War. He constructed it with loving care from a curious collection of miscellaneous building materials, and then painstakingly decorated the inside with innumerable bits of silver paper. Every year in June, on the meadow in front of the chapel, the two-week long **Tollwood Festival** is held. A theater-tent is the venue for performances by numerous cabaret and musical groups, and a whiff of the exotic surrounds the stalls and booths selling arts and crafts, some items purely decorative and others of practical use, as well as culinary specialities from as far afield as Portugal and southern India.

ENGLISCHER GARTEN

What would Schwabing be without its **Englischer Garten** (English Garden) – the largest and one of the most beautiful green spaces to be found in the center of any major city in the world? It is as old as the French Revolution, and has a closer connection with that event than you might think. Until the 18th century, this area along the river Isar was a wilderness of meadows laced by little streams, which served as a hunting ground for the Wittelsbach princes and was out of bounds to the public. Then, after the storming of the Bastille in Paris in 1789, Elector Karl Theodor, already less than popular with the 40,000 citizens of Munich, started to get distinctly nervous. In order to placate his grumbling subjects, he followed the advice of his Minister of War, Benjamin Thompson, (who was later made Count Rumford), and "in great haste" summoned Friedrich von Sckell, the Court Gardener at Schwetzingen. Shortly afterwards he informed his astonished subjects of his plans for a *Volksgarten*, which was intended to promote "a companionable mingling and reconciliation between all classes of society, who may come together here among the beauties of nature." It was to become a people's garden "for the purpose of exercise and recreation," but also

Above: Cycling in the Englischer Garten.
Right: Sun-worshippers at the Monopteros.

ENGLISCHER GARTEN

to promote educational ideals in the spirit of Enlightenment. Today, the Englischer Garten is, without doubt, one of the largest and most beautiful gardens in Germany, perhaps even in the world, and differs profoundly from the strict geometrical proportions of a French baroque garden, through its picturesque and very "English" blend of untrammelled nature and the gardener's art.

Probably the best starting point for our stroll through the Englischer Garten is the university. **Veterinärstrasse** leads straight into the park; bicycles can be rented at this entrance in summer. You cross the **Eisbach** stream, officially called *Schwabinger Bach* at this point. Along its banks in summer you will find the famous nude sunbathers and, of course, the inevitable curious onlookers. If you follow the stream to your right as far as the **Haus der Kunst**, you may on hot days witness a remarkable activity known as Eisbach-surfing. A simple wooden plank is fastened to the bridge by a rope, and then, thanks to the cascading current of the stream, you have non-stop surfing Hawaiian style. Right beside the bridge is the **Rumford Monument**. Not far away, in the middle of a pond behind the Haus der Kunst, is the **Japanisches Teehaus**.

The **Monopteros**, a monument situated on an artificial mound, used to be the meeting-place for Munich's hippies in the 1970s. The short climb up to it is well worth the effort for the beautiful view of the Munich skyline. In the center of the little temple there is a memorial in honor of the founding fathers of the gardens, Elector Karl Theodor and King Max I, commissioned from von Klenze by Ludwig I. Nowadays, in the meadow below, a colorful crowd of New Agers gathers to the music of guitars, bongos and an occasional saxophone. From nowhere in particular, wisps of smoke from joss-sticks waft past, along with the scent of marijuana, and occasionally the wind will carry the oompah-beat of a Bavarian band from the nearby *Chinesischer Turm* (Chinese Tower).

ENGLISCHER GARTEN

The wooden **Chinesischer Turm** was built in 1789-90 after the "original" in London's Kew Gardens, and was used as a lookout tower and music pagoda. It burned down in 1944, but an exact replica was reconstructed in 1951-52.

The five-storyed structure, with a wood-tiled roof, is built with an enchanting delicacy, and from its eaves gilded bells are suspended. In spring, as soon as the first warming rays of sunshine slant down through the bare branches of chestnut trees on to the beer garden tables, an assorted crowd of Munich locals will gather to enjoy their beer. If you want to have a meal in more sophisticated surroundings, you can do so at reasonable prices on the terrace of the nearby inn, also called *Chinesischer Turm*.

With its 6,500 seats, the beer garden at the Chinese Tower is the second largest in Munich, after the *Hirschgarten*. Even if the weather is only half-way decent,

Above: A wintry scene at the Chinese Tower in the Englischer Garten.

people from all over the world, and from every social level, come here. You might see a punk with bright green hair next to an overstressed executive with his tie undone; the bucolic Bavarian beside the somewhat disapproving lady pensioner on holiday from Dortmund. And if you are lucky, you might catch a fire-eater doing his act. For the entertainment of children (and relief for their parents) there is an enchanting wooden carousel in service from April to October.

Provided of course, that you are still capable of walking straight after spending a lengthy break in this Elysium, you should now head north, to **Rumford-Schlössl**, a small castle built by Johann Baptist Lechner in 1791. After that, cross the road which takes buses through the Englischer Garten and you are in the so-called *Hundewiese* (Dog's Meadow), which leads to **Kleinhesseloher See**. This artificial lake with its three small islands was created by Freiherr von Werneck and is a wonderful refuge for ducks and swans. On its western shore is a modern restaurant called the **Seehaus**: inside, the restaurant serves excellent food in a high-class atmosphere; outside, the Seehaus has a lovely and extremely popular – though somewhat pricey – beer-garden, with some tabels along the shore and others set back in the shade. Behind it is a place to hire pedal-boats and rowboats.

Two monuments were erected here to the founding fathers: at the beer garden is a pillar in memory of Friedrich von Sckell, and behind the Seehaus a monument to Freiherr von Werneck, designed by Klenze. Here, a footbridge takes you over the Mittlerer Ring road to the northern section of the Englischer Garten. This much quieter and idyllic part of the park stretches northward for nearly two more miles (3 km) along the left bank of the river Isar. Two popular beer gardens are to be found there: at the beginning the **Hirschau** beer garden, and at the furthest end, the **Aumeister**.

SCHWABING / LEOPOLDSTRASSE

Transport Connections

U-BAHN: U2 to Josephsplatz, Hohenzollernplatz; U3/U6 to Giselastrasse, Münchener Freiheit.
BUS: No. 33 from Münchener Freiheit to Kurfürstenplatz, Nordbad; No. 54 to Giselastrasse, along Hohenzollernstrasse, Münchener Freiheit.
STREETCAR: No. 12 to Scheidplatz, Kurfürstenplatz, Hohenzollernplatz, Nordbad; No. 27 to Nordendstrasse, Elisabethplatz, Kurfürstenplatz, Hohenzollernplatz, Nordbad.

Restaurants / Cafés / Night-life

BAVARIAN with beer garden: **Biergarten am Chinesischen Turm**, Englischer Garten 3, tel. 395029, 11 am to 11 pm, Munich's second-largest, best-known and most colorful beer garden; **Hirschau**, Gysslingstr. 15, tel. 369945, 11 am to 1 am, tranquility in the Englischer Garten, dancing daily from 8 pm, on weekends from 3 pm; **Kaisergarten**, Kaiserstr. 34, tel. 347752, 10 am to 1 am, quiet, small beer garden, hot meals; **Seehaus im Englischen Garten**, Kleinhesselohe 3, tel. 3816130, 10 am to midnight, *the* beer garden of the rich and beautiful, on Kleinhesselohe Lake; **Zum Aumeister**, Sondermeierstr. 1, tel. 325224, Tue-Sun 10 am to 11 pm, northernmost beer oasis in the Englischer Garten, popular with cyclists and staff of nearby Radio Bavaria.
SPECIALITY CUISINE: **Adria**, Leopoldstr. 19, tel. 396529, 10:30 am to 3 am, fresh Italian food for night owls; **Cabus**, Isabellastr. 4 (corner of Neureuthstr.), te. 2710330, stylish crêperie; **Daitokai**, Kurfürstenstr. 59, tel. 2711421, noon to 2 pm (last order) and 6 pm to 10 pm (last order), Japanese, elegant interior, expensive, more economical lunch menu; **Dilan**, Herzogstr. 90, tel. 304713, Turkish; **El Cortijo**, Feilitzschstr. 32, tel. 331116, fine Spanish cuisine in the former "Seerose"; **.egger**, Friedrichstr. 27, tel. 398526, bar-restaurant with international cuisine, good sounds, mixed youngish crowd, small, shady beer garden; **Mama's Kebap**, Feilitzschstr. 7, tel. 392642, daily 11 am to 1 am, weekends usually till 3 am, popular Turkish snack bar with excellent food; **Romagna Antica**, Elisabethstr. 52, 2716355, Mon-Thu 11:30 am to 2:30 pm and 6:30 pm to midnight, Fri-Sat evenings only, Italian, rather expensive, regular haunt of Munich stars, reservation required; **Tantris**, Johann-Fichte-Str. 7, tel. 362061, Tue-Sat noon to 2 pm (last order) and 6:30 pm to 10:15 pm (last order), absolutely top-class gourmet cuisine (two Michelin stars), exclusive and very expensive, reservation advised; **Werneckhof**, Werneckstr. 11, tel. 399936, 6 pm to 1 am, good French cooking, medium prices.

TRENDY CAFÉS with good food: **Bamberger Haus**, Brunnerstr. 2, tel. 3088966, at Luitpold Park; **Café Extrablatt**, Leopoldstr. 7, tel. 333333, Mon-Fri 7 am to 1 am, Sat 9 am to 1 am, Sun 9 am to noon, jet-set café; **Café Münchener Freiheit**, Münchener Freiheit 20, tel. 349080, 6:30 am to 10 pm, open till 1 am in nice weather, breakfast till noon; **Café Schwabing**, Am Kurfürstenplatz, tel. 3088856, 8 am to 1 am, good breakfasts.
ICE-CREAM PARLORS: **Venezia**, Leopoldstr. 31, tel. 395540, has a branch at Kurfürstenplatz; **Rialto**, Leopoldstr. 62, tel. 348279.
TEA SHOPS: **Friesische Teestube**, Pündterplatz 2, tel. 348519, Mon-Sat 10 am to 10 pm, cozy, 150 varieties of tea, breakfast till 2 pm.
BARS / PUBS: **Bunter Vogel**, Herzogstr. 44, tel. 346185, good food; **Heppel & Ettlich**, Kaiserstr. 67, tel. 349359, cabaret in the evenings, children's cinema Sun mornings at 11; **Luigi Malone's**, Leopoldstr. 28a, tel. 395071, cocktail bar, international cuisine; **Roxy**, Leopoldstr. 48, tel. 349292, 8 am to 3 am, fashionable clientele, imaginative cocktails; **Schwabinger Podium**, Wagnerstr. 1, tel. 399482, Oldies und live music; **Shamrock Irish Pub**, Trautenwolfstr. 6, tel. 331081, Mon-Sat 4 pm to 1 am, live music, darts; **Spado's**, Belgradstr. 16, tel. 334379, turbulent *cervezeria* serving tapas; **Waikiki**, Neureutherstr. 39, tel. 2711146, 7 pm to 2 am, cocktails, Asian and Hawaiian food.
DISCOS: **Crash**, Ainmillerstr. 10, tel. 391640, hard rock and Oldies; **Viva**, Leopoldstr. 3, tel. 343535; **Singles**, Leopoldstr. 25, tel. 346358; **Alabamahalle** and **Millenium**, Domagkstr. 33, tel. 3244253.
LEISURE / SPECIAL EVENTS: **Englischer Garten**: The northern part can be reached by the U3/U6 to Universität, Giselastrasse or Münchener Freiheit, the southern part by the U3/6 to Odeonsplatz, by bus No. 53 to the Haus der Kunst.
Olympiapark: Reached by U3 to Olympiazentrum. *Television tower* with viewing platform and revolving restaurant, tel. 30672750. Elevator runs daily 9 am to 11:30 pm; *Olympia Swimming Hall* open daily 7 am to 10:30 pm, Tue & Thu till 6 pm, Mon from 10 am; *Tollwood Festival*, two weeks in June, with cabaret, music and international food.
Münchener Freiheit: *Schwabinger Weihnachtsmarkt*, Christmas Fair (in December).

Post Offices

Post Offices: Agnesstr. 3, tel. 30628423; Leopoldstr. 57, tel. 30628401.

Taxi Stands

Barer-/Schellingstrasse, tel. 2723874. Elisabethplatz, tel. 2721111. Münchener Freiheit, tel. 346364/216142. Siegestor, tel. 216141. Kurfürstenplatz, tel. 2710733. Josephsplatz, tel. 216121.

NEUHAUSEN

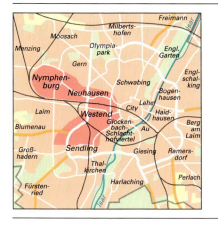

ROYAL SPLENDOR AND EVERYDAY LIFE

NEUHAUSEN
NYMPHENBURG PALACE
WEST END
SENDLING

NEUHAUSEN

Neuhausen is the area lying between Dachauerstrasse, the railroad tracks and Nymphenburg Palace and, despite its name ("Neuhausen" means "new houses"), is older than one might imagine. The first documentary mention dates back to 1163, and it can be assumed that the foundation of Neuhausen may have been as early as the 10th century. In 1662, Elector Karl Ferdinand Maria instructed the Italian architect Barelli to draw up plans for the palace of Nymphenburg – *Schloss Nymphenburg* – to mark the birth of the crown prince, Max Emanuel.

Building began in 1664 and continued until 1758. As was the custom in those days, Nymphenburg Palace was built well outside the city gates. The only other buildings nearby were the servants' quarters. When the heart of the original village was destroyed by fire in 1794, a whole network of streets was then laid out, and at the beginning of the 19th century well-to-do middle-class citizens of Munich moved out of the city and settled in the vicinity of the palace. Thus the Nymphenburger Strasse of today was originally a kind of feeder road, providing access to the palace from the city, and as early as 1876 the first horse-drawn tram ran through the district. The incorporation of Neuhausen into the royal capital of Munich was announced by the City Council on December 27, 1890.

The destruction wrought by war and its aftermath drastically altered the face of Neuhausen once more. The former hunting lodge at Rotkreuzplatz was demolished and the airfield at Oberwiesenfeld closed. Controversial new building projects such as the Kaufhof department store and the increased volume of traffic have both had a detrimental effect, though it must be said that the Kaufhof has brought new life to the district, making it the crystalization point of the entire neighborhood.

In spite of all this, Neuhausen, among the city's many neighborhoods, is still considered to be a good, even a fashionable address in Munich. Especially in recent years it seems to have developed into both the intellectual and the solid, middle-class heart of Munich. Increasing numbers of architects, artists, designers, and teachers are now moving to some of the fine, turn-of-the-century houses in the quarter, and to the small villas to be found in Gern or Nymphenburg.

Preceding pages: Sunset over Nymphenburg Palace. Left: At the wildlife enclosure in the Hirschgarten.

NYMPHENBURGER STRASSE

Nymphenburger Strasse

A good starting-point for a walk through Neuhausen is **Stiglmaierplatz**. The buildings around this seemingly-unplanned square are dominated by the majestic trademark of the world-famous Löwenbräu brewery. The Bavarian lion, surmounts the company's turreted headquarters. The **Löwenbräu-Keller**, with an ample beer-garden and various dining rooms, should not be missed – it offers a sample of the cozy, informal atmosphere which the Germans call *Gemütlichkeit*.

On Nymphenburger Strasse, leading away from the city center, you first come upon the **Courts of Law** (district, state and superior state courts) at No. 16. Diagonally across is Munich's favorite international **Cinema** (No. 31), where German-language as well as American and French films are shown in their original versions. Film fans like to meet at the bar in the spacious foyer, where they pass the time before a film having a cappuccino or an ice cream, or munching on popcorn (for ticket reservations, phone 555255).

A little further along, on the corner of Maillinger Strasse, on the left hand side of the street, you will see the **Wappenhaus**, whose Jugendstil façade is adorned with Munich's coat-of-arms, as well as the coats-of-arms of many foreign countries. The most important building on Nymphenburger Strasse, however, must be No. 64: it is the **Franz Josef Strauss House**, the party headquarters of the CSU which has governed the Bavarian Free State for decades with an apparently unassailable majority.

Visitors to Munich of all ages will be much more interested in seeing the home and winter quarters of Munich's internationally-acclaimed **Zircus Krone** (on the corner of Wredestr. and Marsstr., just a few minutes walk along Pappenheimstr.). This is a circus held in a building, constructed in 1962, shaped like a circus tent where daily, from December to March,

Right: A street festival around the fountain at Rotkreuzplatz.

ROTKREUZPLATZ

top circus artistes, animals and their trainers can be seen. The circus leaves on tour every year in March, at which time the elephants are driven in a picturesque procession along **Arnulfstrasse** to the main station. From March until the following winter season the circus hall is used for other events, particularly rock concerts. Many of the big names of the rock and pop worlds have performed here, from the Beatles and Bob Dylan to Freddie Mercury. Not far from here the **Hackerbrücke**, an architecturally-interesting steel bridge dating from the 19th century, spans the railroad tracks near the Hacker-Pschorr Brewery.

Turning right here, you come to the former container train station just a few steps away, where a large **flea market** takes place all year round (Thu-Sat, 7 a.m. to 6 p.m.; S-Bahn Hackerbrücke). During the Oktoberfest, the grounds here serve as a parking lot, and in December the Winter Tollwood Festival, an alternative Christmas Market with a wide program, sets up shop here (see p. 203).

Around Rotkreuzplatz

Going further along Nymphenburger Strasse, you will cross **Landshuter Allee**, a busy part of the Middle Ring Road. About 100 yards/meters further on you reach what is probably the newest "sub-center" of Munich, the busy **Rotkreuzplatz** square.

High-rise buildings are rare in Munich, so the lofty tower of the **Rot-Kreuz-Schwesternschule** (Red Cross Nursing School) on the square is particularly noticeable. The **Rot-Kreuz-Krankenhaus** (Red Cross Hospital) is attached to it.

Another modern structure is the **Kaufhof** department store, a clinker-construction building which dominates the lively square with its amusing fountain. A number of shops and small fruit and vegetable stands have settled into the area, making shopping trips into the city center hardly necessary any more for many locals. On Thursdays, from 1 p.m., a market is held here, featuring natural and organically-grown foods from the surrounding

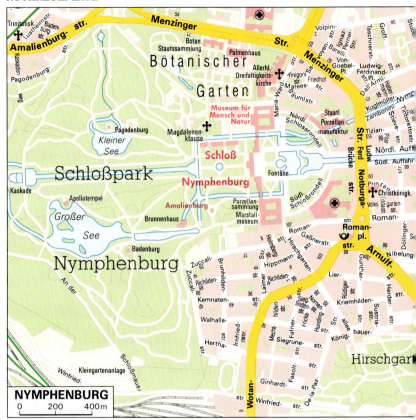

countryside. Handmade presents can also be found at this year-round market.

A landmark on Rotkreuzplatz is **Sarcletti's** (on the corner of Schulstrasse), one of Munich's leading ice cream parlors. If you would rather not stand in line, go to **Venezia**, directly on the square. Diagonally across from Sarcletti's, on Nymphenburger Strasse, next to McDonalds, a small passage leads to **Karl-Albrecht-Hof**. A stone column stands here as a memorial to the Elector of Bavaria, who was also German Emperor. Here, the Italian restaurant **Dai Gemelli** serves delicious *antipasti* and choice Italian wines.

Not far away from Rotkreuzplatz are some of the most popular metting places in the neighborhood: **Café Ruffini**, at Orffstrasse 22, run by a cooperative and offering full breakfasts, Italian-style cuisine and organically-produced wines; diagonally across, **Frundsberg** (Frundsbergstr. 46) has become *the* trendy bar in Neuhausen, offering international cuisine, good wines and cocktails, and even Internet access; **Café Freiheit** at *Platz der Freiheit* (Leonrodstr. 20 corner of Landshuter Allee), and restaurant **Bröding** (Schulstrasse 9). Intellectuals, actors and actresses are regular customers at all four places. In contrast, the **Jagdschlössl** (Hunting Lodge) on Rotkreuzplatz, is adorned, as one might expect, with the appropriate trophies and has a more down-to-earth atmosphere.

HIRSCHGARTEN / NYMPHENBURG

The No. 12 streetcar runs from Rotkreuzplatz to Romanplatz. The neighborhood which lies between Rotkreuzplatz and **Romanplatz** is one of Munich's smartest residential areas, it is therefore well worth making the journey on foot to see some of the beautiful villas and gardens situated beneath tall tress, for example around **Rondell Neuwittelsbach** and **Prinzenstrasse**.

The **Hirschgarten** (Deer Garden) has by far the largest beer garden in Munich, and lies a bit to the south of Romanplatz. It has an interesting history: In about 1780, Elector Karl Theodor had a zoological garden laid out here. The fallow deer for the royal hunt were kept in an enclosure, which still exists today beside the beer garden and still contains deer. This makes it a popular place to bring children and a favorite picnic spot for local people. It is also an ideal location for the *Magdalenenfest*, a festival held here annually in July which attracts visitors as much for its scenery as for the quaint wooden carousel and the many street vendors.

The **Nymphenburg Canal** is only about fifteen minutes' walk from here. This decorative waterway runs straight as an arrow and is spanned by two bridges (only the western bridge near Romanplatz is open to traffic). It leads straight up to the central building of Nymphenburg Palace. The **Hubertus Fountain**, in the form of a belling stag behind a wrought iron trellis, marks the eastern end of the canal, nearest the city. From the fountain there is a view across the two footbridges between the **North and South Avenues** to the main façade of Nymphenburg Palace, with its impressive fountain which is set in a large circular forecourt.

Nearby, at Wendl-Dietrich-Strasse 20, you find Munich's **Jugendherberg** (Youth Hostel). On the way there you pass by the Neuhausen **Mustersiedlung** (Model Housing Estate), built in the 1920s with approximately 1,900 apartments and broad lawns which stretch between Rotkreuzplatz and Arnulfstrasse. **Maria-Trost-Kirche** on Winthirstrasse should be seen; the church where the Irish missionary Winthir, who is said to have converted the people of Neuhausen in about 1000 AD, is buried. A number of other Neuhausen worthies are also buried here, including Oskar von Miller, founder of the German Museum and Johann Baptist Stiglmaier, who cast the "Bavaria" monument.

In winter, the Nymphenburg Canal offers particular pleasure not only to the inhabitants of Neuhausen. This is the season for the traditional sport of curling, for ice-hockey and for skating. The canal

NYMPHENBURG PALACE

linking the palace with the city was built in 1730 as a counterpart to the canal which had been built in the park at Nymphenburg a few years earlier. It is fed by the Würm, a small river in the west of Munich.

NYMPHENBURG PALACE

Nymphenburg Palace is a magnificent sight when approached along the *Nördliche* or *Südliche Auffahrtsallee*, on either side of the Nymphenburg canal. It is a vast baroque construction, about 660 yards (600 m) wide, and the pavilions which make up the complex flank the palace on the left and right in a broad semi-circular sweep.

In 1662, Elector Ferdinand Maria presented to his wife, Henriette of Savoy, the *Schwaige Kemnat* (roughly translated: Alpine Boudoir), to celebrate the birth of their son and heir, Max Emanuel. Increasingly ambitious building projects were continued into the 18th century; side wings were added on, and a large circular palace section now embraces the architecturally-harmonious buildings, waterways and parkland. Over the centuries extensions were planned in ever stricter symmetry, and the canal came to serve as a reflective axis.

The architects Enrico Zuccalli and Giovanni Antonio Viscardi were responsible for the present-day appearance of the palace, which was originally dedicated to the goddess of the hunt, Diana. Zuccalli had already planned the buildings at Schleissheim and Lustheim, as well as the Theatinerkirche. During his long absence from Munich, occupied with the war against the Turks, Max Emanuel entrusted Viscardi with supervising the actual construction work.

Following Zuccalli's death and a long gap in the building program caused by the War of the Spanish Succession, Elec-

*Above: The park of Nymphenburg Palace.
Right: One of the splendid royal coaches in the Marstall Museum.*

NYMPHENBURG PALACE

tor Karl Albrecht put the management of the building of Nymphenburg in the hands of Josef Effner in 1715. Effner was also responsible for the construction of the *Badenburg*, the *Pagodenburg*, and the *Magdalenenklause*, all of which display a French influence.

A tour of the palace itself begins on the first floor and leads first of all to the **Steinerner Saal** (Stone Hall), the two-story banquet hall of the central building with frescos by Johann Baptist Zimmerman. You should also be sure to see the **Gobelin Zimmer** (Tapestry Room), the former bedrooms, the **Wappenzimmer** (Heraldic Room), the **Chinesisches Lackkabinett** (Chinese Lacquer Room) and the **Schönheitsgalerie** (Gallery of Beauty) of King Ludwig I. In contrast to the *Schönheitsgalerie* of Max Emanuel, King Ludwig's beauties include a number of ladies of humble birth, Helene Sedlmayr for instance, the daughter of a Munich shoemaker, and the notorious courtesan Lola Montez, the Spanish dancer, who cost Ludwig his throne. The **Chapel** in the west wing, which was completely renovated as recently as 1992, is also worth a visit.

The summer residences at Nymphenburg can be seen on a short walk through the extensive park which surrounds the palace. It is particularly worth visiting the **Amalienburg**, a charming and quite beautiful little rococo building designed by Franz Cuvilliés the Elder. The Amalienburg was built between 1734 and 1739 as a small hunting lodge for Electress Maria Amalia, while the unique **Badenburg** was built a little earlier, between 1718 and 1721, by J. Effner for Elector Max Emanuel. The **Pagodenburg**, also by Effner, was built beside the Pagodenburg lake as a royal tea pavilion. Also worth seeing are Max Emanuel's hermitage, the **Magdalenenklause**, and a **witch's cottage** designed for the royal children about 1800, but above all the old greenhouses; the **Palmenhaus** (Palm

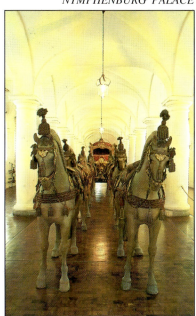

House) and the **Steinernes Haus** (Stone House). The great **cascades** behind it were built by Effner in 1717. The reclining figures symbolize the river deities of the Danube and Isar rivers.

Friedrich Ludwig von Sckell was responsible for the **Palace Gardens** as they appear today. He changed the strictly symmetrical lines of the park, originally laid out in the French style, into a more informal English landscaped garden. Each evening at dusk one can see a regular sight: flocks of crows returning from their forays into the city to roost here for the night.

Nymphenburg Park is just as popular with the human inhabitants of Munich, who enjoy having this beautiful open space right on their doorstep. Where else in the midst of the city – other than in the Englischer Garten – can you walk through such lovely artificially-landscaped nature? At the crack of dawn, panting joggers get their exercise here and in spring, when the first warm rays of sunlight flood through the park, old and

NYMPHENBURG PALACE

young alike come to relax on the benches beside the Steinernes Haus and bask in the long-awaited warm sunshine. Two artificial lakes, cascades and streams, the charming little summer residences, and the Monopterus temple delight the eye of anyone enjoying a leisurely stroll through the park. Refreshments are on hand too, at the **Café Palmenhaus** which has been accommodated in an old greenhouse.

Besides the palace and the park, Nymphenburg also offers four further attractions: three museums and an inn. The Marstall Museum (Royal Stables) and the **Porzellan Museum** (Porcelain Museum) are both to be found in the south wing of the palace. The first Bavarian porcelain factory was founded in 1747 by Elector Max Joseph III. It was originally housed in a small building in the Au district and was subsequently moved in 1761 to a specially-built house on the palace grounds. The fine porcelain was all decorated by hand, and customers had to pay princely prices – as one might expect for porcelain from a royal factory. The **Marstall Museum** boasts a collection of royal coaches and magnificent carriages, as well as portraits of the Wittelsbach family's favorite horses.

The north wing of the palace houses the popular **Museum für Mensch und Natur** (Museum of Man and Nature). Man's relationship to the natural world is portrayed here in a vivid and convincing display, and in a style which particularly appeals to children.

The palace inn, **Zur Schwaige**, to be found in a side wing of the palace, has a shady beer garden and serves both good Bavarian and international food.

The Botanical Gardens

Having made the long journey from the city out to Nymphenburg Palace, you should definitely make time to visit the

Above: Like an impressionist painting – in the park of Nymphenburg Palace. Right: Blutenburg Castle.

Botanical Gardens which adjoin it. The gardens are open all the year round and are easily reached by the No. 17 streetcar. The entrance to the botanical gardens is on **Menzinger Strasse**, just opposite the hospital (*Krankenhaus zum Dritten Orden*). In summer, a small signposted side entrance leads directly from Nymphenburg Park into the gardens. You only have to follow the signs leading in the direction of "Magdalenenklause." The highlight of a visit to these beautiful gardens is without a doubt the **Tropisches Gewächshaus** (Tropical Greenhouse), a filigree confection of glass and steel. Here you can walk through dense forests of ferns, enjoy the magnificent orchids in a humid jungle climate, or admire the immense number of different varieties of cactus.

Blutenburg

It is also worth braving the frequent traffic jams on Menzinger Strasse and Verdistrasse to drive out to the medieval castle of **Blutenburg**. Between 1431 and 1440 Duke Albrecht III of Bavaria had the castle built as a hunting lodge and summer residence. Later on, under Duke Sigismund, this island-like building was expanded to include protective walls, defence towers and a moat fed by the waters of the Würm.

A new chapel was added to the castle in 1488; note the wings of the late-Gothic altar by Jan Polak, who worked in Munich from 1482 on. There are some particularly beautiful small glass paintings, including an *Adoration of Christ* from 1497.

Amongst other things, the Blutenberg is home to the **Internationale Jugendbibliothek** (International Youth Library), which contains 400,000 titles in 110 languages. During the summer months, the popular **Blutenburg Castle Concerts** are held in the inner courtyard. There is also a restaurant which offers you a rare opportunity to enjoy a candlelit meal in the courtyard of a this lovely castle.

WEST END

WEST END

This part of Munich was designated as the 20th City District in 1890. It lies between the Theresienwiese and Barthstrasse on an east-west axis, and between Landsbergerstrasse and the Ganghofer Bridge on a north-south line. The wide-ranging policy of traffic calming introduced in recent years means that the volume of through-traffic has largely been stemmed. It is inadvisable for anyone who is not familiar with this area to visit it by car, as even the locals despair over the confusing one-way system.

The oldest residents call this district **Schwanthaler Höh'** (Schwanthaler Heights). It came into being in the middle of the l9th century, growing up around large construction projects such as the railroad tracks which were laid down to the main station, the *Ruhmeshalle* (Hall of Fame) and several breweries, Hacker-Pschorr and the Augustiner Brewery, for example, all of which have made their mark on the area. Workers came here, some from far away, some from the overcrowded city, and they naturally needed somewhere to live. Most found only poor accommodation where they would frequently have to sleep in shifts. This led, largely through their own initiative, to the creation of the first housing cooperatives. With help from the SPD (Social Democratic Party) and trade unions, large blocks of flats were erected to the west of Ganghoferstrasse. These were for the exclusive use of cooperative members and enabled many families to find cheap accommodation. Indeed, fifth generation members of some of these original families still live here today, comparatively cheaply by Munich standards.

For a long time the West End had a disreputable name as a run-down, disadvantaged, working-class suburb. However, since the mid-1960s it has undergone a fundamental change: thanks to the comparatively favorable rents it enjoyed, it became an attractive proposition for students and foreign workers. Turks, Yugoslavs, Greeks and Italians have brought an unusual and varied atmosphere to the district, and it is now nicknamed "Munich's Kreuzberg" and "Little Istanbul." There is a choice and variety here which is unique in Munich, thanks to the many small fruit and vegetable shops, and the restaurants offering Mediterranean fare.

This multicultural ethnic mix creates problems, too, such as the prevalence of rent-sharks and speculators, but the **Kulturladen West End** (West End Cultural Center) at Ligsalzstrasse 20 can often offer assistance. Neighborhood festivals, entertainment and exhibitions are organized here with different nationalities, children's groups and study groups, and there is also a tenants' advice center which is extremely helpful and prevents, for example, unwanted development in the area. To serve the area's cultural requirements in the stricter sense, there is the **Kulturkeller** on Westendstrasse.

Towards the bottom of **Schwanthalerstrasse**, almost at the foot of Schwanthaler Höh' and in the center of the St.-Paul-Platz, the neo-Gothic basilica of **St. Paul** towers high above the surrounding rooftops. St. Paul's, which has a nave flanked by two side aisles, is one of Munich's best-known churches, not least because visitors to the famous Oktoberfest have to pass it on their way to the *Wies'n*, where the beer festival is held. On December 17, 1960, a low-flying aircraft collided with the main tower of the church and crashed in flames on to a streetcar in Paul-Heyse-Strasse. Forty-nine people lost their lives.

Georg von Hauberisser (1841-1922), the architect of St Paul's, was also responsible for the new town hall at Marienplatz. He himself lived in what is

Left: Lady Bavaria calmly accepts the homage of thousands of tourists.

BAVARIA MONUMENT

probably the finest house in the whole of the West End, **Hauberisser House**, at Schwanthalerstrasse 106, built in 1885.

From here, Schwantalerstrasse climbs gradually up to Schwantaler Höh'. The view on the left is, however, blocked by the monstrous, interlocked-cement-block **Hacker-Pschorr Complex**. A considerable area of Schwanthaler Höh' was sacrificed to this building during the 1960s, and today the vast complex combines shops, appartments and administrative offices. The only consolation offered by this architectural nightmare, which critics have labelled "Munich's Building Sin," is the fact that it contains two large restaurants, **Hackerkeller** and **Pschorrkeller.** Large events and exhibitions are often held here, and in summer you can sit outside: the friendly little beer garden nearby, beneath the trees, has thankfully been allowed to remain.

A few minutes away stands the imposing **Bavaria Monument**, which Ludwig I commissioned. The design of Bavaria with the oak leaf wreath, flanked by a lion, Munich's emblem, was by Ludwig von Schwanthaler. Munich's two master founders, Ferdinand von Miller and Johann Stiglmaier, took seven years to cast the six component parts of the monument from 150 tons of bronze melted down from old cannons. It was a statue of enormous proportions for those days, over 55 feet (18.5 m) high, on a 33-foot-high base which has 60 steps. It was unveiled on October 9, 1850. The "Bavarian Statue of Liberty" can be climbed inside right into the head, and the view of Munich's center from here in good weather is a reward for the 130-step climb.

The perfect setting for the statue is provided by the **Ruhmeshalle** (Hall of Fame; 1843-53), also commissioned by Ludwig I and conceived by Leo von Klenze as the counterpart to the Valhalla of the rival Prussians. The cornice, decorated with designs by Schwanthaler, is supported by 48 Doric columns. The col-

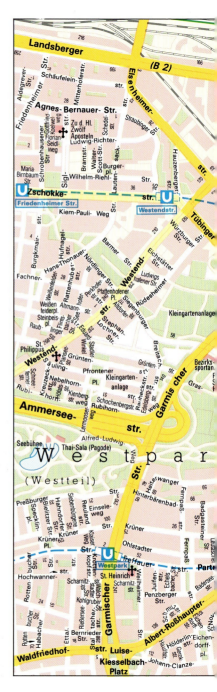

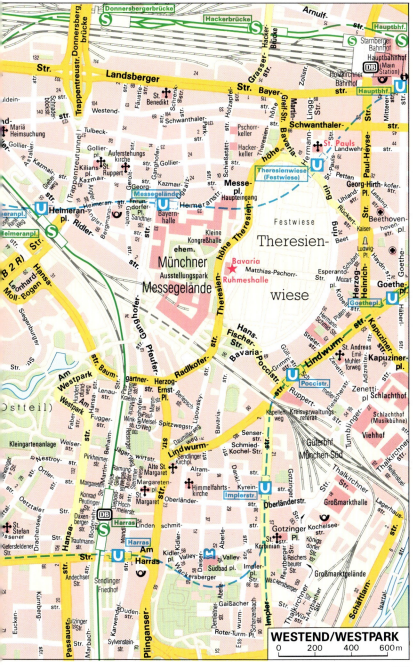

WEST END

onnade houses more than 70 marble busts of significant Bavarian historical figures.

The **Theresienwiese** (Theresa's Meadow) – or *Wies'n* for short – stretches out beyond the Bavaria statue and the Ruhmeshalle. In fact, the "meadow" is not green at all, and every year for two weeks it is the scene of the Oktoberfest. For the remaining 50 weeks the gravel-grey field is used mainly as a parking lot.

Just behind Bavaria and the Ruhmeshalle, between Theresienhöhe, Heimeranstrasse and Ganghoferstrasse, is the old **Messegelände** (Exhibition Grounds), with over 20 exhibition halls and an exhibition area of around 111 acres (45 hectares). Since the Exhibition Grounds were moved to the site of Munich's old Riem Airport in February 1998 (see p. 214), plans are underway for a complete facelift of the old grounds over the next few years. The small park in the middle is all that remains of the original exhibition grounds laid out between 1826 and 1831 by King Ludwig I as a public park in this new quarter of Munich. The construction of about 1,500 new apartments with cultural establishments is planned, as are a school and sites for craftsmem's workshops. A branch of the German Museum – the "Museum for Mobility" – is scheduled to move into the historically-protected exhibition halls, and various public events are planned to be held in the Congress Hall. During a period of transition, smaller exhibitions will be held in the remaining halls.

You can take a rexaing break at **Georg-Freundorfer-Platz**. Thanks to traffic-abatement measures and the construction of the U-Bahn station, a large grassy park with play areas has taken the place of a planned multi-story parking lot. Not far away is another green oasis in the West End; the wooded **Gollierplatz**, where Turkish, Greek, Italian and German children play together without con-

Above: View from Schwanthaler Höh' across to St. Pauls church. Right: The Hacker-Pschorr-Complex looms over Schwanthaler Höh'.

flict or difficulty in a truly multi-cultural society. During the summer months, one of Munich's best flea markets is held here regularly.

Diagonally across from the park is the red clinker brick façade of the **Ledigenheim** (Home for Bachelors), built in the Bauhaus style of the 1920s to solve the problem of homeless drifters. Here, too, is the neo-Romanesque **Church of St. Rupert**, which was built between 1901 and 1903. However, the oldest church in the West End is **St. Benedikt's** on Schrenkstrasse, which dates from 1883. The land for building the church and the church's bells were donated by the Federation of Brewers. Next door to it the city authorities erected the first school in the district, but it was destroyed in World War II. Today, in its place, are a branch of the public library and a youth leisure center.

Just around the corner on busy Landsberger Strasse, the northern boundary of the West End, stands the oldest inn in the area, **Postfranzl**, which was first mentioned in 1820 and is a protected historical building. Seeing the premises today, with its tiny beer garden, one can get more or less of an idea of what Schwantaler Höh' must once have looked like. To the annoyance of many a West Ender, however, the Postfranzl does not stock the noble "Edelstoff" brew of the **Augustiner Brewery**, even though the brewery itself is more or less just around the corner, down Landsberger Strasse.

West Park

This spacious and truly beautiful park lies to the south-west of the West End, between Hansastrasse, Ganghoferstrasse and Fürstenriederstrasse. Sadly, it is divided now by the Middle Ring Road, although the two parts of the park are linked by foot-bridges. This newest of Munich's parks covers an area of about 178 acres (72 hectares) and was laid out for the International Horticultural Exhibition (IGA) of 1983. Publicity from the IGA, combined with the participation

WEST PARK

of a number of citizens' action groups, helped to produce a remarkable, artificially-created natural landscape right in the heart of the city. Hills, small lakes and waterfalls have been so skillfully incorporated into the landscape that one could almost believe the park evolved naturally, and the many artificially-created stretches of water and wetlands have now encouraged swans, ducks, coots and frogs to make their homes here, as well as all sorts of wildlife not normally seen in an urban environment. A **lakeside stage** in the form of an amphitheater is used for open-air concerts and theater performances. Over 200 Nepalese craftsmen created a wooden **Temple** in the park, with adjoining buildings. Not far away a Chinese "scholars' garden," the **Gelehrtengarten**, has been recreated, which makes one want to stop and meditate awhile.

Above: The Thai Pavilion in the West Park.
Right: The memorial to the Blacksmith of Kochel in Sendling.

A gleaming golden Thai **Pavilion** adds to the Eastern flavor in this corner of the park, not surprisingly nicknamed "Little Asia." On a hill not far away is the **Rosengarten** (Rose Garden), which comes alive in summer as people enjoy their *Weissbier* (wheat beer), pretzels and *Steckerlfisch* (fish on a spit). The **Hopfengarten** (Hop Garden) at the other end of the park offers a more peaceful atmosphere, and making your way there you will perhaps pass the **Drachenwiese** (Kite Meadow), a favorite with children, or the idyllically-situated **Seecafé** (Lake Café), where ducks, swans and carp beside the cafés orange tables hope to be thrown a few tidbits.

SENDLING

The district of **Sendling** (or more precisely Obersendling, Mittersendling and Untersendling) lies south of the West Park and extends as far east as the river Isar. Since it was mentioned as early as 782 AD, the village of Sentlinga can justly claim to be more than 300 years older than the city of Munich itself, to which it was eventually annexed several centuries later. Since the early 20th century, Sendling has been an industrial area, particularly Mittersendling and Obersendling. This is the home of Linde Eismaschinen AG, the engineering firm of Deckel, Philip Morris and Siemens, the electrical and electronics giant.

Sendling achieved historic significance in 1705 with the *Sendlinger Bauernschlacht* (Peasants' Battle), when more than 800 peasants from the uplands, resisting forcible recruitment, were butchered by the Austrians during what came to be called the *Mordweihnacht* (Christmastide Slaughter).

The village church of **St. Margaret** (on the corner of Lindwurmstrasse and Plinganserstrasse) was burned down during this conflict but was rebuilt in 1711 in the Upper Bavarian baroque style. In 1830, Wilhelm Lindenschmidt executed a relief on the north wall of the church to commemorate the slaughter. Opposite the church stands a memorial to the man said to have led the peasants into battle, the Blacksmith of Kochel, though this may be more legend than history.

The only working farm still in existence within the boundaries of Munich is in Sendling: *Stemmer Hof*, in the possession of the same family since 1799. For decades now they have resisted the development of their old *Stemmerwiese* (meadow) with the support of various citizens' action groups. The **Jägerwirtstrasse** (Road of the Huntsmen's Innkeeper), along the Stemmerwiese, is a reminder of the olden days when huntsmen and beaters took liquid refreshment together after a successful hunt. From Sendling's maypole in front of St. Margaret's, the old **Blacksmith's Shop** can be seen (today it is an inn). The endless stream of traffic on Plinganserstrasse flows on past here down to **Harras**, once the idyllic heart of Sendling, now a hectic

traffic junction with road, rail, streetcar and bus routes converging here.

To the east of Harras, at the foot of Sendling Hill, lies Munich's "stomach." This is the site of the **Grossmarkthalle** (Wholesale Market Hall), one of the largest covered markets for fruit and vegetables in Europe, where more than 10,000 traders work on approximately 74 acres (30 hectares) to keep Munich supplied with food. Needless to say, this draws a tremendous volume of traffic into the area. The market halls are not especially interesting to visit, so it is best to take the underground U6 from Harras straight back into the city center. It is also possible to make this journey by car or on foot from Harras, down Sendling Hill and along **Lindwurmstrasse**, past Munich's oldest discotheque, the former "Crash" – nowadays called the **Stromlinien Club** – and reach the bulky form of the building which houses the local government offices, the **Kreisverwaltungsreferat**, by way of Goetheplatz and Sendlinger-Tor-Platz.

NEUHAUSEN / NYMPHENBURG

Transport Connections
U-BAHN: U1 to Maillinger Strasse, Rotkreuzplatz.
BUS: No. 32 to Romanplatz; No. 68 to Kemnatenstrasse, Hirschgartenallee, Romanplatz; No. 33 to Rotkreuzplatz, Heimeranplatz, Westpark; No. 83 to Winthirplatz, Rotkreuzplatz; No. 177 to Neuhausen, Volkartstrasse, Rotkreuzplatz.
STREETCAR: No. 12 to Leonrodplatz, Rotkreuzplatz, Renatastrasse and Romanplatz; No. 17 via Arnulfstrasse and Romanplatz to Amalienburgstrasse; No. 20 to Stiglmaierplatz, Lothstrasse and Leonrodplatz.

Restaurants / Cafés / Night-life
BAVERIAN with beer garden: **Augustinerkeller**, Arnulfstr. 52, tel. 594393, "Edelstoff" beer on tap, children's play area; **Hirschgarten**, Hirschgartenallee 1, tel. 172591, beer garden (own picnic food allowed) and restaurant, deer enclosure right beside; **Jagdschlössl**, Nymphenburger Strasse 162, tel. 1689241, robust and earthy; **Löwenbräukeller am Stiglmaierplatz**, Nymphenburger Strasse 2, tel. 526021, central location (own picnic food *not* allowed); **Schlosswirtschaft zur Schwaige**, Schloss Nymphenburg, tel. 174421, good asparagus dishes, high-class atmosphere; **Taxisgarten**, Taxisstrasse 12, tel. 156827, only if the weather is good, the spare ribs with barbecue sauce are very popular, (own picnic food allowed).
TRENDY CAFÉS with good food: **Café Freiheit**, Leonrodstrasse 20 (corner of Landshuter Allee), tel. 134686, "in" place for cool types, good European cuisine; **Frundsberg**, Frundsbergstrasse 46, tel. 164333, 6 pm to 1 am, Sun 10 am to 1 am, ideal for brunch; **Café Neuhausen**, Blutenburgstr. 106, tel. 1236288, bistro flair, with outdoor seating; **Café Ruffini**, Orffstr. 22, tel. 161160, Tue-Sat 10 am to midnight, Sun 10 am to 6 pm, closed Mon, famous for breakfasts, service on the terrasse in summer, Italian cuisine, good table wine. **Sappralott**, Donnersberger Str. 37, tel. 164725, bar-restaurant, music is sometimes loud, open Fri-Sat till 3 am.
SPECIALTY CUISINE: **Agri**, Jutastr. 5, tel. 1235454, 5:30 pm to 1 am, Turkish cuisine, the appetizers are especially good; **Bistro Dai Gemelli**, im Karl-Albrecht-Hof, Nymphenburger Strasse 154, tel. 1675289, Mon-Fri noon to 10 pm, closed weekends; **Broeding**, Schulstrasse 9, tel. 164238, Tue-Sat 7 pm to midnight, this small restaurant serves only one 5-course meal per evening, exquisite, Italian-inspired regional cuisine, own imported Austrian wines, no credit cards; **Khanitta**, Thorwaldsenstr. 19, tel. 1297772, 11:30 am to 2:30 pm and 5:30 pm to 1 am, great Thai food, wide-ranging menu, no credit cards; **Metaxa**, Blutenburgstr. 37, tel. 1294545, 11:30 am to 2:30 pm and 5:30 pm to midnight, closed Sunday, good Greek food, small, shady beer garden; **Ralph's**, Leonrodstrasse 85, tel. 186764, Sun-Tue 6 pm to 1 am, Fri-Sat till 3 am, American cooking, good but expensive cocktails; **Shiraj**, Leonrodstrasse 56, tel. 1293974, Mon-Sun 11:30 am to 3 pm and 6 pm to midnight, Wed 6 pm to midnight, exclusive Indian food; **Shoya**, Gabelsbergerstr. 85, tel. 5236249, Mon-Sat 11 am to 1 am, Japanese atmosphere, in the back room you can eat on your knees in original Japanese style.
ICE CREAM PARLORS: **Sarcletti**, Rotkreuzplatz, Nymphenburger Strasse 155, tel. 155314, 8 am to 11:30 pm; **Venezia**, Rotkreuzplatz 8, tel. 847414, 11:30 am to 2:30 pm and 6 pm to midnight.
DISCOS: **Backstage**, Helmholtzstr. 18, tel. 1266100, directly beside S-Bahn station Donnersberger Brücke; **Tilt**, Helmholtzstr. 12, tel. 1297969, on the grounds of the former container train station, independent music, pop music Fridays.

Museums / Sightseeing
Nymphenburg Palace with the summer residences Amalienburg, Badenburg, Pagodenburg, Magdalenenklause and Hexenhäuschen in the palace gardens. In the south wing of the palace: *porcelain collection* in the **Marstall Museum** (Tue-Sun 9 am to noon and 1 pm to 5 pm), in **Lustheim Palace** (Tue-Sun 10 am to 12:30 pm and 1:30 pm to 4 pm) and in the **Schlossrondell** (Mon-Fri 8:30 am to noon and 12:30 pm to 5 pm, closed holidays, with sales rooms, tel. 17919710). Worth seeing in the north wing of the palace are the **Museum für Mensch and Natur**, Tue-Sun 9 am to 5 pm; **Palace Rooms** are open Tue-Sun 10 am to 12:30 pm and 1:30 pm to 4 pm, and the **Amalienburg** daily from 9 am to 12:30 pm and 1:30 pm to 5 pm; **Badenburg**, **Pagodenburg** and **Magdalenenklause**: Tue-Sun 10 am to 12:30 pm and 1:30 pm to 5 pm (only April to Nov). Entrance fee charged.
Schloss Blutenburg houses the *Internationale Jugendbibliothek* (reading and lending library in 12 languages, free children's films, tel. 89121160). The *Blutenburg Concerts* take place year-round. Info: tel. 8344945 and 9570028. Take the S2 or bus 73, 75 or 76 to Obermenzing.

Leisure Time
Botanischer Garten, Menzinger Str. 65, tel. 17861-310, Nov-Jan 9 am to 4:30 pm, March and October 9 am to 5 pm, April and September 9 am to 6 pm, May-August 9 am to 7 pm, lunch break 11:45 am to 1 pm. The greenhouses close half an hour before the park does, entrance fee, tram 17.
Zirkus Krone, Marsstrasse 43, tel. 558166, has its winter quarters in Munich, shows every evening from December to March. With S1-S7 to Hackerbrücke.

GUIDEPOST WEST END / SENDLING

Post Offices
Romanplatz 1, tel. 53882311; Leonrodstrasse 56, tel. 53882316; Winthirstrasse 4, tel. 53882383.

Taxis
Rotkreuzplatz, tel. 133946 and 216194; Waisenhausstrasse, tel. 216197; Romanplatz, tel. 176288 and 216193; Leonrodplatz, tel. 154141 and 216195.

WEST END

Transport Connections
S-BAHN: S1-S8 to Hackerbrücke.
U-BAHN: U4/U5 to Theresienwiese, Messegelände, Heimeranplatz.
BUS: No. 32 to Messegelände, Kazmairstrasse, Gollierplatz, Trappentreustrasse; No. 33 to Westpark, Heimeranplatz, Trappentreustrasse. (buses stop at the Donnersberger Brücke S-Bahn station.)

Restaurants / Cafés / Night-life
BAVERIAN with beer garden: **Hacker-Pschorr-Keller**, tel. 507004 and 501088, typical Bavarian restaurant with beer garden and live music from 7 pm, open 8 am to 1 am; **Rosengarten im Westpark**, am Westend 305, tel. 575053, daily 9:30 am to 11:30 pm; **Hopfengarten im Westpark**, Siegenburgerstr. 43, tel. 7608846, when the weather is good from 11 am to 10:30 pm, your own picnic food allowed in beer garden.
GREEK: **Stoa**, Gollierstr. 38, tel. 5024613, cozy Greek restaurant, humane prices.
INTERNATIONAL: **Ligsalz**, Ligsalzstrasse 23, tel. 504292, good and economical, Guinness served.
ITALIAN: **Al Paladino**, Heimeranplatz 1, tel. 5025657, 11:30 am to 2:30 pm and 6 pm to 11 pm, closed Sat, fresh Italian food, very good menu of the day; **Speisecafé West**, Tulbeckstr. 9, tel. 505400, small garden in rear courtyard, Italian wines, (jazz) breakfast till 5 pm.
TURKISH: **Antalya**, Bergmannstrasse 50, tel. 501948, belly dancing Fri-Sat from 9 pm, inexpensive Turkish food, closed Monday.
VEGETARIAN: **Gollier**, Gollierstrasse 83, tel. 501673, Mon-Fri noon to 2:30 pm and 5 pm to midnight, Sat 5 pm to midnight, Sunday 12 to 12, lunch buffet, drinks and tasty food from organic farms.
TRENDY BARS: **Ça Va**, Kazmairstrasse 44, tel. 5028584, 5 pm to 1 am, Sat-Sun 10 am to 1 am, Monday is Pasta Day; **Stragula**, Bergmannstr. 66, tel. 507743, cozy dext-door pub in the quarter.
DISCOS: **Nachtwerk**, Landsberger Str. 185, tel. 5783800. In Nachtwerk Club and in Club Nachtwerk 9zig Krad there is something happening every night; from 70s disco to pop to techno.

Sightseeing
The enormous **Bavaria** statue with Ruhmeshalle at Theresienhöhe can be visited Tue-Sun 10 am to noon and 2 pm to 5:30 pm (in winter till 4 pm), entrance fee, U4/U5 to Theresienwiese; the world-famous *Volksfest* and beer spectacle, **Oktoberfest**, takes place at the end of September for two weeks at Theresienwiese (S-Bahn 1-8 to Hackerbrücke or U3/U6 to Goetheplatz).

Post Offices
Post Office 12, Bergmannstrasse 47, tel. 5388-2585, Mon-Fri 8 am to noon and 3 pm to 6 pm, Sat 8 am to noon.

Taxi Stands
Theresienhöhe, tel. 509966; Ganghoferstrasse, tel. 506175 or 216192; Landsberger/Trappentreustr., tel. 216196; Eichstätter Strasse, tel. 572810.

SENDLING

Transport Connections
U-BAHN: U3/U6 to Implerstrasse, Poccistrasse; U6 to Harras, Partnachplatz, Westpark.

Restaurants / Cafés / Night-life
ASIAN: **Mangostin**, Maria-Einsiedelstr. 2 (U3 to Thalkirchen/Zoo), tel. 7232031, excellent Thai specialities in the beer garden, expensive.
BAVERIAN: **Antoniustenne**, Plinganserstrasse 10, tel. 773964, good food and wine, Tue-Fri 16:30 pm to 3 am, Sat till 4 am, Sun 9 pm to 3 am, closed Monday; **Sendlinger Augustiner**, Alramstr. 2, tel. 7470925, good Bavarian food, Thu-Sat beer from wooden keg; **Wöllinger**, Johann-Clanze-Str. 112, tel. 7144651, Bavarian cuisine, rustic decor, small garden; **Zum Flaucher**, Isarauen 8, tel. 7232677, lovely location on the river Isar, with beer garden.
GREEK: **Taverna Korfu**, Boschetsriederstrasse 47, tel. 7854942, cozy, inexpensive.
YUGOSLAVIAN: **Monte Negro**, Implerstr. 23, tel. 776162, 11:30 am to 2 pm and 6 pm to midnight, delicious specialities from Montenegro, good fish.
ITALIAN: **Pasticceria Bussone & Co.**, Thalkirchner Str. 126, tel. 7213164, 6 am to 10 pm, Neapolitan flair at the Grossmarkt.
SOUTH AMERICAN: **La Peseta Loca**, Oberländerstr. 3b, tel. 772845, food and livemusic from Latin-America.
TRENDY BARS: **Substanz**, Ruppertstr. 28, tel. 7212749, beer bar with punk overtones, live music often.
DISCOS: **Stromlinienclub**, Lindwurmstrasse 88, tel. 7460243, British pop, indepentent, etc.

Post Office
Am Harras 2, tel. 776286.

Taxi Stands
Am Harras, tel. 773077; Boschetsriederstr. 5, tel. 216172; Partnachplatz 3, tel. 216170; Ratzingerplatz 5, Tel. 782858.

141

SCHLACHTHOF

SCHLACHTHOF

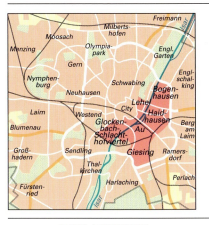

ON THE BANKS OF THE ISAR

**SCHLACHTHOF
GLOCKENBACH
LEHEL
GÄRTNERPLATZ
AU / GIESING
HAIDHAUSEN
BOGENHAUSEN**

SCHLACHTHOF

Beyond the old city walls, **Lindwurmstrasse** runs in a south-westerly direction from Sendlinger Tor towards the *Schlachthof* (slaughterhouse) district. This road used to be an important trade route, sometimes called the *Weinstrasse* (Wine Road) because wine was brought in along it from the south. The tranquility it once enjoyed has now vanished – the volume of traffic, the hectic shopping activity and the racing cyclists, even on the sidewalks, make it immediately obvious that this is one of Munich's main arterial roads.

To the right, between Lindwurmstrasse, Goetheplatz and Pettenkoferstrasse, is the hospital of Ludwigs-Maximilian University. The post office at **Goetheplatz**, built by Robert Verhoelzer from 1931 to 1933, dominates the square. It forms the last link in the chain of postal structures which have helped give Munich its "new building" appearance. Opposite is a five-screen movie theater, the **Royal-Palast**, which is amongst the largest and most modern in the city.

Preceding pages: The Maximilianeum stands at the head of Maximilianstrasse. Left: The Munich Employment Office.

For sports historians, the courtyard behind **Häberlstrasse 11** is interesting to see. The imposing building was erected in 1907-8 for the local men's sports club, and even incorporated a small gymnasium for women to improve their fitness, which was considered very progressive at the time.

An example of modern architecture at **Kapuzinerplatz** can't help but get your attention. This vast building with its clinker brick façade, which fits in with the high red brick walls of the Plague Cemetery diagonally across from it, was completed in 1987 and houses Munich's **Arbeitsamt** (Employment Office). It assembles under one roof a large staff who were formerly scattered all over the city. This is the largest office of its kind in the whole of Germany.

Anyone not seeking a job is instead better advised to visit the **Paulaner Bräuhaus** opposite, a sophisticated Bavarian inn with a large beer garden. It was founded in 1892 as the brewery pub for Munich's most important brewery of the time, Thomasbräu.

The old brewery had to yield to the **Thomashöfe**, a modern residential complex. But brewing continues, however, in fact, right in the middle of the inn, which means that Paulaner serves not only the freshest *Weissbier* in town, but it also

145

SCHLACHTHOF / GLOCKENBACH

serves up the popular brew in small glasses, as well as the familiar large ones.

Munich's **Schlachthof** (slaughterhouse), behind the Arbeitsamt, was built over a century ago under the direction of Max Pettenkofer, an expert in hygiene, and was of a highly advanced design for its day. A brisk trade in meat grew up around the slaughterhouse, which served the whole city, and the business still thrives here today. On the whole, this district has retained much of its original character and there are many old-fashioned bars and small neighborhood shops to be seen on Adlzreiterstrasse, while many houses on **Tumblingerstrasse** and at **Zenettiplatz** are still painted with their original faded trade signs, which lend them a great deal of old-time flair. The gourmet on the lookout for a pork-free refuge will find just that around the corner, at the small but excellent **Italfisch** seafood restaurant on Zenettistrasse.

Above: Street life on Hans-Sachs-Strasse.

Not many people are aware that from 1885 to 1894 Albert Einstein lived at **Adlzreiterstrasse 12**. The little house in the courtyard where the Einstein family lived is no longer there, but his scientific genius is commemorated by a plaque. A visit to the Adlzreiterstrasse Street Festival, which takes place in summer, will help make you appreciate the wide range of cultures which have settled into this quarter; nearly one third of the inhabitants here are foreigners.

At **Thalkirchner Strasse** 48 is Munich's **Dermatology Clinic**. Hiding behind a long, high wall opposite the clinic is the **Alter Südlicher Friedhof** (Old Southside Cemetery), dating back to the year 1788; an inner-city idyll with morbid charm. Its many park benches invite one to take a break amid the small neo-Gothic spires overgrown with ivy that grace the sarcophagi of long-dead mayors; amid gravestones bearing almost illegible epitaphs to a "privateer's wife" or a "battlefield artist"; amid weathered puti of mossy marble that find shade under grand old beech trees. Some famous names are to be seen in the old part of the cemetery: this is the final resting place of the painter Carl Spitzweg, and the scientific pioneers Justus von Liebig and Joseph von Fraunhofer, among others.

GLOCKENBACH

The **Glockenbach** district lies to the west of the cemetery. Its name, meaning "bell brook," derives from a bell foundry which once stood on one of the countless streams that flowed through the city. Street names like **Baumstrasse** and **Holzstrasse** (Tree and Wood Streets) are reminders that this was a district where many of Munich's craftsmen and woodworkers were to be found. The streams, upon which a lot of mills were also built, were used to bring in tree trunks, which had been floated downstream on the Isar

GLOCKENBACH

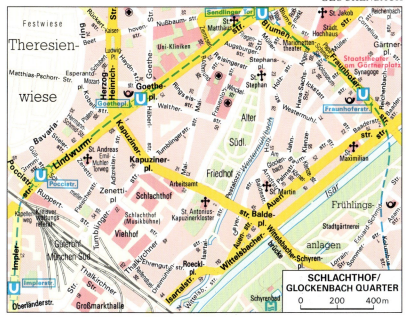

to Munich. They were then lifted out of the water to be dried on land before being further transported into the city.

Probably the prettiest spot in the area is **Am Glockenbach**. The **Westermühl bach** runs through here and along **Pestalozzistrasse**. It is the only remaining stream of what was once a dense network of waterways running through Munich. It lends a cozy, village air to this square with its *Gründerzeit* (late 19th century) buildings, and because of this, the district has become a rather trendy place, where even members of the gay community feel comfortable in the neighborhood's pubs, bars and cafés (for example, **Café Glück**, Palmstr. 4).

Anyone who enjoys rummaging in small boutiques and second-hand shops will be at home on **Müllerstrasse**. Here, and on **Hans-Sachs-Strasse** – which has been historically protected since 1981 because of its neo-renaissance and neo-baroque buildings – you will find avant-garde fashion, old bric-à-brac and expensive designer products. Across from the **Modernes Theater**, a small private stage with a bar, is a cinematic relic with a tendency toward cult or message films, the **Arena**, on Hans-Sachs-Strasse, which still has its hard seats from the 1930s. A popular in-spot, **Faun**, is just a few doors down from here.

By far the most famous drinking-establishment in the neighborhood is the **Fraunhofer**, on bustling **Fraunhoferstrasse**, which forms the boundary with the Gärtnerplatz district. Over a hundred years old and formerly a hunting hostelry, it is now one of the most popular "alternative" pubs in Munich, recently restored to its old imperial glory. The place is always full thanks to the excellent cuisine, friendly service and reasonable prices. For more intellectual pursuits there is a small theater in the courtyard of the Fraunhofer, and a cinema, the **Werkstattkino**, whose movies often raise a ruckus and bring in the full weight of the state.

The vast **St. Maximilian Church** on Auenstrasse can be seen for miles

GLOCKENBACH / LEHEL

around, from the banks of the Isar and across **Wittelsbach Bridge** and **Cornelius Bridge**. The church was built at the end of the 19th century in the Italian Romanesque style.

One expedition worth taking is to the southern edge of the quarter. The atmosphere around Mamma Ferraro's **Eiscafé Italia** on **Roecklplatz**, which welcomes children, is almost Neapolitan. Eyes light up and mouths water when the unmistakable Tomaso comes out balancing his specialties. The only close competition is Ellio's **Ciao** around the corner on Wittelsbacherstrasse. Many a cyclist along the Isar has come to a screeching halt with the thought of Ellio's strawberry mélange sundae. Back on **Ehrengutstrasse**, such popular student meeting places as the excellent Turkish **Yol**, and **Glatz**, known for its delicious crepes, ad-

join the "Italia." The bastion of Indian culinary culture on the square is **Sangam**, which offers excellent Tandoori cuisine served in a beautiful interior of carved, wooden arabesques. Exotic dishes from the French colonial tradition are brought to the table at **Makassar**, just around the corner on **Dreimühlenstrasse**. The herbs of Provence and the rum of the creoles inspire attention-getting creations by the chef. **Americanos**, on Thalkirchnerstrasse, attracts young and hip Tex-Mex fans, who can step on each other's cowboy boots here in the evening.

LEHEL

Of all the districts of Munich, Lehel (pronounced *Lechel*) has the loveliest situation: it is bounded by the Englischer Garten to the north and the green ribbon of the Isar river to the east, while the Hofgarten and the Residenz lie to the west and, close by to the south, Viktualienmarkt.

Above: One of the memorials in the Old Southside Cemetery. Right: St. Anna-Platz in Lehel with the neo-romanesque parish church of St. Anna.

ST. ANNA-PLATZ

Many of the lovely old houses dating back to the early 1870s, the *Gründerzeit*, are still standing here, but the shocking rents can only be afforded by companies and very well-heeled individuals. Small shops and bars are becoming rare here. Yet a pleasant elegant atmosphere can still be felt in this quarter.

Above the U-Bahn station *Lehel*, which is in the center of the district, is **St. Anna-Platz**, where there are two churches dedicated to St. Anne. **Klosterkirche St. Anna** stands almost hidden at the side of the square. Munich's first rococo church, built from 1723 to 1733, is surrounded by monastery buildings which have been occupied by Franciscan monks since 1827.

The church was badly damaged during World War II but, with much sacrifice, was rebuilt and restored to its full glory between 1946 and 1968. The treasures of the church include the high altar by the Asam brothers, which was restored in 1970, and paintings by C. D. Asam. Its younger sister church, the **Pfarrkirche St. Anna** (Parish Church of St. Anne), is rather more staid and dignified. It stands opposite the monastery church, neo-Romanesque in style, the work of Gabriel von Seidl. The square itself, spread out before it, is beautiful, tree-lined and peaceful – quite a rural idyll. Lion Feuchtwanger, one of Munich's greatest writers, spent his childhood here, and in the 1920s wrote *Erfolg* (Success), a novel in which he held up a critical mirror to his native city.

A stroll down Bruderstrasse to Prinzregentenstrasse brings you to the **Haus der Kunst** (House of Art), built by the Nazis. This temple of art, with its formerly antiquated reputation, was given a breath of fresh air in 1994. Director Christoph Vitali has since managed, through magnificent, world-class exhibitions, as well as unusual and effective projects, to bring the museum and its art to the people. Accompanying suitable exhibitions, an additional musical program, running late into the night, is already being organized. To this, opening hours

that are favorable to the museum-going public can also be added (until 10 p.m.). The west wing of the museum houses the **Staatsgalerie Moderner Kunst** (State Gallery of Modern Art), in which expressionist and surrealist artists' works, deigned "degenerate" and removed by the Nazi regime, are on display. The east wing houses Munich's fashionable discotheque **P1**, outside which Munich's "Beautiful People" can still be seen standing in line at three in the morning.

Southwest of the Haus der Kunst is the late-classical **Prince Carl Palace**. Lavishly restored and scarcely used, this is the official residence of the Minister-President of Bavaria. The *Altstadtring* (Inner Ring Road) passes right through the building's "cellar." From the Haus der Kunst, make for the statue of the Angel of Peace, the *Friedensengel*; past the *Eisbach* and the first paths into the Englischer Garten, Lerchenfeldstrasse with the **Prähistorische Staatssammlung** (National Prehistoric Collection) branches off to the left. Bavaria's cultural epochs can be followed here, from the early Stone Age to the late Middle Ages.

Back on Prinzregentenstrasse, a visit to the **Neue Sammlung** (New Collection), with rotating exhibitions on the history of design, is worthwhile. A little further on is the massive edifice of the **Bayerisches National Museum** (Bavarian National Museum). It was erected between 1894 and 1900, at vast expense, by Gabriel von Seidl and furnished in the most magnificent manner as a symbol of Bavarian independence. A visit here is essential, both for folklore and art history (see p. 181 of the "Museums in Munich" section). At the **Schack Gallery** (Prinzregentenstrasse 9), works by Böcklin, Schwind, Lenbach and Spitzweg are exhibited.

The promenade along the Isar begins in front of the Luitpold Bridge at the

Above: Day in, day out, the traffic roars through the "cellar" of Prince Carl Palace. Right: A good place to sit in the sun.

Friedensengel. This will delight your eyes, but not your ears. At the turn of the century, this was one of the best addresses in the city, but now the traffic surges around it, in front of the houses on **Widenmayerstrasse** and behind them again on **Sternstrasse**. Despite this, the façades of these magnificent houses still serve as a reminder of the heyday of Munich's bourgeoisie. A glance at the embankment of the Isar and the cataracts in the river may help you realize how idyllic this quarter once was. Continuing in the direction of Maximilianstrasse, you pass the long complex of the *Bayerische Versicherungskammer* (Bavarian Insurance Association).

On reaching **Maximilianstrasse**, you will be rewarded with a magnificent view of one of Munich's finest streets. On the left, across the Isar, is the **Maximilianeum**, the seat of the Bavarian parliament, where the *Freistaat*'s political decisions are made. It was built between 1857 and 1874 under the direction of Friedrich Bürklein.

On the right, towards the city center, the statue of King Maximilian II, which the people of Munich casually refer to as the **Max Two Monument**, immediately catches your eye. Kaspar von Zumbusch erected the statue in 1875 to honor the king, who not only promoted the arts and sciences, but who also took an interest in social affairs. The arms of the four Bavarian tribes – the Franks, Bavarians, Palatines and the Swabians – are displayed supported by children on its base.

A little further towards the city center, Maximilianstrasse is dominated by two huge buildings influenced by English Gothic, their stature only slightly diminished by the trees in front of them. On the left is the **Museum für Völkerkunde** (Museum of Ethnology) and on the right the seat of the **Regierung von Oberbayern** (Upper Bavarian Government). Both buildings were constructed in the mid-19th century in a "style representing contemporary culture." A visit to the recently-renovated Museum of Ethnology is highly recommended. Here you can

LEHEL

delve into a wide variety of treasures from the Asian, African and Latin-American cultures. Since 1997, the enormous restored murals have been on display. About 100 years ago, 59 artists, among them Franz Defregger, Ferdinand Piloty and Wilhelm Hauschild, decorated this building, at the time planned to be the Bavarian National Museum, with a total of 143 colossal paintings with Bavarian themes: pretty women from Augsburg in renaissance gowns, Barbarossa's marriage in Würzburg and the funeral of Walter von der Vogelweide can now all be viewed by the public (see also "Museums in Munich").

A little further on runs the **Altstadtring** (Inner Ring Road), whose six lanes have cut a broad swathe right across an historic old quarter of the city. Those who want to enjoy a bit of attractive idyl should stroll over to the quarter around **Adelgundenstrasse**, where the city's

Above: The Müllersches Volksbad, a public swimming-pool, beside the Isar river.

poor lived – back when they still had money enough (heading away from the center; behind the Museum of Ethnology). There are the galleries and smart bars that are so typical of Munich hereabouts, however, the area around **Mariannenplatz** still retains quite a peaceful air and its bourgeois character, too. The most noticable feature of Mariannenplatz is **Lukaskirche** (St. Luke's Church), a massive domed building erected in 1893-96, which can be seen from afar.

From here you can cross part of the river by a foot-bridge over to **Praterinsel** (Prater Island). In the building which once housed the **Riemerschmidtschen Schnapsfabrik** (schnaps distillery), regular exhibitions, interesting theatrical productions and "happenings" are held by the artisits who live here. At the home of the *Deutscher Alpenverein* (German Alpine Society), the **Alpine Museum** outlines art, science, the mountains and the society's history from 1760 to 1945. You will also find the largest specialized Alpine library in the world here.

Crossing the **Kabelsteg**, one of the smallest and most beautiful bridges across the Isar (only for pedestrians and cyclists), once arrives at the pebble banks of the river. In summer the shore is crowded with swimmers and sunbathers, naked and half-naked. You can hear the rushing of water over the weir and the cries of the gulls, and can admire the ornate decoration of one of Germany's oldest swimming pools, the **Müllersches Volksbad**, whose Jugendstil architecture and interior decor has fascinated many a visitor. Behind the Volksbad, the elegant chimney of the **Muffathalle**, one of Munich's most popular disco-halls, where concerts are also held, can be seen.

Across the weir on the banks of the Isar, at a small green area beside the Ludwigbrücke, is the **Vater-Rhein-Brunnen** (Father Rhine Fountain), upon whose park benches and fountain steps Munich's forgotten citizens, the destitute and

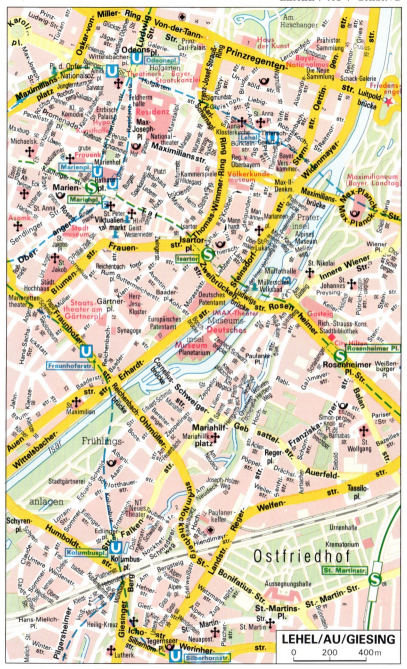

DEUTSCHES MUSEUM

homeless linger. On the other side of the Ludwigbrücke, the **Deutsches Museum** (German Museum) stretches out. The first thing you notice when you look at the museum is the **Kongress Saal** (Conference Hall). Today, the **Forum der Technik** is housed in this building, containing Germany's first IMAX movie theater; this is an immense state-of-the-art large-screen cinema in which spectacular 3-D films dealing with the natural sciences are shown.

The museum itself is reached by walking along the Isar canal, past the museum on the right, and thus on to the island on which the museum stands (see p. 179). The museum complex stretches across its beautiful site on the island. Once inside, it is almost impossible to tear yourself away: time flies by unnoticed while observing and trying out the natural sciences displays and models.

Above: The entrance to the Deutsches Museum. Right: View from Reichenbach Bridge across to the European Patent Office.

In the well-run Käfer delicatessen restaurant you can build up your strength between rounds, and a visit to the museum shop will round out any visit nicely: they have a wide variety of articles on offer, from specialized books and experiment kits to model-building sets.

From **Cornelius Bridge** you get a good view of the gardens in front of the museum, where an original old windmill and a rescue ship are among the displays. From here you get your first good idea of the dimensions of the most-visited Temple of Technology in Germany, indeed, in the world.

On the opposite side of the Isar an extensive, sober-looking building from the 1950s can be seen: the **German Patent Office**.

GÄRTNERPLATZ

Across from the museum, on the other side of the river, begins the neighborhood of **Isarvorstadt**, without doubt the most

colorful and most tolerant quarter in Munich. Here the old-established Munich resident buys his vegetables in the same little corner shop as the homesexual in his skin-tight leather outfit; the aging, health-conscious hippie stands in line at the organic bakery behind a young New Age müsli-muncher; and in the numerous bars, cafés and international restaurants, wild-looking characters sit beside normal-looking locals and over-styled yuppies with cell-phones.

To get from the museum to one of the prettiest squares to be found in the city, **Gärtnerplatz**, with its lovely late-19th century façades, cross Cornelius Bridge. Just past the bridge, a gigatic steel, glass and cement complex rises up on the right: the **European Patent Office**. it is only a hop, skip and a jump from here to Gärtnerplatz. This square is laid out in the shape of a star, planted with robinia and horse chestnut trees and is lit up by lanterns at night. At the edge of the square stands another of Munich's cultural jewels, the **Gärtnerplatz Theater**, built in neo-renaissance style with a columned façade. Originally a traditional folk theater, designed by Franz Michael Reifenstuel and built in 1864-65, these days its programs are largely made up of opera, operetta and ballet.

Take a walk now along **Klenzestrasse** as far as Frauenhoferstrasse, keeping south to the corner of **Reichenbachstrasse** and **Baaderstrasse**, and you will be able to enjoy the "alternative" flair of the lively Gärtnerplatz district with its small shops and boutiques, travel agencies and antique shops, health and esoteric specialty book shops.

Baaderstrasse, which leads directly to **Isartorplatz**, is a varied street with a number of trendy bars and an excellent Indian restaurant on the corner of Buttermelcherstrasse, **Ganga**. If you are now in the mood for a refreshing cocktail, the mercurial Mexican pub, **Joe Peña's**, on Buttermelcherstrasse, has a variety on offer. During Happy Hour, from 6 to 8 p.m., you can get your fill of alcohol-based cocktails for half price, too.

THE AU

IN THE AU

In earlier times, the Isar river acted as a boundary between rich the poor. Well-to-do middle-class citizens defended the west bank tooth and nail against the rabble on the other side of the river. They wanted to have nothing to do with them. The millers, coffin-makers, dyers and day-laborers who lived "over there" were housed in damp, miserably-overcrowded lodgings, in unhealthy low-lying areas, next to the factories and workshops.

The Au (Meadow) was one of these slum districts, and for a long time was only visited four times a year by the rest of the city: three times when the *Auer Dult* fair took place, and a fourth time for the tapping of the strong beer on Nockherberg Hill. This original, charming quarter has gained in attractiveness over the years, through students who can still find inexpensive apartments in older buildings, for example, as well as through those who work for a living and who appreciate the natural atmosphere of the Isar. Quite hidden and rather fast, the **Auer Mühlbach**, the bubbling mill stream which was formerly the life-force of the district because the dye-works, tanneries and mills stood along its course, still bubbles today. It is an idyllic walk along the stream down **Quellenstrasse**, and the myriad scents in the colorful **Rosengarten** (Rose Garden; where, incidentally, a section is devoted to poisonous plants) on the southern edge of the *Schyrenbad*, are unforgettable. Chairs and benches invite visitors to relax, and many residents of the city come here to sunbathe or read. A stroll through the **Flaucher** – as the stretch of green along the Isar in the direction of the zoo is known – is especially nice.

It is best to approach the district from the **Ludwigsbrücke**. Immediately after the Deutsches Museum, turn right onto **Zeppelinstrasse**, which runs along the Isar. One of Munich's most novel cinemas stands where Zeppelinstrasse and Lilienstrasse divide, the **Museums-Lichtspiele**, which not only shows current films in their original versions, but is also the showplace of a rather unusual cult event: for more than 20 years the legendary Rocky Horror Picture Show has been shown here daily; entire Rocky Horror clubs appear for the showings – in full costume and armed with sparklers – to sing along (Rocky Horror Club Munich, tel. 0821 / 665809).

In the quarter behind the cinema you leave urban turmoil behind: ducks float on the river, gulls glide through the air, and the further you walk, the wider the **Isarauen** (Isar Meadows) get until you reach the southern end of the inner city. Idyllic scenes can be observed here: Man and dog (Thomas Mann used the title *Man and Dog* for a story in which he de-

---

*Above: The idyllic, village-like Lilienstrasse.
Right: The broad, cobbled square in front of Maria-Hilf-Kirche.*

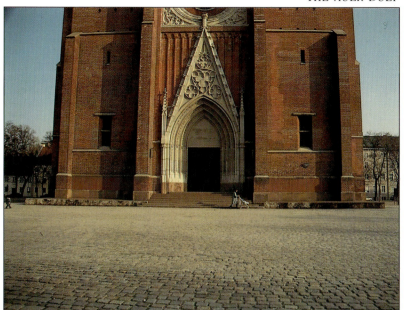

scribes his walks along the Isar), old men quietly playing chess, noisy youths testing their soccer skill on the fields by the Isar and, in winter, cross-country skiers who make use of a trail that runs right through the city.

Karl Valentin, the popular radical Munich comedian and "left thinker," as Tucholsky once called him, was born in the house at **Lilienstrasse 47**. On Lilienstrasse, behind neo-baroque façades now protected as listed buildings, you can still find many homey little shops, and a small French restaurant called **La Marmite**, with outdoor dining in summer.

One block further on, between Sammtstrasse and Franz-Prüller-Strasse, is where the heart of the district beats. Ten houses of the old **Herbergsviertel** district are preserved here; they are protected in the shadow of the Isar's high banks and are filled with new life. Here the weaving-mills and dye works once stood, for which the Auer millstream provided bread and livelihood. At **Franz-Prüller-Strasse 12**, a lopsided house nearly 500 years old used to be the city's plague-house, in which the terminally ill were immured.

The Auer Dult

A little further on lies **Maria-Hilf-Platz**, Munich's largest square after the Theresienwiese. A hundred years ago the farmers of neighboring Giesing were still grazing their cattle here. Since 1796, the week-long **Auer Dult** fair has been held here in the months of May, July and October: market stalls offer wares of every description, and the air is filled with the fragrant aroma of Bratwurst, as well as with the squeaking of a carousel and the cries of imaginative inventors hawking their patented creations. People by the thousands are drawn to the old Au by this fair, where beside organically-grown produce and pottery, knick-knacks and junk can be found – and maybe even a bargain.

The brick-red **Maria-Hilf-Kirche**, which was built in 1831-39 as the first

NOCKHERBERG / GIESING

monumental church outside the Old Town, dominates the scene. For a long time its towers stood without their tops because after the war there was no money for restoration. Today, however, they tower proud and complete above the quarter once again. The stained glass windows here are well worth seeing – they even served as models for the much more famous Cologne Cathedral.

Behind the church lies the **Neudeck** women's prison. It must be especially frustrating to serve a sentence here, for a special aroma often pervades the district – that of the beer mash from the Paulaner Brewery on Nockherberg Hill. Once a year there they hold the "hardest" drinking spree in the city: the **Starkbierfest** (Strong Beer Festival). From the first Saturday before St. Joseph's Day (March 19) people meet in the halls of the historic Salvatorkeller (**Paulanerkeller** nowadays), in order to down great quantities of the dark, sweet, strong beer. This festival lasts for two weeks and has been dubbed "the fifth season of the year" by the people of Munich. The traditional tapping of the barrel is the prelude to all the festivities, an unparalleled Bavarian spectacle, which all leading figures from business and politics, including the Minister-President himself, have to attend in order to have their legs pulled in no uncertain fashion by a guest speaker. The Minister-President takes it all in good heart and, grinning broadly, orders his next drink. This is brought by one of the sturdy waitresses who carry up to twelve liter mugs of beer at a time through the thick clouds of smoke, and the unbelievable noise of three or four brass bands playing at once. But at any time of year a drink or two can enjoyed in the beer garden, which has always been a favorite meeting place for the good people of Au and Giesing.

GIESING

Just as it is Haidhausen, **Giesing** is also a stone's throw away from elegant Harlaching. It was originally settled by farmers and peasants, and then later acquired a reputation for harboring rebellious workers. Here, in 1919, they organized a last stand against the "White Troops" of the counter-revolution and fought to the bitter end.

In the center of the old village, above Nockherberg Hill, between Ichostrasse, Martin-Luther-Strasse and the Tegernsee road, one can still get a good impression of earlier living conditions; crooked houses with low entrances and plasterwork which is crumbling away. This is one of Munich's few districts which has been spared the attentions of speculators.

High above the Isar, the 300-foot-high (95 m) tower of the neo-Gothic **Heilig-Kreuz-Kirche** (Holy Cross Church) rises above district and city as it has since

Above: Bavarian bric-a-brac on sale at the Auer Dult. Right: The Nockherberg leads up to "down-at-heel" Giesing.

1886. The site is actually more beautiful than the church itself, and once marked the start of the steep descent to the Isar.

Giesing has the reputation of being Munich's "Bowery" district, comparable perhaps to London's East End. Few would think of showing friends or strangers around this part of the city and tour buses certainly do not visit it.

The district today centers around the **Telapost** building on Tegernseer Landstrasse, near the U-Bahn exit on Silberhornstrasse. It dates from 1928-29 and is notable for its strict functionality. Many have thought upon seeing it that it was **Stadelheim Prison**, but that is quite a bit further out of town on Stadelheimer Strasse. When an attempt to establish a Soviet-style government in Munich failed, Gustav Landauer and Eugen Leviné were executed there in 1919, and Hans and Sophie Scholl were guillotined at Stadelheim in 1943.

There are happier sights to visit on the way to Harlaching; namely the place where the career of Germany's most famous soccer player, Franz Beckenbauer, began. This is the **"60er" Stadium**, which today is being renovated. Further out of town is the training ground of the 1860 München team, the local rival of FC Bayern, whose training ground is quite close by on **Säbenerstrasse**. Not far from the stadium is an important piece of the district's industrial history, the **AGFA Works**. Until 1982 AGFA, with 4,600 employees, was the largest industrial concern in Giesing. Today, this number has been reduced to 2,000, the other buildings being let to a variety of firms.

Life in Geising is not bad. Most of the housing here is rented and was built in the 1950s and 1960s. Giesing is not exactly beautiful, but it certainly is lively; at **Kaffee Giesing** (Bergstr. 5) dinner can be enjoyed to the sounds of live jazz or blues. **Kukuvaja** (Emersonstr. 1) serves fantastic Greek food until 1 a.m., and **Galerie Mosel und Tschechow**, at Winterstr. 7, shows exhibitions by contemporary artists.

HAIDHAUSEN / GASTEIG

HAIDHAUSEN

When, in 1158, Henry the Lion decreed that the important *Salzstrasse* (salt road) should be diverted from Unterföhring in the north towards the modern center of Munich further south, the new highway led directly through what today is the district of Haidhausen. By way of the Ludwigsbrücke, Roseinheimer Strasse and Innere Wiener Strasse, one arrives at the heart of this old-established quarter.

Haidhausen flourished thanks to the salt trade: inns, as well as wheelwrights, bricklayers, smiths and many other craftsmen and tradesmen moved here. They were often rough types with bad reputations, and the city folk were not about to let them into their "front parlor." Today, however, those who have lived in Haidhausen for many years do not want anyone else moving here. The district is

Above: The Gasteig cultural complex towers defiantly above Rosenheim Hill.

thriving once again, but this time the character of the old quarter is threatened; bistros, "Yuppie" bars, smart apartment blocks, as well as hotels and business complexes are taking over the streets of the district bit by bit. Where friendly little bars and small shops once made older residents feel welcome, computer shops and supermarkets are now springing up. Haidhausen looks set to take over Schwabing's position as *the* fashionable quarter, and will probably soon suffer the same fate. Yet a stroll through the streets and across the squares of this neighborhood, and a glance into its rear courtyards, can still reveal a lot about an older Munich.

Coming from the Isartor across the Ludwigsbrücke stands what seems to be a huge, futuristic fortress. It is in fact the most expensive cultural investment that Munich has made in many years: the **Kulturzentrum Gasteig** (Gasteig Cultural Center). The controversial building, with its shiny red brickwork and tall glass façades, has been called the "culture bunker" by critics. The name *Gasteig* is derived from the Bavarian *gacher Steig*, meaning the steep path to Haidhausen up Rosenheimer Hill. However off-putting the exterior of the building may be, its interior is a complete success. The vast sums of money it cost have, on the whole, been well spent: 6,000 visitors a day come here (many more during the Munich Film Festival in July). The Munich Philharmonic Orchestra has a beautiful concert hall here – the 2,500-seat **Philharmonie** – that is famous for its marvellous acoustics. In the **Richard-Strauss-Konservatorium**, known simply as the *Konz* by the people of Munich, young students are taught all aspects of music, at the city's expense, while Munich's adult education center offers countless courses here which are nearly always fully booked. The Gasteig also houses Germany's largest and most-visited municipal library, the **Stadtbibliothek**,

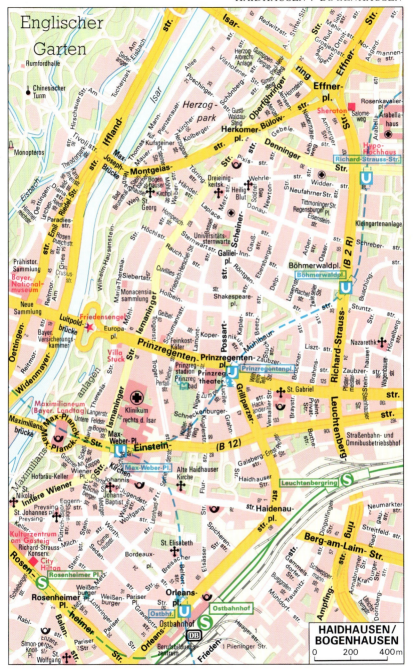

WIENER PLATZ

combined with a large children's as well as a young people's library.

In the **Aspekte Galerie**, exhibitions and shows by Munich artists are splendidly presented. In the courtyard of the Gasteig one can relax over a cup of coffee in summer. Opposite is **Motorama**, a sort of fortress from the 1970s, housing car dealers and supermarkets, with a hotel and the **Liberty** discothèque integrated into the structure.

The City Hilton Complex is the third building which will catch the visitor's eye on Rosenheimer Strasse. It is next to the Gasteig and built in a similar style: a luxury hotel in front, with a complex of posh apartments behind. To make room for this building they tore down a historic, archetypal Munich *Bierkeller*, the *Bürgerbräukeller,* where an (unsuccessful) attempt was made to assassinate Hitler in 1939.

Above: It is not always quite as peaceful as this at Wiener Platz. Right: The fountain at Weissenburger Platz.

Back in the direction of the Ludwigsbrücke and the Isar, an idyllic little spot still survives: the **Nikolai and Loretto Chapel**, hidden amongst the dense woodland covering the Isar embankment. From here the road follows the Isar downstream to the **Müllersches Volksbad** swimming pool, which deserves a visit, whether to plunge into the beautiful Jugenstil swimming hall or to relax in the imposing steambaths.

From here the street at the Gasteig leads to **Innere Wiener Strasse**, and further on to Max-Weber-Platz. Opposite the old residential buildings, largely preserved here, stands the dark and grimy building that once housed the state brewery, the Hofbräuhaus, which was partly burned down in 1987. Many today still maintain that the fire was caused by arson – real estate speculators perhaps – because this site on the Isar embankment, bordered by Wiener Platz, is one of the inner city's prime positions.

The city planners have preserved here one of Munich's few remaining traditional restaurants outside the city center: the **Hofbräukeller**, with its wonderful beer garden laid out beneath the old horse-chestnut trees on **Wiener Platz**. Directly in front of this is a spot of Haidhausen idyll: around a tall blue-and-white maypole stand quaint little kiosks and handsomely-restored old lodging-houses. A few steps further on, on **Grütznerstrasse**, a complete contrast is provided by turreted town houses with bull's-eye panes. Wienerplatz has always been one of Haidhausen's focal points and so it comes as no surprise that the young and chic have *their* café here: **Café Wiener Platz**. If this does not appeal, you should try the nearby **Kytaro**, probably the best Greek restaurant in Munich, with a small beer garden which is always crowded in fine weather.

Behind this the red brick tower of Haidhausen's "cathedral," the **Johanniskirche**, rises like a sharpened pencil. The

JOHANNISPLATZ / ORLEANSPLATZ

church, with its 21 magnificent neo-Gothic glass windows, stands impressively at **Johannisplatz**. The square around it, with its small park and old townhouses, is one of the most pleasant in the whole city and remains fairly immune to the tumult of the traffic around the busy square nearby; **Max-Weber-Platz**. One little surprise on the square is the **Johannis Café**, which stays open until 3 a.m. on weekends, and is frequented by a wide spectrum of people: in the later – or, depending on your point of view, earlier – hours, you might see elderly ladies, hardened drinkers nevertheless, with their even-older admirers, or a suburban gigolo with his date, both dressed to kill; students, writers and alcoholics – in short, the sort of people who add a bit of spice to the district, sitting together around 1950s-style kidney-shaped tables before the backdrop of Matterhorn wall-paper. This place is an absolute must for night owls!

Just around the corner from **Kirchenstrasse** is **Preysingstrasse**, where pedestrians have priority over the traffic, which is reduced to a slow crawl. A historic First World War-era apartment in the **Üblacker House** has been faithfully restored. Turning right at **Wörthstrasse** brings you straight to **Bordeauxplatz**. Planted with trees and lined with old townhouses, this square is reminiscent of town squares in southern France; only the *boules* players are missing.

From here it is not far to **Orleansplatz** with the **Ostbahnhof** (East Station), an important traffic junction for German Rail, and S-Bahn and U-Bahn trains. Here, as at Max-Weber-Platz, the square's character, charm and history have fallen victim to the high volume of traffic. Not even the elaborate re-opening of the Ostbahnhof a few years ago it could disguise the fact that the splashing of the fountain at Orleansplatz is drowned out by the roar of traffic.

Kunstpark Ost was opened at the end of 1996 on the former Pfanni grounds behind the Ostbahnhof (entrance Grafingerstr. 6). This many-faceted, exciting

PARISER PLATZ / WEISSENBURGER PLATZ

multi-media offering has brought new momentum to Munich's often somewhat slack nightlife: the **Colosseum**, a concert hall for 2,000 people, offers ambitious musical events; the three-part **Babylon Complex** houses the Babylon Stage for rock concerts, and various clubs in two halls; there is an Indian-style disco beneath a reflecting starry sky in the **Natraj Temple**. Then there is still the **Incognito** music stage and the 1920s-style **Bongo Bar**, among others. The **Nachtkantine** is a bar in mega-format. The **Cinerama** shows films focusing on independents and the 1960s. If you still haven't had enough, you can always go bargain-hunting at the huge flea market (Fri. 9 a.m. to 8 p.m., Sat. 7 a.m. to 6 p.m.).

From the Ostbahnhof one can wander through what is perhaps the prettiest part of Haidhausen, the *Franzosenviertel*

Above: A bird's eye view of Pariser Platz.
Right: Lively scene at one of Munich's many flea markets.

(French Quarter). In 1871, as an expression of the euphoria brought on by the German victory in the Franco-Prussian war, all the names of the streets and squares here were changed to the names of places in France which had been captured by the Germans. The quarter still has little shops, secluded courtyard cafés, "alternative" galleries and craft shops, squares planted with trees and flowers, quiet corners and a leisurely lifestyle.

Wherever you are in this area, whether on Sedanstrasse, Metzstrasse, Gravelottestrasse, or at the small circular **Pariser Platz**, you will find the local people live as a community, know one another and greet each other whenever they meet. As in other parts of Munich, behind many of the old façades some rather modern luxury appartments are hidden.

A walk through pleasant Haidhausen should finish up at **Weissenburger Platz**. In summer, this round square is a delight with its wonderful floral display around the beautiful fountain at its center. In winter, at the Christmas market here, art objects and sweets can be purchased, and the delicious aroma of roasted almonds, mulled wine and *Lebkuchen* (gingerbread) hangs in the air.

Now it is only a few minutes from here, through the pedestrian zone of tree-lined **Weissenburger Strasse**, to **Rosenheimer Platz**. From the Ostbahnhof or from Max-Weber-Platz, the U-Bahn takes you to Haidhausen's rich neighbor, Bogenhausen.

BOGENHAUSEN

As early as the turn of the century, Bogenhausen was home to the rich and the super-rich. Elegant villas with broad façades dating from the 1870s and the Jugendstil period give character to the streets, for instance in Holbeinstrasse, Mühlbauerstrasse and Prinzregentenstrasse. This is a busy and active district during the day, but at night the streets are empty. Many who work here return to their homes in other parts of Munich, because the high rents here mean that, above all, only lawyers, publishers, consulates and the like can afford to put up their brass plates beside the entrances of these villas. Many landlords own property here but live elsewhere. Still, architecturally, Bogenhausen is one of the jewels of Munich.

On **Prinzregentenplatz** stands the **Prinzregenten Theater**, which was built in 1900-01 by Max Littmann in a combination of classical and Jugendstil styles to provide an appropriate setting for the works of Richard Wagner. It served as Munich's opera venue until the reconstruction of the National Theater. It was closed in 1963 because it had fallen into such a state of dilapidation, but thanks to a group of supporters and patrons it was restored to its former glory and was reopened in 1988. In November 1996, the completely renovated stage was grandly dedicated with a production of "Tristan and Isolde." The theater is at its most

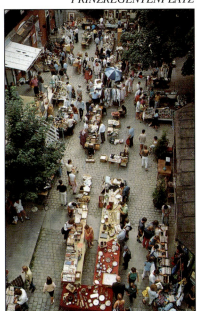

beautiful in the evenings, when its lights are festively aglow and its audience crowds the beautifully-restored foyer and staircase.

A little further towards the Friedensengel, past the **Prinzregentenbad**, the pool which becomes a skating rink in winter, you come upon a very special place: **Feinkost-Käfer**. After *Dallmayr's* in the city center, this is Munich's most famous gourmet temple. Everyone knows *Käfer*, even those who cannot afford to go there. In the *Käferschenke* restaurant, business people and celebrities meet, while in the delicatessen on the floor below you can buy delicious specialities from all over the world.

Diagonally across from Käfer's, on the corner of Ismaningerstrasse and Prinzregentenstrasse, is the famous **Villa Stuck**. It was built in 1897-98 after a design by Franz von Stuck who, after Franz von Lenbach, was probably the most famous painter of his time in Munich. Even in his own lifetime, this Jugendstil villa, which also received a studio build-

FRIEDENSENGEL

ing in 1913-14, was regarded as a work of art in which Munich society liked to meet. Today it belongs to the city of Munich. In its interior, Jugendstil fans wander about in throngs to view the rooms and works of art created by von Stuck; even the turgid and sensual painting *The Sin*, once considered to be provocative, can be seen here. Part of the museum is used for large, sometimes thematically unusual, art exhibitions. In addition, Villa Stuck also houses one of Munich's most exclusive Chinese restaurants, **Tai Tung**.

Looking out from the sculpture of the spear-hurling Amazon in front of Villa Stuck over Prinzregentenstrasse towards the city center, the shiny gold winged **Friedensengel** (Angel of Peace), one of Munich's most-photographed monuments, catches your eye. It gazes patiently down on the traffic swirling around its feet. The gilded angel stands 20 feet (6 m) high, supported on a slender column above a classically styled base, into which four mosaics representing the blessings of peace are inset. In one hand the angel holds an olive branch and in the other hand a statue of the Greek goddess Athene. The Friedensengel was erected in 1896 to celebrate the 25th anniversary of the Franco-Prussian war as a memorial to peace. From here, there is an excellent and pleasing view of the architectural harmony of the lower part of Prinzregentenstrasse, which sweeps down to Prince Carl Palace.

Möhlstrasse, *the* street in Bogenhausen, branches off from **Europa-Platz** to the east of the Friedensengel. Here are the magnificent villas built for brewery owners, industrialists and the nobility at the turn of the century, each in its tasteful garden setting. Today, they have been taken over mainly by consulates and offices.

Turning right along Siebertstrasse will bring you to **Holbeinstrasse**. The fine Jugendstil houses here are all protected as historic monuments. Look particularly at No. 7, which was built in 1907 and is probably the best example of Munich's upper-middle-class style of domestic architecture. Further along the street lies **Shakespeareplatz**, lined with trees and ornate houses. But even here, in a place ideally suited for homes with families and children, the situation is unchanged: the names on the brass plates are almost exclusively those of agencies, offices or companies. Going back along **Possartstrasse** brings you to Prinzregentenplatz once again.

Arabella Park lies three stations further on from here, on the U4 underground line. Its development was begun in 1965, when bulldozers moved in to plough up the fields and meadows which had previously covered the area. Today, around 50,000 people live and work in Arabella Park, and its skyscrapers intrude

Above: Eternally poised for take-off – the Angel of Peace. Right: The Hypobank – an effective example of modern architecture.

ARABELLA PARK

on Munich's skyline. Life here is not completely work-orientated though, and there are places for strolling, shopping and stopping off for a cup of coffee around **Rosenkavalierplatz**. Here stands one of Munich's most unusual cinemas, the *Cadillac*, in whose foyer you can admire a real Cadillac limousine. There are some nice restaurants around, and the public library on the square provides Munich artists a venue for exhibiting their works in a separate, airy room.

One of Germany's leading publishing houses, Burda-Verlag, has its offices here; while nearby the bureaucrats in the Ministry of the Environment try to find some light in the darkness of the worsening ecologicial situation of the world.

The rather unimaginative façade of the **Sheraton Hotel**, in standard grey concrete, and the "oldest" of all these new high-rise buildings, the more imaginative **Arabella House**, do not seem to impress those who live here very much one way or the other; yet people do seem to enjoy living in this uncompromisingly modern environment.

The Bavarian **Hypobank** also seems to feel quite at home here, and shows it, too; they had this shining aluminum highrise built from 1975 to 1981. It is cold and fascinating at the same time. After the Olympic Tower, this is the tallest structure in the city.

If by now you have had more than your fill of modern architecture, take a No. 154 bus down to **Mauerkircherstrasse**, one of the favorite haunts of Thomas Mann and also of Germany's richest man, Herr Flick. Walk along **Thomas-Mann-Allee** (where the famous author lived at No. 10 until the Nazis drove him out) and enjoy the peacefulness of the river; take your time and watch the people with their dogs, the joggers and the cyclists along by the Isar as you come upon them.

Returning by way of **Pienzenauerstrasse**, you will see **Herzog Park**. Until

the late 19th century there were just open fields and woods here, until 1892 when it was decided to extend the city boundaries. This was the hour of the birth of the best residential area in the whole city, where even today the stylish and wealthy live – and pay the corresponding price!

The No. 20 streetcar or the bus will take you past the venerable old bridge, **Max-Joseph-Brücke**, back to Schwabing or into the center of Munich, but as a conclusion to this tour, visit **Bogenhausener Kirchplatz**, where the little onion dome of the church of **St. Georg** stands guard over one of the loveliest – if not *the* loveliest – cemeteries in the city. It was originally the parish church of the village of Bogenhausen, with a pulpit by Ignaz Günther. A number of famous sons and daughters of Munich lie buried along the wall which surrounds the church; including actors Carl Wery and Liesl Karlstadt, authors Erich Kästner, Annette Kolb and Oskar Maria Graf, and filmmaker Rainer Werner Fassbinder, to name but a few.

SCHLACHTHOF GLOCKENBACH GÄRTNERPLATZ
Transport Connections
U-BAHN: U3/U6 to Goetheplatz, Poccistrasse, Implerstrasse; U1/U2 to Fraunhofer Strasse.
BUS: No. 31 to Implerstrasse, Aberlestrasse, Poccistrasse. Bus No. 58 to Goetheplatz; Bus No. 52 to Baldeplatz and Gärtnerplatz.
STREETCAR: Nos. 17, 18 and 27 to Fraunhoferstrasse.

Restaurants / Cafés / Night-life
BAVARIAN: **Paulaner Bräuhaus**, Kapuzinerplatz 5, tel. 530331, 10 am to 1 am; **Wirtshaus im Schlachthof**, Zenettistr. 9, tel. 765484, Fri till 3 am, beer-garden till midnight.
INDIAN: **Tandoori**, Baumstrasse 6, tel. 2012208; **Ganga**, Baaderstr. 11, tel. 2016465, 11:30 am to 3 pm and 5:30 pm to midnight.
TURKISH: **Schwimmkrabbe**, Ickstattstrasse 13, tel. 2010080, 5 pm to 1 am, specialities, belly-dancing weekends; **Yol**, Ehrengutstr. 21, tel. 779562, 5 pm to 1 am, fantastic appetizers and prawns, Wed, Fri, Sat, Sun belly-dancing.
MEXICAN: **Joe Peña's**, Buttermelcherstr. 17, tel. 226463, 5 pm to 1 am, restaurant and popular cocktail bar.
GOURMET: Glockenbach, Kapuzinerstr. 29, tel. 534043, Tue-Fri noon to 1:30 pm and 6 pm to 1 am, Sat 7 pm to 1 am (hot food till 9;30 pm), gourmet dishes, awarded a Michelin star; **Italfisch**, Zenettistr. 25, tel. 776849, Mon-Fri 11:30 am to 1 am, Sat 6 pm to 1 am (hot food until 10 pm), closed Sunday and holidays, fine seafood; **Makassar**, Dreimühlenstr. 25, tel. 776959, 6 pm to midnight, French-Creole cooking.
BARS: **Ballhaus**, Klenzestr. 71, tel. 2010992,Sun-Thu 10 am to 1 am, Fri-Sat 10 am to 3 am, sushi bar from 6 pm, trendy café-restaurant; **Café Glück**, Palmstr. 4, 2011673, very cozy, organically-produced foods; **Faun**, Hans-Sachs-Str.17, tel. 263798, Fri-Sat till 3 am, wholesome cooking, inexpensive; **Forum**, Corneliusstr. 2, tel. 268818, Sun-Wed 8 am to 1 am, Thu-Sat 8 am to 3 am, with sidewalk café, tasty breakfasts; **Fraunhofer**, Fraunhoferstr. 9, tel. 266460, 4:30 pm to 1 am, Bavarian inn, well-mixed crowd; **Glatz**, Ehrengutstr. 15, tel. 764589, popular "alternative" spot; **Pacific Times**, Baaderstr. 28, tel.20239470, 5 pm to 1 am, exotic food, good selection of cocktails; **Rothmund**, Rothmundstr. 5, tel. 535015, 10 am to 1 am, good menu of the day.
GAY BARS: **Morizz**, Klenzestr. 43, tel. 2016776, 7 pm to 2 am, Fri-Sat till 3 am, sterling club atmosphere, heteros are also welcome, European and Thai cuisine; **Nil**, Hans-Sachs-Str. 2, tel. 265545, 3 pm to 3 am; Ochsengarten, Müllerstr. 45, tel. 266466, 8 pm to 1 am, Fri-Sat till 3 am, Munich's traditional leather bar; **Vita S.**, Morasstr. 16, tel. 2913310, Tue-Sun from 6 pm, women only, serves food.
ICE CREAM PARLORS: **Ciao**, Wittelsbacherstr. 16, tel. 778778; **Italia**, Ehrengutstr. 23, tel. 763219.

Post Offices
Fraunhoferstrasse 22a, tel. 53882573; Goetheplatz 1, tel. 53882612.

Taxi Stands
Baldeplatz, tel. 216171; Goetheplatz, tel. 536017; Reichenbachplatz, tel. 2161331.

LEHEL
Transport Connections
U-BAHN: U4/U5 to Lehel. *BUS:* No. 53 to Königinstrasse, Friedensengel, Prinzregentenstrasse.
STREETCAR: No. 19 to Nationalmuseum, Lehel, Maxmonument.

Restaurants / Cafés / Night-life
BAVARIAN: **Mariannenhof**, Mariannenstr. 1, tel. 220864, Mon-Fri 11 am to 1 am, Sat-Sun 6 pm to 1.
INTERNATIONAL: **Alaska**, Mariannenstr. 3, tel. 293100, Mon-Sat noon to 2:30 pm and 6 pm to midnight, Japanese, sushi; **Chesa Rüegg**, Wurzerstr. 18, tel. 297114, Mon-Sat noon to 3 pm and 6 pm to midnight, Swiss cuisine; **Halali**, Schönfeldstr. 22, tel. 285909, Mon-Fri noon to 3 pm and 6 pm-1 am, Sat 6 pm to 1 am, German nouvelle cuisine, fish, lobster, game, reservation advised; **Roma**, Maximilianstr. 31, tel. 227435, Italian.
SEAFOOD: **Austernkeller**, Stollbergstr. 11, tel. 298787, Tue-Sun 6 pm to 1 am, closed Mon, fresh oysters, high prices.
CAFÉS / BARS: **Café Muffathalle**, Zellstr. 4, tel. 484978, Mon-Wed 6 pm to 1 am, Thu-Sat 6 pm to 3 am (disco from 10 pm), Sun 10 am to 1 am; **Egon's Bar**, Setzstr. 12, tel. 29161076, daily till 3 am; **Schumann's**, Maximilianstr. 36, tel. 229060, Sun-Fri 6 pm to 3 am.

Leisure Time
SWIMMING / SAUNAS: The Jugendstil **Müllersches Volksbad**, Rosenheimerstr. 1, tel. 23613026. Take S1-S8 to Isartor.
DANCING / CONCERTS: The Muffathalle behind the Volksbad is a culture and dance temple today, Zellstr. 4, tel. 294500, *CINEMAS:* IMAX cinema of the German Museum (nature and music films), reservation advised; MAXX, Isartorplatz 4, tel. 21238080; in original version at Museumlichtspielen, Lilienstr. 2, tel. 482403.

Post Office
Thierschstr. 3, tel. 53882713.

Taxi stands
Königinstr., tel. 285968; Max-Monument, tel. 294041; National Museum, Prinzregentenstr., tel. 297045.

GUIDEPOST AU / GIESING / HAIDHAUSEN / BOGENHAUSEN

AU / GIESING
Transport Connections
S-BAHN: S1, S2 to Giesing. *U-BAHN:* U1 over Kolumbusplatz to Mangfallplatz; U2 to Giesing. *BUS:* Nos. 44 and 45 to Giesing; Bus No. 52 to Maria-Hilf-Platz and Kolumbusplatz. *STREETCAR:* No. 25 to Silberhornstr.; No. 27 to Maria-Hilf-Platz, Giesing.

Restaurants / Cafés / Night-life
BAVARIAN: **Paulanerkeller am Nockherberg**, Hochstrasse 77, tel. 4599130, daily 9 am to midnight, strong beer, beer-garden; **Wirtshaus in der Au**, Lilienstr. 51, tel. 4484100, Mon-Fri 5 pm to 1 am, Sat-Sun/holidays 10 am to 1 am, Sunday jazz brunch, good prices;
INTERNATIONAL: **Alpenhof**, Alpenplatz 1, tel. 6914512, Tue-Sun 11:30 to midnight, Italian; **La Marmite**, Lilienstr. 8, tel. 282242, Mon-Fri from 7 pm, French; **Outback**, Weissenburgerplatz, tel. 48997880, from 6 pm, Australian cuisine, lamb, shark steaks; **Poseiden**, Säbenerstr. 9, tel. 6926241, 11 am to 3 pm and 5 pm to 1 am, Greek.
CAFÉS / CLUBS: **Kaffee Giesing**, Bergstr. 5, tel. 6920579, Mon-Sat 2 pm to 1 am, Sun 10 am to 1 am, bar with international cuisine, music every evening (jazz, blues, piano); **Kafe Zentral**, Schwaigerstr. 10, tel. 657372, 8 am to 1 am, seating outside in good weather.

Leisure Time
Auer Dult: Thrice-annual fair at Maria-Hilf-Platz. In May called the *Maidult*, in July the *Jakobidult* and in October the *Kirchweihdult*. In March the *Starkbieranstich* (tapping the strong beer) takes place in the **Salvatorkeller** on **Nockherberg Hill**, followed by 16 days of uninterrupted beer-drinking!

Post Offices
Tölzerstr. 5, tel. 6121436; Balanstr. 385, tel. 687423; Chiemgaustr. 83, tel. 41228901; Haushamerstr. 3, tel. 41228902.

Taxi Stands
Candidplatz, tel. 216184; Giesing station, tel. 6914077; Ostfriedhof, tel. 6916238; Wettersteinplatz, tel. 216183.

HAIDHAUSEN / BOGENHAUSEN
Transport Connections
S-BAHN: S1-S8 to Ostbahnhof, Rosenheimer Platz. *U-BAHN:* U4/U5 to Max-Weber-Platz; U4 to Prinzregentenplatz; U5 to Ostbahnhof. *BUS:* No. 51 to Max-Weber-Platz, Rosenheimer Platz; Nrs. 53 and 54 to Prinzregentplatz and Ostbahnhof; No. 56 to Ostbahnhof; No. 44 to Richard-Strauss-Strasse, Böhmerwaldplatz; Nos. 88 and 188 to Arabellapark and Effnerplatz. *STREETCAR:* No. 18 to Deutsches Museum, Gasteig and Max-Weber-Platz; No. 19 to Max-Weber-Platz and Ostbahnhof.

Restaurants / Cafés / Night-life
BOGENHAUSEN: **Bogenhausener Hof**, Ismaninger Str. 85, tel. 985586, 6 pm to 1 am, closed Sun, very elegant. **La Vigna**, Wilhelm-Diess-Weg 2, tel. 931416, noon to 2:30 pm and 6:30 pm to 11 pm, Italian; **Käfer-Schänke**, Prinzregentenstr. 73, tel. 41680, Mon-Sat 12 noon to midnight, exclusive; **Mifune**, Ismaninger Str. 136, tel. 987572, Mon-Fri noon to 2 pm and 6 pm to 11 pm, Sat-Sun 6 pm to 11 am, luxurious Japanese.
HAIDHAUSEN: *BAVARIAN with beer-garden:* **Hofbräukeller**, Innere Wiener Str. 19, tel. 4487376, open 9 am to midnight; **Zum Kloster**, Preysingstr. 77, tel. 4470564, Mon-Sat 10 am to 1 am, Sun 6 pm to 1 am.
SPECIALITY CUISINE: **Bernard & Bernard**, Innere Wiener Str. 32, tel. 4801173, 7 pm to1 am, crêpes; **Kytaro**, Innere Wiener Str. 36, tel. 4801176, 5 pm to 1 am, Greek, reservation advised; **Lisboa Bar**, Breisacher Str. 22, tel. 4482274, 6 pm to 1 am, Portuguese; **Maria Passagne**, Steinstr. 42, tel. 486167, 7 pm to 1 am, sushi, music and 60s decor; **Namaskar**, Rosenheimer Str. 113a, tel. 4480962, 11:30 am to 2:30 pm and 5:30 pm to 1 am, Indian; **Restaurant im Gasteig** (in the City Hilton), Rosenheimer Str. 15, tel. 48042302, tasty, inexpensive midnight buffet from 10 pm to midnight – ideal after a Gasteig event; **Ritzi**, Maria-Theresia-Str. 2, tel. 4701010, art deco café and restaurant with fine Italian and thai food; **Rue des Halles**, Steinstr. 18, tel. 485675, 6:30 pm to 1 am, French cuisine.
TRENDY BARS AND CAFÉS: **Atlas**, Innere Wiener Str. 2, tel. 4802997, breakfast till midnight, good food, in-spot; **Drehleier**, Rosenheimer Str. 123, tel. 482742, 7 pm to 1 am, music, cabaret, inexpensive food; **Hinterhof-Café**, Sedanstr. 29, tel. 4489964, Mon-Sat 8 am to 8 pm, Sun from 9 am, muesli and sandwiches. **Jam**, Rosenheimerstr. 4, tel. 484409, good food, average prices; **Johannis Café**, Johannisplatz 15, tel. 4801240, Sun-Wed, 11 am to 1 am, Fri-Sat till 3 am; **Café Wiener Platz**, Innere Wiener Str. 48, tel. 4489494, 8 am to 1 am.
DISCOS: **Liberty**, Rosenheimerstr. 30, tel. 484840, for 60s and 70s fans.
KUNSTPARK OST: Grafingerstr. 6, info-telephone 49002928, enormous area with bars and clubs, incl. the **Bongo Bar**; Fri-Sat **Metropolitan Night Club** from 11 pm; **Colosseum**, concerts; **Heizkraftwerk** and **Ultraschall II**; techno discos; **Natraj Temple**, disco; **Nachtkantine**, giant bar.

Post Offices
Kirchenstr. 4; Orleansplatz 7; Arabellastr. 26.

Taxi Stands
Max-Weber-Platz, tel. 4704002; Prinzregentplatz, tel. 479931 and 216155; At the Gasteig, tel. 216123; Ostbahnhof, tel. 216153.

THE ISAR

THE SHIMMERING ISAR

Other great cities of the world have beautiful rivers, too – Paris has the Seine, New York the Hudson and Vienna the Danube – but the Isar is far more than just a river for Munich. It is the city's natural center, from which everything is either "left or right of the Isar." Its banks serve as beach and playground, as a place to meditate or simply to get a bit of fresh air, and the paths along the river are especially popular with joggers and dogs.

In times past it did not serve the city's leisure requirements to quite the same extent. In the 19th century the public health pioneer, Max Pettenkofer, advised that Munich's sewage should be drained into the Isar in an attempt to improve the insanitary conditions which had brought plague and cholera to the city.

Preceding pages: Ancient glory in the Glyptothek. Above: Munich life at the "Flaucher." Right: A rafting trip on the Isar – a spectacular way to experience the river.

Isaria, the "Wild One," was the name given to the unbridled river which originated high up in the Karwendel mountains and then found its way over rocks and pebbles down to Munich. It was a dangerous river, with rapids and shallows which were the undoing of many a logger who was accompanying mighty tree trunks down the river to be cut up and used in the big town. However, that was long ago.

Today, broad stretches of the Isar within the city are lined with concrete banks; it is rather lazy and lacks temperament. Only in early spring, when the snows melt, can one still get some idea of the Isar's former might: then it spills over its high banks, and the usually turquoise-green waters of the river thunder over the little weir above the Deutsches Museum in a foaming brown torrent. The city council is always talking about restoring the Isar to is natural state, but little has so far come of this. The people of Munich do not seem to mind – they love their Isar just as it is, even when in summer it is often no more than a mere trickle, lapping at the gleaming white expanses of its gravel banks; they can always find an opportunity to spend a few quiet or a few lively hours on the Isar.

A really spectacular way to experience the river is on a *Flossfahrt* (raft trip) from Wolfratshausen to Munich. What used to be hard labor for the loggers of old, has today become a favorite pastime for staff outings. The rafts drift down the Isar, accompanied by jazz groups or brass bands, with free beer and chemical toilets provided on board. Bookings for this often have to be made six months in advance! (Info and bookings from bavaria euroraft, Heubergstr. 6a, 82441, Ohlstadt, tel. 08841 / 7751; fax 79413).

A bicycle ride along the banks of the Isar is certainly more beautiful and more peaceful. There are over 60 miles (100 km) of cycle paths from north to south (and vice versa, naturally). On both sides of the river there are tempting green paths, meadows and gravel banks and, of course, marvellous shady beer gardens such as the *Mühlenwirt* at Schäftlarn to the south of Munich, or the *Aumeister* to the north.

It is no longer advisable to bathe in the river, but this does not seem to deter many people – the turquoise waters of the river are just too tempting, and as soon as the warm weather arrives, the beaches of the Isar are crowded with swimmers and sunbathers, from the *Pupplinger Au* at Icking down to the *Eisbach* in the Englischer Garten. It is far more inviting than an outdoor pool, is more friendly – and it's free. And the *Flaucher*, with its wide gravel banks, weirs, park and beer garden, forms the focal point of this wonderful natural leisure resource.

The local bard, Willy Michl, sings of the "Shimmering Isar, where all the nudists are..." – echoing the thoughts of the Müncheners who love to see people bathing naked in the middle of the city. The Isar thus divides the citizens of Munich:

nudists sunning themselves on Prater Island below the Deutsches Museum, and the voyeurs on the bridges striving for a better view!

Often, when the summer lies heavily and lazily over Munich, the banks of the Isar resemble an army camp. Smoke rises from a hundred barbecues, barrels of beer are rolled out and tons of sausages are consumed. A multitude of people drink into the night, and at least a few don't wake up until the next morning, surrounded by the trash of yesterday's party. An invitation to a riverside party like this is a social "must" during the summer.

But the Isar is especially beautiful not only in summer: the light green of spring, the reddish yellow of chestnut trees in autumn and the gleaming white of the first winter snows contrast with the turquoise-colored waters of the Isar – a true feast for the eyes! And that is why Müncheners come to their river all year round. They all meet here; the people of Giesing, Haidhausen, Schwabing and Bogenhausen.

MUSEUMS IN MUNICH

Munich really owes its reputation as the home of some of Europe's most important museums to the Wittelsbach's passion for collecting. The art treasures they amassed over the centuries form the basis of the collections that can be seen in Munich's large museums, and Ludwig I built magnificent royal "temples of art" to house them: the *Glyptothek* (Museum of Sculpture), *Staatliche Antikensammlung* (State Antiquities Collection) and the *Alte* and *Neue Pinakothek* (Old and New Museums of Art). These remain obligatory destinations for any art-lover to visit.

Today public finance, wealthy individuals and companies fulfill the role once occupied by royal patrons. Museums receive considerable funding, and their collections are continually being expanded and enriched by spectactular purchases and gifts. If you are particularly interested in contemporary art, you should not forget the many commercial galleries in Munich, which formerly made up for the lack of representation of contemporary art in the public galleries. Now, however, – financed primarily through public funds – a third *Pinakothek* for modern art is slated to be opened in 1999, in which four Munich museums of 20th century art will be united.

Around Königsplatz

"I want to make Munich into a city that will give so much credit to Germany's honor that a person does not know Germany if he has not seen Munich." This was the ambition of Ludwig I, who saw his dream begin to be realized when, in 1816 as Crown Prince, he laid the foundation-stone for the **Glyptothek**. De-

Left: One of the treasures of the Alte Pinakothek – "Alexanderschlacht" by Albrecht Altdorfer.

signed by von Klenze, the building grew up around a square inner courtyard, with a free-standing four-winged section in the style of an Ionic temple. On its completion in 1831 this was the most important example of classical architecture at the time and it caused quite a sensation. Its collection of sculptures is world-renowned and stands comparison with those of the Louvre and the British Museum: it contains figures from the pediment of the temple of Aphaia in Aegina, the early Greek *Kuroi*, and the *Barberinian Faun*, to name only a few of the outstanding pieces of Greek and Roman sculpture on display here.

Opposite the Glyptothek stands the **Staatliche Antikensammlung**, housed in the windowless, late-classical building which bounds the southern side of Königsplatz. This museum was also built on the initiative of Ludwig I to house an extensive collection of Athenian vases from the 6th and 5th centuries BC, Greek and Roman terra-cottas, and Greek, Roman and Etruscan bronze, jewellery and glass.

At the western side of Königsplatz, on the corner of Luisenstrasse, is the **Städtische Galerie im Lenbachhaus**, the city-owned art gallery in the villa which was once the home of Franz von Lenbach, Munich's "prince of painters." He built it between 1887 and 1891 in the Florentine renaissance style. The main focus of the extensive collections here lies in the 19th century (Lenbach, Corinth, Slevogt) and the 20th century, with numerous works from the Jugendstil period and by the group of artists known as the *Blauer Reiter* (Blue Rider), including Marc, Macke, Münter, Jawlensky and Klee. More than 500 works make up the Kandinsky collection. Regular exhibitions of contemporary art are also held here. In addition, the **Kunstbau**, a gallery belonging to Lenbachaus, has been established in the Königsplatz U-Bahn station.

The next large museum near Königsplatz is the **Alte Pinakothek**, between

MUSEUMS

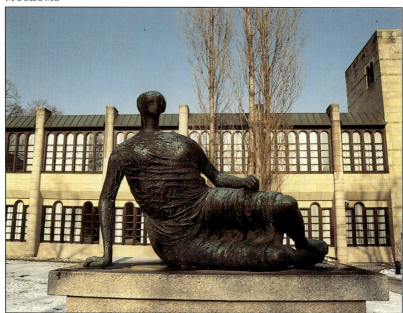

Arcisstrasse and Barerstrasse. It was reopened in 1998 after extensive renovations. The Alte Pinakothek is counted among the six most important picture galleries in the world today.

Commissioned by Ludwig I, it was built by von Klenze from 1826 to 1836. On its completion it was hailed by Wölfflin as an "artistic masterpiece of perfect proportions." Sadly, the bombs of World War Two destroyed the 24 statues of famous artists by Ludwig Schwanthaler which lined the south façade, as well as the interior frescos by Peter Cornelius. Inside, though, one of the most important collections of Western art from the 14th to the 19th centuries awaits art lovers from all over the world.

The basis of the collection was created by Wilhelm IV with a series of historical paintings he acquired in 1530. One of the most famous works in this group is the *Alexanderschlacht* (Alexander's Battle) by Albrecht Altdorfer. Maximilian I inherited the Wittelsbach passion for collecting, and purchased works by Albrecht Dürer, including *The Four Apostles*. Elector Max Emanuel had a particularly keen interest in Dutch and Flemish art, buying works by Van Dyck and Breughel, and later Karl Theodor contributed paintings by Rubens (including *The Descent into Hell).* Max IV Joseph introduced the French masters to Munich. With secularization, rich treasures from churches and monasteries were added to the collection. Ludwig I himself became known as a collector of pre-Raphaelite art. In the 19th and 20th centuries the major banks funded the purchase of futher valuable works.

Directly opposite, separated by broad lawns and Theresienstrasse, stands the **Neue Pinakothek** – a rather strange-looking building that combines neo-renaissance and post-modernist influences, with its rows of arched windows, inset walls and creased copper roofs. It

Above: Henry Moore's "Large Reclining Woman" in front of the Neue Pinakothek.
Right: Art-fatigue in the Neue Pinakothek!

was built in 1975-81, and is often dubbed "Palazzo Branca" after its architect, Alexander von Branca.

The interior is arranged around two inner courtyards; the visitor turns a lot of corners, goes up and down staircases. What you see on this tour is a varied collection of European painting from the late 18th to the beginning of the 20th centuries. Again it was Ludwig I who laid the foundations of the collection, which was originally housed in a mid-19th century building which was destroyed in the Second World War.

The eye can scarcely take in some of the gigantic, history-dense canvases, from Piloty's *Thusnelda in the Triumphal Procession of Germanicus,* which measures 21 by 15 feet (ca. 5 x 7 m), to Spitzweg's *The Poor Poet*, from Friedrich's *Mountain Landscape* to Feuerbach's *Medea*, from Degas' *Girl Ironing* to Van Gogh's *View of Arles.* In the park near the main entrance is a likewise enormous sculpture by Henry Moore, *Large Reclining Woman*.

Around Marienplatz

Museums of a very diffrent kind can be found during a stroll around Marienplatz. On Neuhauser Strasse, about mid-way between Karlsplatz and Marienplatz, is the **Deutsches Jagd und Fischerei Museum** (German Hunting and Fishing Museum) which, although hidden by a church façade, is easily recognized by the bronze sculptures of a wild boar and a fish at its entrance. The façade itself was originally part of St. Augustine's church, which in 1803 was converted into a tollbooth during secularization. Among the curiosities on display are rows of stuffed heads from prize stags which stare with glazed eyes at the stucco decoration of the early- baroque vaults; and elegant sleighs stand beneath the crystal chandeliers in the choir of the former chancel. There is also a real rarity to be seen here – a whole collection of *Wolpertingers* – legendary creatures found only in Bavaria, which the museum guide will tell you, are "allergic to *Kölsch* (a north-

MUSEUMS

German beer), parties of tourists and republicans."

The Gothic tower of the former city fortifications, close to the Old Town Hall at Marienplatz, today houses the **Spielzeug Museum** (Toy Museum) in four small rooms. The museum was founded by the caricaturist Ivan Steiger. Adults enter at their own peril, for the old toys standing in neat rows in their glass display cases might possibly evoke an instant wave of nostalgia. The smallest doll in the world can be seen here, as can toys made of wood, paper and lead, and mechanical toys of all sorts, from 1780 to the present day.

On your way to the Stadt Museum on St. Jacobs-Platz, you pass the **Ignaz Günther House** (Oberanger 11, entrance opposite the Stadt Museum). In this Gothic gabled house the famous court sculptor of the rococo period, Ignaz Gün-

Above: The Hunting Museum is the only place in the world where Wolpertingers can be seen. Right: Chamber pots for all tastes.

ther (1725-77), lived and worked. At the rear second entrance to the house on Oberanger street, is a Madonna, a copy of the original by Günther which now hangs in the Bavarian National Museum. Only the downstairs rooms and the Gothic hall on the first floor are open to the public. The rooms provide a proper setting for exhibitions which generally have a theme connected with the history of the city.

Diagonally across the square is the **Stadt Museum** (City Museum), housed in the former city armory and the royal stables which were attached to it. In this unique, diverse and lively museum, besides interesting rotating exhibitions, priority is given to exhibits which are related to Munich's history. Twenty rooms have been furnished in faithful detail to illustrate fashions in cultivated living from the 17th to the 20th centuries.

Among the greatest treasures of the museum are ten of the original sixteen figures of morris dancers carved by Erasmus Grasser, a master of the late-Gothic period, who fashioned this set of figures from lindenwood for the banquet hall of the Old Town Hall. Anyone truly interested in Munich's history should have a look at the medieval model of the city created by master woodworker Jakob Sandtner. Various specialized departments within the museum are also worth a visit, such as the photographic and film museum, the second-largest collection of musical instruments in Europe, a costume and textiles collection, a puppet theater collection, and a small brewery museum (see also p. 67).

If you need to relax after such a heavy diet of historical exhibits, walk through the attractive food market – Viktualienmarkt – as far as Westenriederstrasse, where one of Munich's most original museums awaits you. This is the **ZAM** (*Zentrum für aussergewöhnliche Museen*: Center for Unusual Museums). There is, indeed, a great deal here that is unusual, not to say absurd. For instance, in the

Chamber Pot Museum there are 2,000 exhibits from two millennia, the oldest of which dates back to Rome in the 2nd century BC. The Bourdalou room shows a collection of portable potties for woman in need. In the Lock Museum you can see creaking padlocks and medieval chastity-belts. Then there are museums of corkscrews, pedal-cars and Easter bunnies, as well as the Sissi (the last Austrian empress) Museum.

If your appetite for oddities is still not satisfied, it is not far to the **Valentin Museum**, diagonally across from the tower of the Isartor gate. A sign at the entrance announces that admission is free "to 90-year-olds, if accompanied by their parents." On display here is the intellectual legacy of Munich's by far most-famous comedian and popular entertainer, including his "winter toothpick" trimmed with fur, his snow-sculpture ("unfortunately melted"), and the hook on which he hung up his original career as a carpenter. In a tiny pub at the top of the tower you can have a cup of coffee and enjoy what is said to be the best *Weisswurst* in Munich.

The Fascination of Technology

From the Isartor, walk along Zweibrückenstrasse to the bridge across the Isar, and you come to Munich's most famous museum, the **Deutsches Museum** (German Museum). Situated on an island in the middle of the Isar, this massive building contains a total of 164,000 square feet (50,000 sq m) of exhibition space. If you spent only one minute at each exhibit, it would still take you 24 12-hour days to cover the museum!

Plans for this gigantic "survey of achievement" in science and technology were drawn up at the end of the 19th century by Oskar von Miller, and in 1906 the foundation-stone was laid by Kaiser Wilhelm II, though construction was not competed until 1925 (archiect: Gabriel von Seidl). Since then, the Deutsches Museum has attracted millions of visitors from all over the world. Almost every

MUSEUMS

Above: Technology on display in the aviation hall of the Deutsches Museum.

tourist who comes to Munich goes to see this unique collection covering every field of the natural sciences and technology, supplemented by diagrams, models, dioramas, films and re-created experiments (see also p. 154).

Here you can take away miniature bricks which are turned out by a model brick-works, or see what happens when a member of the staff is put into a "Faraday Cage," a cage-like metal screen, which is then bombarded by a 220,000-volt flash of lightning with an ear-splitting crack; you can quietly ponder over the movement of a Foucault pendulum or let yourself get lost in the revelry of childhood dreams at the sight of the gigantic model railroad.

In the basement, the adits and shafts of a coal-mine have been reconstructed in the basement, while in the planetarium the universe glides in majestic silence above your head. In the aviation hall, one of the world's first jet planes, the ME 262, is on display. The world's first automobile, built by Carl Benz in 1886, is also on display. The museum shows you what a 17th century "computer" looked like in the days of Newton and Leibniz, as well as under what "primitive" experimental conditions the atom was first split by Otto Hahn and Fritz Strassmann in 1938.

Germany's first IMAX screen – 52 by 72 feet (16 x 22 m) – has been set up in the **Forum der Technik**. Films on subjects as diverse as Alsaka, polar bears, New York and the Rolling Stones are shown here.

A branch museum – the **Flugwerft Schleissheim** – was opened in 1992 at the northern edge of Munich. It contains the restored historic airplane factory built here between 1912 and 1919. Its 26,000 square feet (8,000 sq m) of exhibition space extend the air and space collection of the museum island. The vertical take-off plane, which used to stand in front of the Deutsches Museum, can now be seen here.

Odeonsplatz – Prinzregentenstrasse

Another group of museums can be visited on a walk starting from Theatinerstrasse, over Odeonsplatz to the south side of the Hofgarten.

Strolling along Theatinerstrasse from the direction of Marienplatz, one could easily overlook the entrance to the **Kunsthalle der Hypo-Kulturstiftung** (Art Gallery of the Hypo-Bank Cultural Foundation) set among the row of exquisite and expensive shopfronts. This gallery offers a broad spectrum of exhibitions: from the art of Sudan to German expressionism.

The obelisk in front of the entrance to the banquet hall of the Residenz points the way to the **Staatliche Sammlung Ägyptischer Kunst** (State Collection of Egyptian Art), where items from the Glyptothek and other collections are brought together in stuccoed renaissance rooms. In obtaining its new acquisitions, the museum has specialized primarily in three-dimensional sculpture, as opposed to friezes and reliefs. There are also mummy portraits and sarcophagi, as well as a facial fragment from the huge statue of Echnaton.

For those to whom ancient Egypt is somewhat too distant, a little further on, in the northern part of the Hofgarten arcade, is the entrance to the **Deutsches Theater Museum**. There was originally a memorial here to the court actress Clara Ziegler (1844-1909), and it subsequently developed, in the course of time, into an acknowledged institution specializing in the world history of theater, with building plans for theaters, designs for stage sets, costumes, masks, props and stills from famous productions.

Only a short distance away, through the underpass beneath the Altstadtring, where Prinzregentenstrasse begins, is the grey **Haus der Kunst** (House of Art) with its Doric-columned façade. It was opened in 1937 by Reich Propaganda Minister Josef Goebbels as the "House of German Art," with an exhibition of works by Nazi artists. Today, interesting and international world-class exhibitions attract visitors young and old during extremely obliging opening hours (weekdays until 10 p.m.).

In the museum's west wing is the **Staatsgalerie Moderner Kunst** (State Gallery of Modern Art), with a fine collection of works by artists who were banned by the Nazis and are now world-famous. Here you can admire paintings by the German expressionists Beckmann, Heckel, Kirchner, Nolde and Schmitt-Rottluff alongside Braque, Picasso, Chirico, Ernst, Mirò, Dalí and Magritte.

Two museums dedicated to Bavarian themes stand side by side on the left hand side of Prinzregentenstrasse (No. 3) going towards the Isar. The origins of the **Bayrisches National Museum** lie once again with the Wittelsbach enthusiasm for collecting, this time Bavarian art and handicrafts. Today, it is considered one of the foremost museums of European sculpture, folk art and folk crafts, with items from the early Middle Ages to the present day. This includes a unique collection of Nativity scenes from all over the continent.

Housed in a side wing is the museum's complementary "modern" counterpart, the **Neue Sammlung** – containing Europe's largest design collection; all sorts of hisorical everyday articles, from flat-irons to gasoline pumps, are documented here.

A visit to the **Prähistorische Staatssammlung** (State Prehistoric Collection) – just around the corner at Lerchenfeldstrasse 3 – gives an insight into the prehistory and ancient history of Bavaria, with archaeological discoveries from the Stone Age to the Roman Empire to the Middle Ages. Among the museum's treasures are three Carolingian columns, a stucco relief and fresco fragments from the *Sola* basilica at Solnhofen.

MUSEUMS

Back on Prinzregentenstrasse, in the building at No. 9, is the **Schack Gallery**. Here you can see the bequest of Count Schack (1815-94), containing works by late-Romantic German artists including Schwind, Spitzweg, Lenbach, Feuerbach, Böcklin and Marées.

The last port of call on this tour, which you can make after crossing the Isar and walking up the hill beneath shady trees and past the glimmering gold Friedensengel, is the neo-classical **Villa Stuck**. This house was built in 1897-98 after a design by Franz von Stuck, the master of the house and so-called "painter prince." The villa is worth visiting not only for the rotating exhibitions which are held in the studios, for the original furnishings in the living rooms, the paintings of Franz von Stuck, and even the house itself, seen as a synthesis of the arts, are also all well worth a visit.

Above: The imposing entrance to the Museum of Ethnology.

Other Museums

Another important museum in the city center is the **Staatliches Museum für Völkerkunde** (State Museum of Ethnology) on Maximilianstrasse. Apart from the many exhibitions staged here, this museum, with its approximately 300,000 exhibits from Asia, Africa and Latin America, is the second-largest museum of its kind in Germany, after the one in Berlin. It emerged from the 1782 "collection of curiosities," assembled by the dukes and electors of Bavaria.

In 1990 the **Museum Mensch und Natur** (Museum of Man and Nature) opened its doors in a wing of Nymphenburg Palace. Using the latest museum-pedagogical methods it vividly explains biological and geographical themes.

The **BMW Museum**, a 120-foot-wide (40 m) silvery, windowless "concrete dish" beside BMW's headquarters, displays the firm's cars, motorcycles and aircraft engines in a highly-polished exhibition.

MUSEUMS

Collections of Paintings

State and city museums are closed on Mondays. Information on Munich's museums is available on the Internet at http://www.munich-online.de
Alte Pinakothek, Barer Str. 27, tel. 23805215/6. **Neue Pinakothek**, Barer Str. 29, tel. 23805195, streetcar No. 27 from Karlsplatz (Stachus), U2 to Theresienstrasse. 10 am to 5 pm (except Mon), Tue and Thu till 8 pm (both museums). **Schack Gallery**, Prinzregentenstr. 9, tel. 23805-224, U4/U5 to Lehel, Wed-Mon 10 am to 5 pm. **Haus der Kunst**, tel. 21127-0, Tue-Fri 10 am to 10 pm; Sat-Sun/hol 10 am to 6 pm. **Staatsgalerie für moderne Kunst**, tel. 21127137, Prinzregentenstr. 1, 10 am to 5 pm (except Mon), Thu 10 am to 8 pm. **Städtische Galerie im Lenbachhaus**, Luisenstr. 33, tel. 2330320, U2 to Königsplatz, Tue-Sun 10 am to 6 pm. Special exhibitions in **Kunstbau** in U-Bahnhof Königsplatz. **Villa Stuck**, Prinzregentenstr. 60, tel. 4555125, U5 to Prinzregentenplatz, Tue-Sun 10 am to 5 pm, Thu till 8 pm. **Kunstraum München**, Viktor-Scheffel-Str. 20, tel. 348920, Tue-Fri 2 pm to 6 pm, Sat 11 am to 2 pm; contemporary art, U3/U6 Münchener Freiheit. **Kunsthalle der Hypo-Kulturstiftung**, Theatinerstr. 15, tel. 224412, daily 10 am to 6 pm, Thu till 9 pm; rotating exhibitions, U3-6 to Odeonsplatz.

Art and Cultural History

Bayerisches National Museum, Prinzregentenstr. 3, tel. 211241, U4/U5 to Lehel, 9:30 am to 5 pm, (except Mon). **Neue Sammlung (Design Museum)**, Prinzregentenstr. 3, tel. 227844, U4/U5 to Lehel, 10 am to 5 pm. **Staatliche Münzsammlung (Coin Collection)**, Residenzstr. 1, tel. 227221/2, U3/U6 and U4/U5 to Odeonsplatz, 10 am to 4:30 pm. **Staatliche Graphische Sammlung (Graphics Collections)**, Meiserstr. 10, tel. 5591490, U2 to Königsplatz, Tue-Thu 10 am to 1 pm, Wed also 2 pm to 4:30 pm, Thu 2 pm to 6 pm, Fri 10 am to 12:30 pm, closed holidays.

Antiquity / Non-European Cultures

Glyptothek, Königsplatz 3, tel. 286100, with U2 to Königsplatz, Tue, Wed, Fri, 10 am to 5 pm, Thu noon to 8 pm. **Prähistorische (Prehistoric) Staatssammlung**, Lerchenfeldstr. 2, tel. 293911, streetcar No. 53, dialy 9 am to 4 pm (except Mon), Thu till 8 pm. **Staatliche (Antiques) Antikensammlung**, Königsplatz 1, tel. 598359, U2 to Königsplatz, Tue and Thu-Sun 10 am to 5 pm, Wed noon to 8 pm. **Staatliches Museum für Völkerkunde (Ethnology)**, Maximilianstr. 42, tel. 2101360, Tue-Sun 9:30 am to 4:30 pm. **Staatliche Sammlung Ägyptische Kunst (Egyptian Art)**, Residenz, entrance Hofgartenstr., tel. 298546, with U3/6 and U4/5 to Odeonsplatz, Tue-Fri 9 am to 4 pm, Tue also 7 pm to 9 pm, Sat-Sun/hol 10 am to 5 pm.

Munich History

Münchner Stadt Museum, St.-Jakobs-Platz 1, tel. 233-22370, U3/U6 and all S-Bahns to Marienplatz, daily 10 am to 5 pm (except Mon), Wed till 8:30 pm. **Pasinger Fabrik**, August-Exter-Str. 1, tel. 8341841, Tue-Fri 4 pm to 8 pm, Sat-Sun 2 pm to 8 pm; contemporary exhibitions focusing on Munich, S3-6 and S8 to Pasing.

Special Museums

Alpine Museum, Praterinsel 5, tel. 2112240, Tue, Wed, Fri 1 pm to 6 pm, Thu 1 pm to 8 pm, U4/5 to Lehel. **Deutsches Jagd und Fischerei (Hunting and Fishing) Museum**, Neuhauser Str. 53, tel. 220522, U3/U6, all S-Bahns to Marienplatz, daily 9:30 am to 5 pm, Mon and Tue till 9 pm. **Deutsches Theater Museum**, Galeriestr. 4a, tel. 2106910, Tue 10 am to noon, Thu 2 pm to 4 pm, closed holidays, U3/U6 to Odeonsplatz. **Feuerwehr (Fire Dep't) Museum**, Blumenstr. 34, tel. 2353-3186, U1/2 and U3/6 to Sendlinger Tor, Sat 9 am to 4 pm only. **Jüdisches (Jewish) Museum**, Maximilianstr. 36, tel. 297453, Tue, Wed 2 pm to 6 pm, Thu 2 pm to 8 pm. **Kartoffel (Potato) Museum**, Grafinger Str. 2, tel. 404050, Tue-Thu by appointment, Fri 9 am to 6 pm, Sat 11 am to 5 pm. **Kinder und Jugend (Children's) Museum**, in the Hauptbahnhof (entrance Arnulfstr. 3), tel. 2609208. **Museum Mensch und Natur (Man and Nature)**, Schloss Nymphenburg, tel. 176494, streetcar Nos. 17 und 12, Bus No. 41 to Schloss Nymphenburg, 9 am to 5 pm (except Mon). **Puppen (Doll) Museum**, Gondershauserstr. 37, tel. 3228950, Mon, Thu 11 am to 5 pm, U6 to Freimann. **Spielzeug (Toy) Museum**, Alter Rathausturm, Marienplatz, tel. 294001, daily 10 am to 5:30 pm, U3/U6 alle S-Bahns. **Valentin Musäum**, Isartorturm, tel. 223266, all S-Bahns to Isartor, Mon, Tue, Sat 11:01 am to 5:29 pm, Sun 10:01 to 5:29 pm. **ZAM** – Center for Unusual Museums, Westenriederstr. 26, tel. 2904121, all S-Bahns to Isartor, daily 10 am to 6 pm.

Technical Museums

BMW Museum, Petuelring 130, tel. 3822-3307, U3 to Olympiazent., daily 9 am to 5 pm. **Deutsches Museum**, Museumsinsel 1, tel. 21791, all S-Bahns to Isartor, daily 9 am to 5 pm. **Forum der Technik**, Museumsinsel 1, tel. 211250, with IMAX Theater, and Planetarium with laser shows. **Flugwerft Schleissheim**, Effnerstr. 18, daily 9 am to 5 pm, tel. 3157140. S1 toward Freising, Oberschleissheim station. **Siemens Museum**, Prannerstr. 10, tel. 636-32660, all S-Bahns to Karlsplatz (Stachus), U4/U5 to Odeonsplatz, Mon-Fri 9 am to 5 pm, Sun 10 am to 5 pm, every 1st Tue of the month till 9 pm, electro-technology.

SHOPPING

SHOPPING

You will have no problem spending money in Munich – there is a cosmopolitan range of shops, and the prices are commensurate. It is possible to buy almost anything here as long as one can afford it – from an engraved beer tankard to the latest fashionable extravagance from an exclusive couturier.

In Munich it is not only the very rich who make an uninhibited display of their wealth, even people earning quite modest salaries are highly fashion-conscious and intent on improving their image. However, you do need to be familiar with the geography of Munich's shopping districts. The two main areas for shopping are in the inner city: the large department stores (Hertie, Kaufhof, Karstadt's Haus Oberpollinger) are to be found between Karlsplatz and Marienplatz in the pedestrian zone along Neuhauser Strasse and Kaufingerstrasse, while chic little shops with a vast selection of attractive clothes, jewellery, shoes and accessories are to be found in the smaller side-streets and on Sendlinger Strasse close by.

However, if you have a taste for international *haute couture,* and a checkbook to match your taste, you should head for those elegant shops on Maximilianstrasse, Theatinerstrasse and Residenzstrasse, and the designer boutiques on nearby Brienner Strasse. At the beginning of this area, a few yards from Odeonsplatz, the **Luitpold Block** houses about thirty shops and boutiques in a rather luxurious atmosphere. If you have any change left after shopping here, you can use it to sweeten up your life a bit in the palm garden of Café Luitpold.

Despite prophecies to the contrary, Schwabing continues to thrive as a lively shopping area. Brave little boutiques continue to open up to the right and left of the "tourists' mile" on Leopoldstrasse, especially the section between Herzogstrasse and Münchener Freiheit. Imaginative and amusing clothes to suit every taste and purse, as well as classically elegant fashions, are also to be found along Hohenzollernstrasse.

Munich has a wide selection of international fashion, and almost every one of the great names of the fashion world is represented here: **Valentino** (Kardinal-Faulhaber-Strasse 15) and, close by, **Chanel** (Brienner Strasse 10). **Kenzo** is at Maximilianstrasse 22, and **Missoni**, for extravagant knitwear, is at Amiraplatz 3. The most famous tailors in Munich are **Rudolph Moshammer** at Maximilianstrasse 14 and **Max Dietl** at Residenzstrasse 16.

Ludwig Beck, at the corner of the Rathaus, is not merely just another department store: its offerings also include unusual clothes and a vast selection of suitable accessories, as well as exquisite natural cosmetics.

Oben: The atrium of the Hertie department store. Right: Elegant boutiques abound on Theatinerstrasse.

SHOPPING

The best shops for quality traditional Bavarian clothing are **Loden-Frey** (Maffeistrasse 7-9) and **Wallach Haus**, which also sells folk art, at Residenzstrasse 3.

A pair of traditional made-to-measure leather shorts, fashioned from soft deerskin, can be bought at **August Strauss**, Heiliggeiststrasse 2. Then there are three shops which stock good-quality Bavarian souvenirs – **Etcetera** (Wurzerstrasse 12), **Dirndlkönigin** (Residenzstrasse 18) and **Niedermaier** (Goethestrasse 23). **Mändler** (Theatinerstrasse 7) sells rather saucy and expensive clothes, but the most famous shops for "freaky" fashion are **Kookai** (Sendlinger Strasse 41), **Bla Bla Boutik** in Asamhof at Sendlinger Strasse 26, **Nicowa**, at Leonrodstrasse 21 (attractive furniture and colonial-style articles are sold in the basement), all branches of **Hallhuber** (there are two just in the pedestrian zone) and **Tricia Jones**, at Siegesstrasse 24. Matching shoes for your new fashions can be found at **New Shoes** and **Lewy**, both of which are on Leopoldstrasse.

Three of the biggest sports shops in Munich are all quite close together: **Sport Scheck** (Sendlinger Strasse 85), **Sport Schuster** (Rosenstrasse 1-6), and **Sport Münzinger** (Marienplatz 8). In one of these shops will be able to find those new hiking boots, the right ski clothes or a good tennis racquet.

There are two excellent delicatessen shops in Munich: **Dallmayr** (Dienerstrasse 11) and **Feinkost-Käfer** (Prinzregentenstrasse 49). If you find these too expensive, try the outdoor markets at **Viktualienmarkt** or the quieter **Elisabethplatz** in Schwabing. Game can be purchased at the **Zerwirkgewölbe**, near the Hofbräuhaus, the oldest shop of its kind in Germany (Ledererstrasse 3). **Elly Seidl** (Maffeistrasse 1 and Karlstor 2) and **Confiserie Leyssiefer** (Asamhof) are famous for their exquisite chocolates, while **Zechbaur** (corner of Residenzstrasse and Perusastrasse) is the place to go for fine cigars. **Hugendubel** at Marienplatz and at Karlsplatz has the largest selection of titles for bookworms.

ALL ABOUT BEER

Munich enjoys an undisputed reputation as the world's beer capital. Though the world's biggest breweries are no longer to be found here, seven breweries in the city nurture a fine reputation, and their beer is famous throughout the world, even though many loyal men of Munich will grudgingly admit that the northerners brew better beer.

In 1516, because the recipes used for making beer then were so terrible, Duke Wilhelm IV issued his *Reinheitsgebot*, a decree to regulate the degree of purity of the beverage, and the quality of Bavarian beer we know today is a result of this. The brewers of Munich use only barley, hops, water and a little yeast; but for economic reasons they may well feel that their interests are no longer best served by this regulation.

Above: In a Bavarian hop garden. Right: Now all I need is some customers!

Whether you prefer *Helles* (lager beer), *Dunkles* (dark beer) or *Weissbier* (wheat beer), is just a matter of taste. *Bock* and *Doppelbock* are strong beers with about eight percent alcohol and almost twenty per cent original "wort." *Pils* (Pilsner beer), has established itself in Bavaria, but in return for this, Bavaria's most unique beer, *Weissbier*, has conquered the north of Germany.

The first *Bock* beer of the year is drunk on the Sunday after Ash Wednesday outside the city walls at the **Forschungsbrauerei** in Perlach. Those who prefer taking to the hills climb the **Nockherberg**, which rises above the district of Au, for a drink of *Salvator* in mid-March, the "fifth season of the year" in Munich. A favorite drink in the heat of summer is the *Radlermass* (half beer, half lemon soda) and the *Russenmass* (half wheat beer, half lemon soda; a "Mass" is a liter beer mug).

The real beer strongholds, however, are the **Löwenbräu-Keller** at Stiglmaierplatz, the **Paulanerkeller** on Nockherberg Hill and the **Hofbräuhaus am Platzl**. If you prefer to drink in a more refined atmosphere, go to the good, middle-class *Stuben* (neighborhood pubs) but, if you enjoy a robust place, try a *Schwemme* (more of a beer hall).

Great beer can also be enjoyed in any of the 4,000 restaurants in the city; in the **Peterhof** at Marienplatz, for example, where (as a plaque at the entrance points out), the *Weisswurst* (veal sausage) is supposed to have been invented, or the **Donisl**, left of the town hall, which stays open 24 hours a day during the *Fasching* carnival. There is also **Paulaner im Tal** (formerly Bögner) and the **Weisses Bräuhaus** diagonally across from it, and the oldest pubs in Munich, the **Hundskugel** (Hotterstrasse 18) and the **Altes Hackerhaus** on Sendlinger Strasse. If you want to drink with local celebrities, try the **Franziskaner** behind the Neues Rathaus (New Town Hall).

Beer gardens

In good weather the people of Munich always turn to their gardens – or, to be more precise, their beer gardens. This Bavarian institution, which is not quite like anything else in the world, has its own particular history.

Because beer has always been a very sensitive substance which quickly spoils in the summer heat, it must be kept in cool, dark cellars. To enhance the cooling effect of the cellars, spreading, shady chestnut trees were planted in the ground above, since their dense foliage afforded good protection against the heat of the sun. The inhabitants of Munich soon appreciated how pleasant it was to sit beneath these trees when the sun was too hot and enjoy a cool drink of beer. In those days, beer was drunk from glazed earthenware mugs – *Keferlohern* – which kept the beer cooler for a longer time. Nowadays, these have mostly been replaced by glass mugs. The one-liter *Mass* is the measure which is offered in a genuine beer garden, still the accepted measure of beer.

The price of beer has always been a cause for complaint among Munich's drinkers. Chronicles tell of a 66-year "war" which ensued when the price of a measure of beer was raised by a half *Kreuzer*. It began in 1844, when the angry populace demolished a number of breweries, and ended in 1910, when brewery inns were burnt down.

Unfortunately, there are still some bartenders who apparently do not know what the correct measure of beer should look like. The "Mother of the Bavarian *Mass*" still exists today, a wonderful oak container dating from the 18th century, which can be seen in the museum of local history and culture in the town of Neuburg an der Donau.

Locals and visitors alike cherish the custom of being allowed to take one's own food along to eat in a beer garden. This dates back to a decree by Ludwig I. Innkeepers complained that brewers were allowed to sell food with their beer

ALL ABOUT BEER

in some of their beer gardens, which was ruining the innkeepers' own business. The king was of the opinion that the best solution (and one with which everyone was equally unhappy) was that all of his subjects should be allowed take his own food to the beer garden and eat it at a bare table. This tradition has survived to the present day.

By far the largest beer garden in Munich is in the **Hirschgarten** (at Hirschgartenallee 1), in the Neuhausen district. It is situated in a large park and has quite an eventful history. The park's land was once used to rear pheasants, then for growing hops and, still later, it was planted with mulberry trees in an attempt to build up a silkworm farm. Finally, an area of 100 acres (40 hectares) was enclosed as a game preserve, which still exists today.

The **Concordia-Garten** (Landshuter Allee 165) is likewise in Neuhausen.

Above: Be prepared to pay when served!
Right: Typical scene at the Hirschgarten.

Here one can enjoy a beer beneath the shade of horse-chestnut, birch, and maple trees. Another beer garden to be recommended is the **Taxis-Garten** (Taxisstrasse 1), which is not far away from here and which attracts a generally younger crowd. The second-largest and probably the best-known beer garden is the one at the **Chinesischer Turm** (Chinese Tower) in the Englischer Garten. Here, in good weather, there is always a hectic throng of walkers, joggers, dog owners, cyclists, students and, of course, tourists from all over the world. If you need to get your breath back after this, take a leisurely ride in a horse-drawn carriage from here through the park. Close by is the rather smarter beer garden at **Kleinhesseloher See**, where you can enjoy a drink whatever the weather.

The **Osterwald-Garten** (Keferstrasse 12), located at one of the many entrances to the Englischer Garten, must be mentioned as a typical example of an old Schwabing beer garden. Not far away is the **Hirschau** (Gyslingstrasse 15), with a friendly, pleasant and cozy atmosphere beneath the ancient horse-chestnut trees. Going further north there is the **Aumeister** (Sondermeisterstrasse 1) and, crossing over to the other side of the Isar, you will find **Sankt-Emmerams-Mühle** (St. Emmeram 41), which has, to the regret of many, been taken over by the chic set.

There are other much-frequented beer gardens on the right bank of the Isar, but closer to the city center, such as the **Hofbräukeller** at Wiener Platz, which has been a favorite meeting place for many Müncheners for over 100 years. High above the district of Au is the erstwhile **Paulanerkeller** (formerly Salvatorkeller; Hochstrasse 77), famous for its strong beer festival in March. The **Menterschwaige** by the Isar (Menterschwaigstrasse 4) is where no less a personage than King Ludwig I used to celebrate his May festivals.

If you would rather stay in the center of Munich, try the **Augustiner-Keller** (Arnulfstrasse 52) – many of its regular customers will tell you it is like a second home to them in the summer! Lots of prominent locals can be found here; even Munich's well-known newspaper columnist Sigi Sommer had his regular table in the beer garden until his death in 1995. The *Fischer-Vroni* stand in the beer garden is reckoned to cook the best grilled fish in town: the tasty *Steckerlfisch*, which is generally mackerel and is served whole on a long spit.

The **Löwenbräu-Keller** (Nymphenburgerstrasse 2), built in 1882, has lots to offer with its traditional beer garden, and there is a good view across Stiglmeierplatz from the restaurant's upper terrace. The **Augustiner-Grossgaststätte** (Neuhauserstrasse 16) is a little older, and one can sit far into the night in its inner courtyard. The most famous pub in the world is, however, without a doubt, the **Hofbräuhaus am Platzl**, which was built more than 400 years ago. The pleasant sound of splashing water from the lion fountain in the beer garden is lost here amidst the bewildering babel of languages spoken by visitors from all over the world. At the southern edge of town is the **Waldwirtschaft Grosshesselhohe**, which attracts jazz fans and excursionists. From inside town you can take a pleasant bicycle ride along the Isar to get here. The beer and spareribs taste even better after the ride! When the weather is good, internationally-acclaimed Dixieland jazz bands play in the beer garden.

In Munich, the beer garden is an institution. It may be true that you sometimes have to fight for a place to sit, but then the beer tastes good, the day's stress melts away, even social differences seem to disappear; people sit together in harmony, drinking and discussing, seldom stopping at just one *Mass*.

Regarding complaints by nearby residents of noise, a Munich court has ruled: "A beer garden lies in the higher public interest, therefore, a certain amount of tolerence must be allowed."

THE OKTOBERFEST

It all began with the marriage of the Bavarian crown prince Ludwig (later King Ludwig I, who so enriched Munich's architectural heritage) to Princess Therese von Sachsen-Hildburghausen. Since Ludwig was quite prepared to give his blessing to such profane things as popular festivals ("because they express something of the national character which is passed on to our children and our children's children"), he happily accepted the suggestion put forward by Dall'Armi, his bowling-club companion, that the wedding festivities should conclude with a horse race. That was on October 12, 1810, and it was such a great success that it was decided to repeat the event every year thereafter. The *Oktoberfest* was born, and what was once just entertainment provided by the monarch for his subjects has since become the largest popular festival in the world – and a huge money-making business.

Nearly 200 years have passed since the day when the *Theresienwiese* (Therese Meadow) received its name in honor of the royal bride – now it is simply called the *Wies'n* by the people of Munich. In the first decades of the *Oktoberfest,* the entertainments on offer were of a modest nature; two swings and a carousel, and beer was available in small booths.

Nowadays preparations begin in the summer because, while the huge festival tents and Ferris wheels, roller-coasters and various other fairground rides may not be architectural masterpieces, it still requires great technical expertise to erect them. The booths and stalls, on the other hand, are put up in a matter of days. Ten large festival tents stand for 16 days like a city within the city, surrounded by all the stalls selling tobacco, sweets, sausages and fish rolls, pretzels and souvenirs, and a distinctly incongruous milk pavilion.

Above: Six million visitors anually surge across the "Wies'n." Right: The proper music gets things off to a good start.

OKTOBERFEST

Nearly six million visitors quaff about five million liters of beer in the 16-day period. Hundreds of thousands of roast chickens and 80 entire steers are consumed, and thousands of pounds of fish and miles of bratwurst find their way into the stomachs of *Wies'n* visitors. Trying to decide on entertainment is no easier than selecting a meal: there are 45 different rides, from the roller-coaster to the Ferris wheel, 70 stalls with games, shooting-galleries and much more. In total there are around 640 different attractions – the largest popular festival in the world.

The Müncheners love their *Wies'n* and the Oktoberfest, and at 12 noon on the opening Saturday, when the canon-salute sounds as a prelude to the festivities, it draws the crowds like a magnet– even the people who have sworn never to go again because of the price of the beer or the dubious standards of the barmen, or because of the crowds or the dangers of the fairground rides – all of which, of course, are described in exaggerated superlatives.

But the old Bavarian character still survives here, if you know where to look. For example, there is *Vogel-Jakob* with his incomparable birdsong imitations – a reminder of the old *Wies'n* traditions, as is the flea circus, where the performers must be scrutinized under a magnifying glass. *Haut den Lukas* is a stand where muscular swains can try their strength at swinging the hammer, and blush when roundly beaten by a slip of a girl. You can still witness Frankenstein's monster and his companions rising from their coffins, or take a ride in the swaying carriages of the ghost train, while terrifying groans and rattling skeletons come at you from all sides.

There are the sensational attractions like *The Loop*, *Calypso*, *The Devil's Wheel*, *The Crinoline* – a sort of shaking turntable – and *The Toboggan*, like an ancient conveyor belt whose end can only be reached with the greatest diffi-

culty imaginable. There is also the largest mobile organ in the world – the *Orchestrion* – with over 1,000 pipes. Since 1872, the first beer of the festival has always been poured at *Schichtl's*, and this has given Munich a popular saying: *Auf geht's beim Schichtl.*

People of every nation and from every continent meet and rub shoulders here, and of the six million visitors to the festival each year, "only" 1.3 million are actually from the Munich area itself. Each evening bedlam reigns in the beer tents. The comparatively comfortable booths, or "boxes," are booked months in advance, mostly by companies for corporate entertainment.

On the tables and benches you will see Australians, Canadians and Italians dancing their way to the kind of beery heaven that they can never find in their home countries. Many thousands of liters of beer flow down throats on the *Wies'n* with every toast of *Prosit der Gemütlichkeit,* and every rousing rendition of *Oans, zwoa, gsuffa!*

MUNICH FOR KIDS

Above: Penguins and children stroll together at Hellabrunn Zoo.

MUNICH FOR KIDS

Munich especially for kids: there are really quite a lot of things for them to see and do here: for example, the **Theater für Kinder** (Dachauerstr. 46, tel. 595454, U1 to Stiglmaierplatz) offers fairy tale plays to dream and laugh with for little theater-goers from four years of age on up, and in the **Marionette Theater**, marionettes even perform opera in the afternoons (Bumenstr. 29a, tel. 265712, U-Bahn/S-Bahn Marientplatz); part highbrow, part comical plays for older kids are put on at the **Theater der Jugend – Die Schauburg** at Elisabethplatz (tel. 23721-365; streetcar No. 27 to Elisabethplatz).

In Schwabing there are two movie theaters which show children's films: **Kiko**, in the theater-bar Heppel & Ettlich (Kaiserstr. 67, tel. 349359, streetcar No. 27 to Kurfürstenplatz) every Sunday at 11 a.m., and Saturdays at 11 a.m. in **Forum 2** (Nadistr. 3, U3 to Olympiazentrum). Classic films that also appeal to children are shown on weekends at the **Stadt Museum** (St. Jakobsplatz, U-Bahn/S-Bahn Marienplatz). Shown on a giant screen, impressive documentary nature films (for example, about sharks, penguins or the Serengeti desert) attract crowds young and old daily to the **IMAX** cinema (Museuminsel 1, tel. 21125-180, S-Bahn Isartor, reservation advised).

Those who are ready to reach for the stars will most certainly get their money's worth at the **Planetarium** next door. This is the largest and most modern one of its kind in the world. And for those who want to explore the fields of natural science and technology a little more in-depth, and who are interested in learning the specifics about everything from railroads to aircraft, musical instruments to ships and chemical laboratories, or who want to wander through a re-created mine, the **Deutsches** (German) **Museum** is only a few steps away (Museuminsel 1,

MUNICH FOR KIDS

tel. 21791, S-Bahn to Isartor). The museum's friendly attendants are happy to answer questions and to explain the function of exhibits. Classic car fans will like the **BMW Museum** (see p. 183), and the **Kinder und Jugend Museum** in the Hauptbahnhof puts on some exciting events (for example, a "Dress Up Like Dracula" day).

Rattling suits of armor, Bavarian farmhouse rooms and a unique collection of nativity scenes, on the other hand, can be seen at the **Bayerische** (Bavarian) **National Museum** (see p. 183), and a large collection of dolls is on display in the **Stadt** (City) **Museum**. The petting corner of the **Deutsches Jagd und Fischerei** (Hunting and Fishing) **Museum** in the pedestrian zone is a big hit with youngsters – and not only on rainy days – while in the splendid area around Nymphenburg Palace and the palace gardens, the pedagogically well set up **Museum Mensch und Natur** (Man and Nature), has plenty of interest on offer.

Children and adults who like toys should not miss a visit to the **Spielzeug** (Toy) **Museum** inside the Old Town Hall at Marienplatz. An exhibition of very odd things can be seen at **ZAM** (the Center for Unusual Museums; see p. 183), for example, a collection of 2,000 chamber pots, a variety of different pedal-cars, and an Easter bunny collection.

An exciting look behind the scenery of television and movie production is offered on the 90-minute tour of **Bavaria Film Studios** in Geiselgasteig, south of Munich (tel. 6493767, U2 to Silberhornstrasse, then streetcar No. 25 to Bavaria Filmplatz). During the winter months, circus fans will not be disappointed by the afternoon shows at **Zirkus Krone** (tel. 558166, S-Bahn to Hackerbrücke).

Those who want to get a closer look at chimpanzees, leopards and giraffes should head to **Hellabrunn Zoo** (tel. 625080, Siebenbrunner Str. 6, U3 to Thalkirchen/Tierpark). The very young are delighted by the soft fur of the llamas and kid goats in the petting zoo. (Warning: just pet the animals, do not feed them; otherwise the excitable goats might jump on top of your kids!); older children enjoy the elephant and pony rides and the adventure playground. Further **Adventure Playgrounds** can be found in Schwabing at Elisabethplatz (U2 to Hohenzollernplatz), in Neuhausen at Hanebergstr. 14 (U1 to Rotkreuzplatz), and in West Park (Bus 33 to West Park), where an artificial waterfall has delighted many a child. While their parents are enjoying a cold mug of beer in the beer garden, kids can mess around in enclosed playgrounds, for example, in the **Hirschgarten** park (streetcar Nos. 12 and 17 to Romanplatz), at the **Chinese Tower** in the Englischer Garten (Bus No. 54 to Chinesischer Turm), in the **Flausch** beer garden (U3 to Thalkirchen) or in the **Augustiner-Keller** at Arnulfstrasse 52 (U-Bahn/S-Bahn to Hauptbahnhof).

When the weather is good, a walk through the Englischer Garten can take you past the **carousel** at the Chinese Tower and to the Kleinhesseloher Lake (U3/6 to Münchener Freiheit). **Row boats** can be rented here, as well as at the Olympia Lake in Olympia Park (U3 to Olympia Park). **Munich from above** can be seen from the top of the Olympia Park Television Tower, at Marienplatz from the tower of the New City Hall or the the south tower of the Frauenkirche. A fabulous view of Viktualienmarkt can be had from the tower of Alter Peter, though you have to climb a few steps first.

Munich's outoor pools, all of which have playgrounds and wading pools, are recommended to water rats in the summer months. The giant water slide at Michaelibad is a favorite, as is the wave pool at Cosimabad (also open in winter as an indoor pool). The indoor pools at Cosimabad, Giesing-Harlaching and Forstenrieder Park have heated baby's wading pools.

CULTURAL LIFE

CULTURAL LIFE IN MUNICH

"Art blossoms, Art has come to power, Art waves her rose-twined scepter over the city and smiles..." This is how the writer Thomas Mann described Munich in 1902 in his novella *Gladius Dei*, which is also the source of the much-quoted saying "Munich shines."

Mann's appreciation of the cultural scene in Munich was enthusiastic, but at the same time had ironic undertones, for now, as then, the quality of the opera, theater and concerts on offer here can range from dizzyingly sublime heights to the depths of provincialism. One thing, however, can always be counted on; the audience will be large. Years ago, people used to camp out before the box offices on Maximilianstrasse in order to get tickets to the National Theater, the Cuvilliés Theater or the Kammerspiele Theater. These days, tough, in the age of the fax machine, the cell phone and the flood of ticket outlets, the lines may have been reduced, but it is still obvious that Müncheners are just as passionately enthusiastic about the theater and concerts as ever.

Munich has enjoyed a considerably long and passionate relationship with the opera and its composers: Mozart celebrated his first triumph with *Idomeneo* at the Munich Opera; the premiere of Richard Wagner's *Meistersinger* was held here, and Wagner himself conducted the prelude to *Parsifal* at the Munich Opera for his greatest fan and admirer, King Ludwig II. The third darling of Munich's opera-going public is Richard Strauss who, in 1901, captured the hearts of Munich with *Feuersnot*.

Many illustrious names have conducted, directed and performed here at the Bavarian State Opera in the **National**

Preceding pages: Inside a beer-tent – the Bavarian idea of heaven. Left: Sometimes even Munich gets the blues.

Theater on Max-Joseph-Platz. On the list of the world's top operas, the Munich Opera is certainly counted among the top-ten, thanks not least of all to the efforts of its director, Peter Jonas. He is the one who is responsible for the interesting, sometimes rather controversial productions which take place here, and he has connected the names of internationally-known singers, such as Waltraud Meier, Cheryl Studer, Robert Hale and James Morris to the renowned opera house.

The National Theater was originally built in 1818, but was subsequently destroyed twice and was rebuilt both times. It is today the most important classically-designed theater in Germany. The grandiose auditorium holds 2,000 people and provides a suitably formal setting for operatic productions. The Bavarian State Ballet also performs here, which has happily now been revived, after a troubled decade, under the direction of former ballerina Konstanze Vernon.

The highlight and climax of each opera season in Munich is the annual **Opernfestspiele** (Opera Festival) in July. Tickets for this event are much sought after, and in spite of their high prices (up to DM 300) are quickly sold out.

Right beside the National Theater, though not nearly as magnificent, stands the **Residenz Theater**. After numerous changes in directorship, the theater's last two directors, Beelitz and Witt, have managed to attract large numbers of visitors through their exciting classical, as well as contemporary, productions.

Some of the productions of the National Theater and of the National Opera Company are staged in the **Cuvilliés Theater**, the most lovely rococo theater in the world. It was created by François Cuvilliés and was constructed from 1751 to 1753 in extravagant and sumptuous magnificence, and is rightly called the "jewel" of the Residenz. The repertoire of the Cuvilliés Theater includes the wonderfully evocative reading of Lud-

CULTURAL LIFE

wig Thoma's *Die Heilige Nacht* (Christmas Eve), which is staged before Christmas each year.

To the rear of the Residenz are the former stables of the old royal court, which today house an additional stage for the use of the National Theater and the National Opera. Happily, experimental theater productions, which the more traditional theaters prefer to avoid, are often staged here in the cool hall of the **Marstall Theater**.

The formal opening of the **Prinzregenten Theater** on Prinzregentenplatz took place in 1901, coinciding with the production of Richard Wagner's *Meistersinger*. The theater had to be closed down in the 1960s, owing to its delapidated condition, and was reopened after nearly 20 years in 1988. Thanks to the tireless efforts of director August Everding, as well as numerous Munich sponsors and

Above: The beautifully restored National Theater. Right: Rococo splendor in the Cuvilliés Theater.

citizens, the theater's freshly-renovated stage could be re-dedicated in good old Wagnerian tradition in 1996 with the production of "Tristan and Isolde."

The **Staats Theater am Gärtnerplatz** has a wide repertoire which includes opera, operetta, ballet and musicals, and in recent years has enjoyed increasing success.

The **Kammerspiele** on Maximilianstrasse is certainly one of Germany's most famous theaters. On few other stages can you see productions whose cast boasts artists of the caliber of Heinz Bennent, Rolf Boysen Thomas Holtzmann, Gisela Stein or Cornelia Froboess. Since 1983, the manager and artistic director here has been Dieter Dorn. Apart from the classics, which are given a new lease of life when performed in this setting, many more modern plays have been produced at the theater in recent years, such as *Drang*, by the Schwabing playwright and actor Franz Xaver Kroetz. George Tabori is one of the people who have breathed new life into

CULTURAL LIFE

Munich's theaters with his productions of the works of Samuel Beckett. Though some of the productions may be considered to be a little too avant-garde, there are always those productions which people come to see for the quality of the acting and the ingenuity of the stage sets alone.

The ensemble of the Kammerspiele theater also runs the **Werkraum** (Workshop) in Hildegardstrasse, where a new generation of talent has an opportunity to stage demanding and often avant-garde productions.

The **Volks Theater** (People's Theater) at Stiglmaierplatz is deceptively named, for its choice of productions, which lies in the hands of the artistic director Ruth Drexel, is often a long way from the simple, Bavarian tradition; but a great deal of skill and dedication goes into the productions, which range from Shakespeare to contemporary German playwrights like Patrick Süskind.

The greatest variety is to be found at the **Gasteig**, Munich's vast "palace of culture" up on Rosenheimer Hill, which includes experimental theater, dance, performance art, and film and music festivals. Famous names such as Friedrich Gulda and Ivo Pogorelich have performed here on more than once occasion, and there are smaller venues too, where young artists can bring their talent to the public's attention, be it in the Richard Strauss Conservatory, the Carl Orff Hall, in the Small Concert Hall or in the Black Box. In addition, the **Munich Philharmonic Orchestra** found a home for itself in the Gasteig. The new principal conductor and successor to Sergiu Celibidache, after some degree of back and forth, will be James Levine, from New York, beginning in September 1999.

Speaking of orchestras: no other German city can boast five internationally-acclaimed orchestras. Apart from the Munich Philharmonic, there is the **Bavarian State Orchestra** (conductor Zubin Mehta), the **Bavarian Radio Symphony Orchestra** (conductor Lorin Maazel), the **Munich Radio Orchestra**,

CULTURAL LIFE

and finally the **Munich Symphony Orchestra**. There is no shortage of concert halls in Munich for this wealth of artistic talent, making for a lively amount of artistic competition; whether it be in the Philharmonic Hall, the Hercules Hall, the Cuvilliés Theater, the National Theater or the large broadcasting studio of Bavarian Radio. Not to be forgotten amid so much symphonic shine are the **Munich Bach Orchestra** and the **Munich Bach Choir**, which both came to fame under the direction of Karl Richter, who died in 1981.

Light Entertainment Theater and Bavarian Folk Theater

If your German is good enough to handle sophisticated light comedy, you are recommended to go to the **Komödie im Hotel Bayerischer Hof** (Promenadeplatz) or to the **Kleine Komödie** at the

Above: A concert at the Philharmonie. Right: Another kind of cultural life in Munich.

Max II Monument. The quality of the productions may tend to vary, but one can be assured of a pleasant evening in the company of actors who were probably in a television sitcom or series the previous evening. The **Deutsches Theater** on Schwanthalerstrasse was formerly the venue for glittering *Fasching* balls, and variety artists from all over the world appeared here. Today, both visiting and resident companies stage musicals at the theater, from *The Phantom of the Opera* to *West Side Story*.

Folk-entertainers were a peculiar feature of Bavarian cabaret in Munich at the turn of the century and right up to the time of the Nazis in the 1930s. They would perform their broad farce, comic parodies and sketches to entertain their audiences in bars and cafés. Karl Valentin was the most famous name to emerge from this genre and its traditions. The famous **Platzl** became the main venue for this type of entertainment. It survived, across from the Hofbräuhaus, until 1995, when it closed due to poor profitability.

CULTURAL LIFE

In its place today is a branch of the **Planet Hollywood** restaurant chain where, among other things, you can enjoy a piece of Arnold Schwartzenegger's famous apple strudel (he's one of the owners of the chain).

Popular Bavarian theater can be enjoyed by locals and tourists alike at **Georg Maier's Gasthof Iberl** in Solln, and it is refreshing to see the versions of traditional Bavarian melodramas put on by amateur acting groups in the **Max Emanuel Brewery** in Schwabing, with plays like the tragi-comic *Wahre G'-schicht vom Wildschütz Jennerwein* (The True Story of Jennerwein the Poacher). Contemporary folk-singers from the **Münchner Isar-Brettl** are best heard at the *Augustiner* on Neuhauser Strasse.

Independent Theater

In Munich there are between fifty and sixty independent theater groups and many small private theaters; probably more than in New York. One of the original ones is **Theater 44** on Hohenzollernstrasse. They used to concentrate on Sartre and the Theater of the Absurd, but nowadays have moved on to more fashionable productions of modern plays. The **Modernes Theater** – Modern Theater by name and in its productions – also offers entertaining performances of the classics. At the **Theater am Sozialamt** (TamS for short), one can often see visiting international companies. From time to time the program will have a gentle surrealist touch to it, but then returns to a more down-to-earth vein of contemporary social criticism.

Among the newer small theaters which help form the exciting and colorful Munich cultural scene, the **Team Theater Tankstelle** is inspired toward expressionist productions. They also, however, present witty classic pieces. In the **Team Theater Comedy** next door, unique and original musical and singing evenings take place.

Every year at the **open-air stage** of the **West Park** are refreshing stagings of

CULTURAL LIFE

Shakespeare comedies and Karl Orff's *Carmina Burana*, as well as outdoor movies. The **Pathos Transport Theater** has an approach to the classics which is against the conventional grain, and also does new avant-garde productions.

The **Pasinger Fabrik** has a wide-ranging repertoire, including Strindberg productions and interesting interpretations of Shakespeare. Four theater groups appear here alone, and this "creative factory" is also open for interesting exhibitions and special events (for example, the Munich School Theater Festival takes place here).

The **Theater links der Isar** (Theater on the Left Bank of the Isar) covers everything from the classics to modern drama, and many school parties come here for their first experience of the theater on a small stage. Engaging theater with young, ambitious actors and aften featuring guest performers is offered by the **NT**; the **Neues Theater**, in Giesing.

Satirical Reviews and Cabaret

The fame of Munich's **Lach und Schiessgesellschaft** ("Laughing and Shooting Company") has spread far beyond the city itself. The home of Germany's most-famous satirical revue, founded in 1956 by Sammy Drechsel, is on the corner of Haimhauserstrasse and Ursulastrasse, in the heart of Schwabing. It enjoyed wide popularity on television for many years with its cast of Hans Jürgen Diedrich, Dieter Hildebrandt, Barbara Noack and Jürgen Scheller. Unfortunately, only Hildebrandt remains of the original cast, but performances by the "Lach und Schiess" are still generally sold out.

Political satire can also be seen in Schwabing at the **Rational Theater** on Hesseloherstrasse, directed by Rainer Uthoff. High-quality satirical reviews have been presented at Occamstrasse 8 since 1994 by the **Lustspielhaus** of Bavarian television actor Bruno Jonas. Another Schwabing institution is a bar called **Heppel & Ettlich** on Kaiserstrasse, which has a theater in the back room with cabaret, entertainers and poets reading from their works.

A little off the beaten track in the north of Munich is the **Am Hart** inn, where an "alternative" audience meets to eat and drink; in summer they gather in the beer garden. In the evenings one can watch a satirical review, so-called "ashcan cabaret," in the **Hinterhof Theater**.

The large old hall of the **Wirtshaus am Schlachthof** is often filled by entertainers like Bavarian cabaret original Ottfried "Otti" Fischer, but also hosts musicians of international standing as well. Newcomers are given their chance in the **Ox** inside the Schlachthof.

Above: Unsophisticated is the word to describe the Münchner Volkssängerbühne in the Max-Emanuel restaurant. Right: ...unlike the Munich Film Festival in the Gasteig.

CULTURAL LIFE

Comedy, parody and cabaret can also be seen on the small stage of the **Theater im Fraunhofer**. In Haidhausen's **Drehleier**, local cabaret greats like the Bauer, Beier, Zauner trio perform.

Rock, Pop and Festivals

Rock and pop greats from all over the world often appear in Munich, generally in the **Olympiahalle**, in the **Rudi Sedlmayr Halle**, in the **Muffat Hall**, or at **Zirkus Krone**, as well as in the **Colosseum** or **Babylon** inside of **Kunstpark Ost**, behind the Ostbahnhof, which opened in 1996. Megastars like Michael Jackson and Tina Turner also have the **Riemer Reitstadion** and the **Olympia Stadium** at their disposal. In summer, the sounds from concerts ranging from jazz to rock can be heard in the **Theatron** at the foot of the Olympic swimming pool.

The **Tollwood Festival**, which is held on the Olympia Hill in June, pulls in more and more visitors every year. There are performances by theater groups in various tents. Concerts of anything from jazz to Alpine rock, cabaret, jugglers and magicians are all included in the program. Handicrafts from all over the world are sold in an alternative kind of bazaar from noon until midnight, and tasty tidbits, likewise from all aover the world appeal to the eye and the nose. This colorful and ethnically-characterized market fair takes place with a Christmasy touch in December as **Winter Tollwood** on Arnulfstrasse at the Häckerbrücke (on the grounds of the former container train station).

The week-long **Munich Film Festival** takes place in late June/early July at various cinemas around the city. This is not only a cultural, but also a social event. Alongside retrospectives and mainstream films, which are shown in the program venues, audiences are also delighted by interesting, engaging low budget films by filmmakers from the Third World, for example, cultural minorities (such as American Indians) or the more-polished American Independents.

NIGHT-LIFE

MUNICH BY NIGHT

Munich is often called Germany's "secret capital," but when it comes to night-life, it seems Munich cannot make up its mind if it wants to be world class or just a provincial backwater. Anyone from Berlin, a city that never sleeps, would have no hesitation in calling Munich the latter, and certainly night-life here is somewhat modest for a metropolis, even a Bavarian one. The sophisticated visitor might even find this a reason for moving on, taking with them a memory of Munich as a village that happens to have a million inhabitants. Yet there is no lack of people with money to spend, so perhaps the reason lies in the Bavarian character – if drinking in a beer garden until eleven o'clock at night is their idea of a good night out. It certainly has a lot to do with the rigid enforcement of the law with regard to closing-times. The "closed" area laws have forced Munich's bordellos out to the edge of town. The "clubs," as these establishments are known, now have such erotic addresses as "in the industrial zone of Moosfeld."

The customs of Munich's night-life scene are more stringent than probably anywhere else in the world: either you are part of the scene and are greeted by the doorman like an old friend, or you have the right "look" and are allowed in. If neither is the case, then in all probability you will only see Munich's best night-spots from the outside. The rule of thumb is: If you look as if you don't earn your money yourself, you get in.

The "In" Places to Go

For many years now, Munich's most exclusive night-spot has been **P1** in the *Haus der Kunst*, and today belongs to Michael Käfer, the son of Munich's delicatessen king, Gerd Käfer. It is the tradi-

Above: The Park Café awaits an onslaught of customers. Right: Charles Schumann and his team of bartenders.

NIGHT-LIFE

tional rendezvous for the rich and famous – Mick Jagger and Boris Becker have both been seen here – as well as Munich's most beautiful girls, who are more often than not just passing through.

The brightly-lit **Park-Café**, at the edge of the old botanical gardens, is another favorite spot where, night after night once the café's beer garden has closed, a hand-picked, select few crowd in and dance to often deafening music into the small hours.

The **Nachtcafé** at Maximilianplatz opens a little earlier, at seven o'clock in the evening, and when live jazz is played, the bar is open through the night until five in the morning; before the introduction of the night bus and streetcar service in 1994 (see also p. 248), the place served for some as a waiting room for the first U-Bahn train in the morning – in fact, breakfast is served for those who wish to restore their energy after an exhausting night on the town.

Kay Wörsching has created his own glitzy world at **Kay's Bistro** at Viktualienmarkt, where the fantastic decorations change with the seasons. Munich's jet-setters who frequent this bistro attach only secondary importance to the food – to see and to be seen is what they really come here for.

Cocktails for the Discerning

Harry's Manhattan Bar (formerly Harry's New York Bar) on Falkenturmstrasse is famous for its name alone. It is just a few minutes away from the Hofbräuhaus, and its opening marked the introduction of the American-style bar to Munich. The piano plays while pretty girls and well-heeled men of various ages sip their drinks.

The cocktails are just as good at **Schumann's**, which is a short distance away on Maximilianstrasse, and which was started up by Charles Schumann, a former bartender at Harry's. The bar is frequented particularly by journalists and lawyers, film and television people; stars and starlets who have their regular tables here and watch in comfort as the crowd presses around the bar each evening.

The **Egon Bar** on Seitzstrasse is somewhat wild and, like the **Wunder-Bar** on Hochbrückenstrasse (between the Hofbräuhaus and the Tal), attracts a much younger crowd of night owls. There is a candy kiosk in the Wunder-Bar, and the cocktails here are not bad either.

A Mexican bar with a touch of Hemingway is **Julep's** in Haidhausen. It has bare brick walls and boasts a menu of 150 different cocktails, any one of which can be speedily prepared to order.

Other bars which are definitely worth mentioning are **Maximilians Nightclub** at Maximiliansplatz, the **Havana-Bar** on Herrnstrasse and the **Madrigal-Bar** on Maximilianstrasse, and of course there are the bars and nightclubs in the large hotels: the **Piano Bar** and **Night Club** in the Bayerischer Hof hotel, the **Piano Bar** in the Park Hilton and the **Vibraphon Night Club** in the Sheraton.

Places to Say You Have Been

Schwabing's Leopoldstrasse is where you stroll up and down to see and be seen. It is here that the actress Iris Berben runs her fashionable rendezvous, **Roxy**. On warm afternoons, people sit at tables out on the pavement and sip their cappuccinos, in the evening it is cool, in both senses of the word, to have your drinks inside.

Many people begin their evening at the **Café Reitschule**, which always has a faint smell of horses (*Reitschule* means "riding school") and is for many the first stop on the way to a long night out. If the company inside the café is not interesting enough for you, you can watch the riders put their horses through their paces through a large window. Hungry customers will be certain to find something satisfying on the café's extensive menu. Exclusive dining is offered by Munich's newest "in" restaurant: **Lenbach**, owned by delicatessen mogul Käfer, is without a doubt *the* place to go in Munich at the moment.

Discotheques and Club Halls

The city's longest-surviving discotheque is **Crash**, at Ainmillerstrase 10, where loud rock music and a young crowd are its emblem. In **Liberty** (Rosenheimer Strasse 30), teenagers shove each other around to classic rock from the 60s and 70s. **Soul City**, at Maximilianplatz 5, with its gay café-discotheque, is the meeting place of good-looking men and (sometimes) beautiful women.

The Munich club hall scene offers a colorful program of parties, disco nights and pop concerts, generally on the premises of former factories. Techno freaks normally make their way to **Ultraschall II** or the **Heizkraftwerk**, both of which are located in Kunstpark Ost. **Millennium** and the **Alabamahalle**, on the grounds of a former army caserne, both offer deafening music (Domagkstasse 33).

More moderate sounds can be heard at the **Muffathalle** and the **Atomic Café**. At **Nightflight** (with restaurant, bars, gaming room and swimming pool; located at the new airport), you can take off for an exciting evening. "New Age" youth prefer **Tilt** (Helmholtzstrasse 12), with its "Orange Disco." Also worth checking out is the calendar of events at the **Feierwerk**, the **Nachtwerk**, the **Pulverturm** and **Kunstpark Ost**, with its discotheques **Babylon**, **Keller**, **K41** and **Natraj Tempel** (from 11 p.m.).

Jazz and Classics with Wine and Beer

Live music of all kinds, with a frequently changing program, is played in

Right: Music by candle-light – a taste of Munich's night-life.

many of Munich's bars, including the well-known **Kaffee Giesing**, which was run by singer-songwriter Konstantin Wecker until 1993. The jazz, blues and rock on offer here attract a varied audience. Admission is sometimes charged.

Light jazz and heavy mugs of beer are available at the popular **Waldwirtschaft Grosshesselohe**, which has a large beer garden. Winter in Munich means a musical late-morning drink every first Sunday of the month at the "Wawi," as it is called, with excellent jazz fare from 11 a.m. to 3 p.m.

Top-quality jazz music can be heard at one of Europe's leading jazz clubs, the **Unterfahrt** in Haidhausen. The Sunday jazz *Frühschoppen* (late-morning drink) at 11 a.m. is a popular way to pass the time. The Unterfahrt, along with the **Theater rechts der Isar**, the **KIM** children's cinema and the **Freies Music Zentrum**, moved to the subterranean Einsteinhalle – which is listed as a historically-protected building – at Max-Weber-Platz (U4/5 to Max-Weber-Platz).

For a select glass of red wine to the strains of Chopin and Schubert, try the classical inn **Mariandl** located at Goethestrasse 51.

The Schwabing Scene

The old Schwabing tradition of *Künstlerlokale* (places where artists would spend most of the day) sadly belongs to the past. Now the character of this part of Munich is pretty much like the entertainment district of any big city, with its fast food restaurants and tourist bars. Leopoldstrasse has, over the years, been taken over by smart little cafés and boutiques. Some of the old bars have survived and new ones have joined them – these are mostly described in the chapter entitled "The Myth of Schwabing."

Three bars in Maxvorstadt should be mentioned here since they have become local institutions in Munich. The first of these is the traditional **Alte Simpl** on Türkenstrasse. It has repeatedly been pronounced dead, but is still popular with

NIGHT-LIFE

prominent Müncheners. Only a few steps along the street is **La Bohème**. This one-time left-wing rendezvous is no longer a place to meet prominent locals, but is still the haunt of Schwabing's night owls, who lounge on the sofas and armchairs, eating pizza and spaghetti and drinking beer. Diagonally opposite is the cozy **Charivari**, which is always filled to bursting when the evening performance at the nearby *Türkendolch* cinema ends and the Bohème closes for the evening.

Dinner at Midnight

When the hour is late, and you have had your fifth cocktail or have been dancing until you're ready to drop, it often happens that you are suddenly overwhelmed with hunger. Have no fear – in Munich there is a restaurant to suit every taste, no matter what time of night you want to eat.

An inexpensive Schwabing restaurant is the **Adria** on Leopoldstrasse, where not only taxi drivers tank up on pizza or pasta until three in the morning. Likewise open unti 3 a.m., **Noodles**, on Maximilianstrasse, serves a predominantly young clientele and, during the week, night owls fly to **Munix** on Amalienstrasse. Appetites are satisfied to the sounds of live music in the **Nacht-Café** until five a.m.

If you prefer good, simple Bavarian food, you will find it being served until 3 a.m. at the **Bräuhaus zur Brezn** on Leopoldstrasse. Whoever has an appetite at a still later hour can head to **Weintrödler** on Brienner Strasse, which stays open until 6 a.m. You can also round off the night's revelry with coffee and a *Schmalznudel* (a Bavarian pastry) at **Café Frischhut** at Viktualienmarkt, which is very much recommended. From 5 a.m. onwards, this is where the early-rising market traders meet up with every possible kind of straggler returning home after hitting Munich's night spots.

Advance Ticket Sales

Tickets for various events in Munich (including the Opera and cocnerts) can be obtained from ticket sales outlets. Here is a selection of some of them: **Abendzeitung München**, Sendlinger Str. 10, tel. 267024; **Gasteig**, Rosenheimer Str. 5 (tel. 480980, ticket reservations: 54818181); **Hertie** am Stachus (tel. 557232), in Schwabing (tel. 336659); **Kaufhaus Beck** at Rathauseck, tel. 299901; **Kaufhof** at Marienplatz (tel. 2603249), at Stachus (tel. 5125248); **Kiosk at Marienplatz underground** (tel. 264620); **Karstadt** am Dom (EG), tel. 29025499.

STATE AND CITY THEATERS

Altes Residenz Theater (Cuvielliés Theater), Residenzstr. 1, tel. 2185-1940, U3/6 to Marienplatz; **Bayerische Staatsoper** (Bavarian State Opera; National Theater), Max-Joseph-Platz, tel. 2185-1920, U3/6 to Marienplatz; **Theater im Marstall**, Marstallplatz, tel. 2185-1920, S-Bahn and U3/6 to Marienplatz; **Prinzregenten Theater**, Prinzregentenplatz 12, tel. 2185-2959, U4 to Prinzregentenplatz; **Residenz Theater**, Max-Joseph-Platz 1, tel. 2185-1940, S-Bahn and U3/6 to Marienplatz; **Staats Theater am Gärtnerplatz**, Gärtnerplatz 3, tel. 2016767, U1/2 to Fraunhofer Str.; **Münchner Kammerspiele**, Maximilianstr. 26, tel. 2372-1328, S-Bahn and U3/6 to Marienplatz;

Werkraum der Münchner Kammerspiele, Hildegardstr. 1, tel. 2372-1328, S-Bahn and U3/6 to Marienplatz; **Schauburg - Theater der Jugend**, Franz-Joseph-Str. 47, tel. 23721-365, streetcar No. 27 to Elisabethplatz; **Deutsches Theater** (German Theater), Schwanthalerstr. 13, tel. 55234355, U/S-Bahn to Stachus; **Münchner Volks Theater**, Brienner Str. 50, tel. 5234655, U1 to Stiglmaierplatz. **Gasteig - Black Box**, Rosenheimerstr. 5, tel. 480980, reservations - 54818181, S-Bahn to Rosenheimer Platz.

COMMERCIAL THEATERS
VARIETY / CABARET

Blutenburg Theater (crime dramas), Blutenburgstr. 35, tel. 1234300, U1 to Maillingerstraße; **Colosseum**, Grafinger Str. 6 (in Kunstpark Ost), tel. 49002928, U/S-Bahn to Ostbahnhof;

Drehleier, Rosenheimer Str. 123, tel. 482742, S-Bahn to Rosenheimer Platz, popular music and cabaret stage with solid gastronomic offerings;

Feierwerk e.V., Hansastr. 39, tel. 7693600, S7 and U4/5 to Heimeranplatz. Experimental theater with newcomers.

Hinterhof Theater, Wirtshaus am Hart, Sudetendeutsche Str. 40, tel. 3116039 (from 5 pm), U2 to Am Hart. Traditional cabaret-bar with beer garden; **Lustspielhaus**, Occamstr. 8, tel. 344974, U3/6 to Münchener Freiheit. High-class variety; **Georg**

GUIDEPOST CULTURE AND NIGHT-LIFE

Meier's Iberl Bühne, Wilhelm-Leibl-Str. 22, tel. 794214, S7 to Solln. Traditional Bavarian theater, reservations necessary; **Komödie im Bayerischen Hof**, Passage Promenadeplatz, tel. 292810, S-Bahn and U3/6 to Marienplatz. Comedies with star names; **Kleine Komödie am Max-II**, Maximilianstr. 47, tel. 221859, U4/5 to Lehel. Hot material with stars and starlets; **Modernes Theater**, Hans-Sachs-Str. 12, tel. 225473, U3/6 Sendlinger Tor. Exciting theater between comedy and tragedy; **Münchner Lach- und Schießgesellschaft**, Haimhauserstr., tel. 391997, U3/6 to Münchener Freiheit. Germany's most-famous cabaret; **Münchner Volkssängerbühne**, Max-Emanuel-Brauerei, Adalbertstr. 33, tel. 2715158, advance ticket sales - 142758, U3/6 to Universität, traditional Bavarian; **NT - Neues Theater**, Entenbachstr. 37, tel. 650000, U1/2 to Kolumbusplatz. Unusual pieces with engaging young actors, guests; **Pasinger Fabrik**, August-Exter-Straße 1, tel. 8341841 (from 4:30 pm to 8:30 pm)), S-Bahn to Pasing. Experimental theater; **Pathos Transport**, Dachauerstr. 110 d, tel. 184243, days - 123557, streetcar Nos. 12, 20, bus No. 33 to Leonrodplatz; **Peter Steiners Theaterstadl**, Wieskirchstr. 2, tel. 6903671, S1/2 to Giesing. Bavarian theater known on television, Reservations necessary; **Reithalle**, Hess Str. 132, tel. 1291933, streetcar Nos. 12, 20; **TamS – Theater am Sozialamt**, Haimhauserstr. 13 a, tel. 345890, U3/6 to Münchener Freiheit. Engaging theater with international guests; **Theater bei Heppel & Ettlich**, Kaiserstr. 67, tel. 349359, streetcar No. 27 to Kurfürstenplatz. Kabarett; **Theater Blaue Maus**, Elvirastr. 17a, tel. 182694, U1 to Maillingerstr. Young, engaging theater; **Theater im Fraunhofer**, Fraunhoferstr. 9, tel. 267850, U1/2 to Fraunhoferstr. Small rear-courtyard theater with high-quality performers; **Theater links der Isar**, Auenstr. 19, tel. 2022895 (from 6 pm), U1/2 to Fraunhoferstr. Classical theater; **Team Theater Tankstelle**, Am Einlass 2a, tel. 2604333, U/S-Bahn to Marienplatz; **Team Theater Comedy**, Am Einlass 4, tel. 2606636, U/S-Bahn to Marienplatz. Vienna coffee house atmosphere with song and music; **Theater 44**, Hohenzollernstr. 20, tel. 3228748, U3/6 to Münchener Freiheit; **Wirtshaus im Schlachthof**, Zenettistr. 9, tel. 765448, U3/6 to Poccistr.

CLASSICAL CONCERTS

Current info can be found in the yellow monthly program entitled "Munich in ... (month)" available from the Tourist Office.

Herkulessaal und **Max-Joseph-Saal der Residenz**, tel. 220868, S-Bahn and U3/6 to Marienplatz; **Philharmonie** and **Kleiner Konzertsaal im Gasteig**, Rosenheimerstr. 5, S-Bahn to Rosenheimer Platz, tel. 48098614, information tel. 480980; **Blutenburg-Konzerte**, Schloss Blutenburg, München-Obermenzing, tel. 9570028, 939933.

Night-life

RESTAURANTS / BARS: **Adam's City**, Pacellistr. 2, tel. 294455, Mon-Fri till 6 am; **Adria**, Leopoldstr. 19, tel. 396529, 10 am to 3 am; **Alter Simpl**, Türkenstr. 57, tel. 2720699, 9 pm to 3 am, Fri-Sat till 4 am; **Nil**, Hans-Sachs-Str. 9, tel. 2603431; Sun-Thu 7 pm to 2 am, Fri-Sat 7 pm to 3 am (gay); **Bräuhaus zur Brez'n**, Leopoldstr. 72, tel. 390092, 9 am to 2:30 am; **Charivari**, Türkenstr. 92, tel. 282832, till 3 am, Fri-Sat till 4 am; **Club Morizz**, Klenzestr. 43, tel. 2016776, till 2 am (mainly gay); **Egon Bar**, Seitzstr. 12, tel. 29161076; **Epikero**, Detmoldstr. 2, tel. 3510869, Mon-Sat 11 pm to 5 am, Sun 1 am to 5 am; **Harry's Manhattan Bar**, Falkenturmstr. 9, tel. 222700, Mon-Sat till 3 am; **Havana Club**, Herrnstr. 30, tel. 291884, Sun-Wed till 1 am, Thu-Sat till 2 am; **La Bohème**, Türkenstr. 79, tel. 2720833, till 2 am; **Maximilian's Nightclub**, Maximiliansplatz 16, tel. 223252; **Nachtcafé**, Maximiliansplatz 5, tel. 595900, till 5 am; **Night Club in Bayerischen Hof**, Promenadeplatz. 2, tel. 2120-994, Sat-Sun till 3 am; **Park Café**, Sophienstr. 7, tel. 598313, till 4 am; **Planet Hollywood**, Platzl 1, tel. 29030500, 11 am to 1 am; **Schmalznudel** (Café Frischhut), Prälat-Zistl-Str. 8, tel. 268237, 5 am to 2 pm; **Schumann's**, Maximilianstr. 36, tel. 229060, Sun-Fri till 3 am; **Trader Vic's**, Promenadenplatz 2-6, tel. 21200, till 3 am; **Weintrödler**, Brienner Str. 10, tel. 283193, till 6 am; **Wunder-Bar**, Hochbrückenstr. 3, tel. 295118, till 3 am.

DISCOTHEQUES / CLUB HALLS: **Alabamahalle**, Domagkstr. 33, tel. 3244253; **Atomic Café**, Neuturmstr. 5, tel. 2283054, Sun-Thu 9 pm to 3 am, Fri-Sat 9 pm to 4 am; **Backstage**, Helmholtzstr. 18, tel. 1266100, Tue-Thu 10 pm to 3 am, Fri till 5 am, Sat 9 pm to 5 am, Sun 8 pm to 1 am; **Crash**, Ainmillerstr. 10, tel. 391640, Fri-Sat 9 pm to 4 am, Sun, Tue-Wed till 1 am, Thu till 3 am; **Feierwerk**, Hansastr. 39, tel. 7693600; **Kunstpark Ost**, Grafinger Str. 6, info: 49002928, various stages, discos and night events from 11 pm, with no closing time; **Liberty**, Rosenheimer Str. 30, tel. 484840, Fri-Sat 9 pm to 4 am, Sun, Tue- Wed 9 pm to 1 am, Thu 9 pm to 2 am; **Millennium**, Domagkstr. 33, tel. 3244253; **Muffathalle**, Zellstr. 4, tel. 294500; **Nachtwerk**, Landsbergerstr. 185, tel. 5704344, Sun-Thu 10 pm to 4 am, Fri 10 pm to 5 am, Sat 10 pm to 6 am; **Nightflight**, Wartungsallee 9, Flughafen München II, tel. 97597999, daily from 9 pm, no closing time; **Pulverturm**, Schleissheimerstr. 393, tel. 3519999, daily 10 pm to 4 am; **Soul City**, Maximiliansplatz 5, tel. 553301, Wed-Sun 10 pm to 4 am; **Tilt**, Helmholtzstr. 12, tel. 1297969, Wed-Sat 9 pm to 4 am.

EATING OUT

EATING OUT

While it is true to say that beer is a basic form of nourishment in Munich, even Müncheners have a certain sensibility to higher things, which means occasionally sampling the rich and varied gastronomic delights on offer in this "northernmost Italian city." So when the inevitable museum-fatigue sets in, where should the footsore visitor start looking for a good relaxing meal?

The Home Cooking of Munich and Bavaria

On just about every street corner in the city you can buy a delicacy that was probably invented in Munich – the *Leberkäs-Semmel* (meat-loaf roll) which, like *Weissbier* (wheat beer), has long since begun moving into northern parts of Germany. However, the classic Munich speciality, *Weisswürste* (veal sausages), served with a slightly sweet mustard, should preferably be eaten sitting down and, by tradition, should be enjoyed before the stroke of midday. If you have chosen one of the city's large beer gardens in which to recuperate, a less well-known Munich delicacy is recommended – *Steckerlfisch* (fish on a spit), usually a mackerel straight from the charcoal grill.

It is one of the many clichés about this city that its inhabitants eat nothing but *Schweinsbraten* (roast pork) and *Ochsenfleisch mit Meerrettich* (beef with horseradish). Certainly they enjoy these dishes, especially when served up with cabbage and bacon salad – but not every day. Opinions differ about the quality of Munich's potato dumplings, but everyone agrees on the excellence of its *Semmelknödel* (bread dumplings).

To find out which of these appeals to you more, you must sample them for

Above: Someone who clearly likes Bavarian food. Right: Gourmets' dreams come true in Tantris.

EATING OUT

yourself. There are plenty of opportunities to do so along the well-trodden tourist path, for example in the cosy ambience of **Augustiner-Bräu**, in the **Peterhof** next door, or in the robustly Bavarian **Weisses Bräuhaus**. These restaurants are all to be found within the confines of the old inner city, as is **Paulaner im Tal** (formerly Bögner), one of Munich's oldest hostelries, junior only to the **Hundskugel** and the **Altes Hackerhaus**. Nor should you overlook the **Franziskaner**, typical of a more patrician style while still very Bavarian. In Schwabing there is without a doubt only one establishment which is comparable to those mentioned above; **Gaststätte Leopold** on Leopoldstrasse.

Star Wars

Year in, year out, the feared testers from the Michelin Guide visit temples of *haute cuisine* to taste and pass judgment. Once again, **Tantris** has been awarded two of the prized stars. The **Hilton Grill** in the Park Hilton was given one star, as was the top-class Italian resaurant **Massimiliano**, the **Preysing Keller** in Haidhausen, **Gasthaus Glockenbach** near the Isar and **Boettner** in the city center.

Hans Haas, of the **Tantris** restaurant in Schwabing, was chosen "Cook of the Year" in 1995. Haas is the master of the kitchen in which his specialties, including his famous *Stuffed Catfish*, is lovingly prepared. Health-conscious gourmets head to **Gasthaus Glockenbach**, where Karl Ederer serves up refined recipes featuring organically-produced meat from his own farm in Glonn.

Movie stars and crowned heads of state – from Peter Ustinov to Princess Margaret of England – pay royal prices to enjoy a meal at **Boettner** on Pfisterstrasse. Fish (Danube catfish and turbot), crab, lobster, lamb and venison are all featured on the menu here. Loden-suited Bavarian parliamentary buddies, however, are more likely to be encountered at **Käfer** in Bogenhausen. Martin Breuer of the **Königshof** hotel-restaurant is striving

EATING OUT

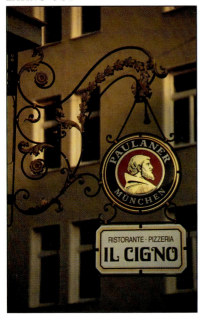

for Michelin stars at his establishment, whose overflowing neo-rococo ambience makes it, in a certain sense, the Asam church of Munich's restaurants.

The World is Your Oyster

Munich has always considered itself "The Gateway to the South" in a culinary as well as a geographic sense. So it is no surprise that Italian cuisine gained a foothold here long before any other German city had its "Italian 'round the corner," and it has been continuously popular ever since. Just about every nieghborhood in town has its favorite Italian restaurant, to which customers flock from all over Munich, for example, **Il Mulino** in Schwabing, where you can enjoy your pizza or pasta beneath shady chestnut trees in summer. **Casa Mia**, at the edge of the Schlachthof quarter on Maistrasse, is

Above: One of the multitude of Italian restaurants in Munich.

both good and inexpensive. The oldest Italian eatery to have achieved cult status is the **Adria** (Leopoldstrasse 19), a restaurant that is popular with the late-night crowd.

Two popular Spanish restaurants in Munich are **Centro Espagnol** (Daiserstrasse 20) and **La Tasca** (Mettinghstrasse 2). It is not just the excellent Spanish food at reasonable prices that attracts Müncheners and Spaniards alike in droves to these places; they come for the relaxed atmosphere as well.

The ultimate Greek restaurant in Munich is **Kytaro** (Innere Wiener Strasse 36), with its covered courtyard. And if you want to dance the *sirtaki* after your meal, you should go to the **Agora** on Lindwurmstrasse.

Good French food need not be expensive, and this is proved by **Le Bousquérey** (Rablstrasse 37), but if your are prepared to spend a good deal more, try **Rue des Halles** (Nr. 18 Steinstrasse).

If you are looking for a Japanese restaurant, **Matoi** on Hans-Sachs-Strasse serves excellent dishes, as does **Shoya** on Gabelsbergerstrasse. At **Daitokai** (Kurfürstenstrasse 59), exquisite, inexpensive several-course meals are on offer at lunch-time. Sushi, those elegantly-presented Japanese snacks, can be sampled both in the noisy and dimly-lit **Ballhaus** restaurant (Klenzestrasse 71) and the serene and comfortable **Tokami** (Rablstrasse 45).

Whoever likes light Indonesian cuisine will be well taken care of at **Garuda** (corner of Theresienstrasse and Schleissheimer Strasse). Thai food fans will like the friendly **Khanitta** in Neuhausen, with their wide-ranging menu and justifiable prices.

South Indian *massala dosa* or true-to-the-original *butter chicken* are among the choices at **Tandoori** (Baumstrasse 6), Munich's "oldest serving Indian restaurant," which specializes in traditional dishes from the clay *tandoori* oven.

RESTAURANTS

BAVERIAN: **Altes Hackerhaus**, Sendlinger Str. 14, tel. 2605026, 9 am to midnight; **Augustiner-Bräu**, Neuhauser Str. 16, tel. 55199257, 9 am to midnight; **Franziskaner**, Perusastr. 5, tel. 2318120, 8 am to midnight; **Hundskugel**, Hotterstr. 18, tel. 264272, 9:30 am to midnight; **Paulaner im Tal** (formerly Bögner), Tal 12, tel. 219940-0, 9 am to midnight; **Straubinger Hof**, Blumenstr. 5, tel. 2608444, 9 am to 11 pm, Sat till 3 am, closed Sun; **Weisses Bräuhaus**, Tal 10, tel. 299875, 8 am to midnight.
FRENCH: **Le Bousquérey**, Rablstr. 37, tel. 488455, 6 pm to 1 am; **Rue des Halles**, Steinstr. 18, tel. 485675, 6:30 pm to 1 am, closed weekends; **Tokami**, Rablstr. 45, tel. 448926, Mon-Sat noon to 2:30 pm and 6 pm to midnight.
GOURMET: **Boettner**, Pfisterstr. 9, tel. 221210, 11 am to 11 pm (last order 8:30 pm), Sat 11 am to 3 pm, closed Sun; **Gasthaus Glockenbach**, Kapuzinerstr. 29, tel. 534043, Tue-Fri noon to 1:30 pm and 6 pm to 1 am, Sat 7 pm to 1 am (last order 9:30 pm); **Königshof**, Karlsplatz 25, tel. 551370, 6:30 am to 10:30 am, noon to 2:15 pm and 6:45 pm to 11:15 pm; **Massimiliano**, Rablstr. 10, tel. 4484477, daily 12:30 to 2:30 pm and 7 pm to 11 pm, closed Sat pm; **Käfer-Schänke**, Prinzregentenstr. 73, tel. 41680, Mon-Sat noon to midnight, closed Sun; **Tantris**, Johann-Fichte-Str. 7, tel. 362061, Tue-Sat noon to 2 pm (last order) and 6:30 pm to 10:15 pm (last order).
GREEK: **Agora**, Aberlestr. 1, tel. 765976, 11 am to 1 am; **Kytaro**, Innere Wienerstr. 36, tel. 4801176, 5 pm to 1 am; **Metaxa**, Blutenburgstr. 37, tel. 1294545, 11:30 am to 2:30 pm and 5:30 pm to midnight.
ITALIAN: **Adria**, Leopoldstr. 19, tel. 396529, 10:30 am to 3 am; **Il Mulino**, Görresstr. 1, tel. 5233335, 11:30 am to midnight; **Casa Mia**, Maistr. 26, tel. 5328734, 11:30 am to 2:30 pm, 5:30 pm to 11:30 pm.
INDIAN: **Tandoori**, Baumstr. 6, tel. 2012208, Mon-Fri 5:30 pm to midnight, Sat-Sun/hol noon to midnight; **Ganga**, Baaderstr. 11, tel. 2016465, 11:30 am to 3 pm and 5:30 pm to midnight; **Namaskar**, Rosenheimerstr. 113a, tel. 4480962, 11:30 am to 2:30 pm and 5:30 pm to 1 am.
INDONESIAN: **Garuda**, Theresienstr. 87, tel. 525936, Tue-Sun 11:30 am- 2:30 pm & 6 pm-11 pm.
JAPANESE: **Daitokai**, Kurfürstenstr. 59, tel. 2711421, noon to 2 pm (last order) and 6 pm to 10 pm (last order); **Matoi**, Hans-Sachs-Str. 10, tel. 2605268, 6:30 pm to midnight; **Shoya**, Gabelsbergerstr. 85, tel. 5236249, Mon-Sat 11 am to 1 am.
SEAFOOD: **Italfisch**, Zenettistr. 25, tel. 776849, Mon-Fri 11:30 am to 1 am (hot meals till 10 pm), closed Sun/hol.
SPANISH: **Centro Espagnol**, Daiserstr. 20, tel. 763653, 5:30 pm to 1 am; **El Espagnol**, Pariserstr. 46, tel. 488496, 5 pm to 1 am; **La Tasca**, Mettinghstr. 2, tel. 168201, 6 pm to 1 am, closed Wed.
THAI: **Khanitta**, Thorwaldsenstr. 19, tel. 1297772, 11:30 am to 2:30 pm and 5:30 pm to 1 am; **Mangostin**, Maria-Einsiedel-Str. 2, tel. 7232031, three Asian restaurants under one roof, with beer garden.
VEGETARIAN: **Buxs**, am Viktualienmarkt, Frauenstr. 9, tel. 296384, Mon-Fri 11 am to 8:30 pm, Sat 11 am to 3:30 pm; **Gollier**, Gollierstr. 83, tel. 501673, Mon-Fri 11:30 am to midnight, Sat 5 pm to midnight, Sun noon to midnight; **Café Ignaz**, Georgenstr. 67, tel. 2716093, Mon-Sat 10 am to 10 pm, Sun 9 am to 10 pm; **Jahreszeiten**, Hertie-Schmankerlgasse am Stachus, tel. 594873, regular business hours; **Prinz Myshkin**, Hackenstr. 2, tel. 265596, Sun-Thu 11 am to midnight, Fri-Sat till 1 am.
VIETNAMESE: **Cô-Dô**, Lothringer Str. 7, tel. 4485797, 6 pm to 1 am.

OUTSIDE MUNICH

NORTH: **Bräustüberl Weihenstephan**, Weihenstephan 1, Freising, tel. 08161/13004. *NORTHWEST:* **Schlosswirtschaft Weyhern**, near Odelzhausen, tel. 08134/394, closed Mon-Tue in winter. *SOUTH:* **Gasthaus Fischmeister**, Ambach, Seeuferstr. 31, at Starnberger See, tel. 08177/533, closed Mon; **Hoisl-bräu Promberg**, between Beuerberg and Penzberg, tel. 08856/2535, closed Mon-Tue; **Jägerwirt**, Kirchbichl, between Dietramszell and Bad Tölz, tel. 08041/9548, with beer garden, closed Mon, Thu; **Klosterbrauerei Reutberg**, Bräustüberl, 83679 Sachsenkam, beer garden, between Holzkirchen and Bad Tölz, near Kirchsee, tel. 08021/8686; **Klosterbräu**, tel. 08178/3694, beer garden; **Rittergütl**, rural beer garden with good food and a view of the mountains, Irschenhausen, tel. 08178/3803; **Gasthof Schmuck**, Arget, tel. 08104/1777, closed Wed; **Gasthaus Steinbacher**, Steingau, between Otterfing and Bauernrain, tel. 08024/4249, closed Tue-Wed; **Waldgasthof**, in Buchenhain, tel. 7930124, south of Pullach, beer garden. *EAST:* **Alter Wirt Oberpframmern**, tel. 08093/1045, closed Thu; **Brauereischänke Aying**, Münchnerstr. 2, Aying, tel. 08095/1345, closed Thu; **Schlossgaststätte Falkenberg**, 85665 Falkenberg, tel. 0809/9604, rural beer garden with chestnut trees, between Moosach and Grafing; **Landgasthof Forstwirt**, Harthausen, tel. 08106/36380, hotel and beer garden, expensive, between Putzbrunn and Oberpframmern. *SOUTHWEST:* **Schlossbräustüberl Seefeld**, Graf Törring Str. 1, Seefeld at Pilsensee, 08152/78922, beer garden; **Kloster Andechs**, Herrsching am Ammersee, tel. 08152/376281, closed Mon-Tue, very popular destination for outings, excellent dark bock beer.

MUNICH, CITY OF FAIRS

Over the centuries, Munich developed from an early customs and trading point "near the monks (*Mönchen*)" into a hub of mercantile activity with important markets on Schrannenplatz (the Marienplatz of today) and in the *Dulten* or fairs of Au and Haidhausen. Farmers and craftsmen gathered here from miles around to buy and sell their wares.

One of the first commercial trade fairs was a highly-successful exhibition held in the "Glass Palace" in 1854, which attracted some 200,000 visitors. Another significant event was "Munich 1908," which took place on the newly laid-out fair ground above Theresienwiese (and which served as Munich's exhibition ground from 1964 until 1998).

What was originally planned as an all-purpose fair ground became, after World War Two, the site for prestigious specialized trade shows. Since then, the number of fairs, exhibitors, visitors and exhibition halls has grown relentlessly. The annual calendar of events includes high-tech shows (*Systec, Systems, Electronica, Laser*), exhibitions of consumer and capital goods (*Drinktec, Hokumak, Ceramitek, Modewoche*) and of the products of skilled trades. With 45 fairs and exhibitions in 1998, Munich is one of the "Big Five" trade-fair cities in Germany.

With the opening of the C-B-R (Caravan and Boat International Travel Market) trade fair in February 1998, a new exhibition era began in Munich on the grounds of the former Reim airport. The Bavarian capital now greets the trade visitor with 460,000 square feet (140,000 sq m) of exhibition space in 14 halls, served by a solar energy system with a maximum output of one megawatt. New to Munich are the Intermot motorcycle trade fair and the Materialica trade fair for new materials. Heim und Handwerk (Home and Crafts) is the Eldorado of do-it-yourselfers.

Above: The new Munich exhibition center in Riem. Right: The BMW building.

MUNICH'S "SILICON VALLEY"

In the last forty years, Munich and the surrounding region have been able to develop into an important center of high-tech industry, particularly microelectronics. The many infrastructure improvements introduced for the Olympics in 1972 have contributed to this growth, and it has also been greatly helped by the excellent leisure facilities which the Isar Valley could offer to those sought-after specialists, who hitherto had only been found in the famous Silicon Valley near San Francisco. They were attracted by the skiing in the nearby Alps, the unique lively atmosphere of the beer gardens, the lakes in the alpine foothills, ideal for swimming, sailing and wind-surfing and, of course, the remarkably rich choice of cultural activities.

When the giant Siemens company decided to move into electronics and set up their research center in Neu-Perlach, it had the additional effect of drawing in a large number of other advanced companies in the same sector. Nearly every important multi-national firm now has a production facility or some other presence in the Munich area. In 1996, Siemens alone employed nearly 39,000 people in Munich.

Deutsche Aerospace (DASA), based in Ottobrunn, has for a long time been involved in air and space travel, whether with the Airbus, various helicopters or the Tornado fighter. Their turbines and engines are produced by MTU. While Krauss-Maffei in Allach is Germany's oldest manufacturer of locomotives, it also assembles the Leopard II tank. Siemens is responsible for their radar systems, as well as a huge range of electrical and electronic equipment.

One of Bavaria's largest chemical companies, Wacker GmbH, has its presence in Munich with an imposing headquarters building in Neu-Perlach, but in terms of numbers employed,

vehicle-building takes second place after the electronics industry (Siemens). MAN's range of products now reaches far beyond the trucks it is best known for. Admirers of the white and blue emblem of BMW will not fail to notice the company's headquarters; modeled somewhat on a four-cylinder engine, it is one of Munich's most original landmarks.

Munich has three very large research establishments in the Max Planck Institute for Plasma Physics, the Center for Space Medicine Research and the German Aerospace Research Association. Over 500 conferences held each year are proof of a lively exchange of scientific opinion and knowledge.

The German and European Patent Offices, the German Federal Patent Court, and other relevant institutions are located here, thus underlining Munich's importance as a leading center for scientific research and technology. The two universities and the Technology Center help to ensure a steady stream of new young scientific talent.

SKIING

ON THE SKI SLOPES

Long ago, when things were very different, Munich was known for its skiers – the people who "went into the mountains" as the saying is here. On weekends, a gang of them would take their *Brettln* (wooden skis) and their backpacks and catch the train to Wallberg, Sutten, Kreuzeck or some other little mountain village; then climb for half a day up the slopes and, after a picnic lunch, tired but happy, they would ski down the mountain which they had dragged themselves up all morning.

But today all that has changed and the Münchener now has to share "his" mountains with hundreds of thousands of "lowlanders." Now everyone is doing it, or thinks they ought to be doing it: skiing and all that goes with it – the jet set winter fashions, the suntan, knowing

Above: After hours of waiting at the ski lift, the blissful downhill run. Right: "Föhn" weather for the Oktoberfest.

about every new lift and *piste* in the remotest valley, the ski fever and the pre-ski exercises – in short, that state of winter excitement which is brought on as if by a virus at the beginning of November, reaches a peak around Christmas, remains virulent until Lent and does not begin to fade until Easter.

A veritable epidemic of this infection grips the entire city, from where it is often only an hour's drive to the nearest ski slopes. That is how quickly you can get from Munich to Lenggries, Garmisch, Spitzingsee or Sudelfield. Those are only the most important of the resorts close to the city, the "local" mountains where you will find row upon row of open-air bars, self-service cafés ("apple strudel caves") and tea-time discos.

Of course, the skiers of Munich have long since become jet setters too, as much at home in the Zillertal, the Arlberg and St. Moritz as they are in the mountains on their own doorstep.

Munich's skiing fans are not deterred by the inevitable traffic jams on the roads to and from the mountains, nor by the long lines for chair-lifts and gondolas. The more crowded the slopes and mountaintop restaurants, the greater seems the thrill of the sport.

At six o'clock on a dark winter morning, at the train station and outside the big sports shops which run special ski buses, you can hear a scraping, clattering noise; it is the day ski-trippers in their hefty plastic ski boots.

When they arrive on the slopes that are now glistening in the morning sun, the sleepy young skiers emerge like brilliantly-colored butterflies. Every color and texture dazzles, every belt and pair of goggles flashes and sparkles. The only pure white to be seen is that on the mountain peaks. Then they line up for the lift, like a long multicolored necklace, inching their way forward, waiting hours for the few minutes bliss of the downhill run – a carnival clad in zany hats.

THE NOTORIOUS FÖHN

There are many days when the sky over Munich is a bright, clear blue, delicately veiled by a few isolated, wispy scraps of cloud. On such days the temperature, even in winter, climbs to spring-like levels and the mountains seem to stand at the very gates of the city, inviting you to climb them – the clear air creates such a staggering visibility. Most people would dream of weather like this; but the Münchener just gets grumpy – the taxi-driver thinks he's surrounded by idiots who should have their licenses taken away on the spot; the secretary spills coffee on her boss' desk. "I'm sorry," she says, "I don't know what's the matter with me. It must be the Föhn again." Schoolchildren sink into an absent-minded stupor: "Gee, how can anyone remember all this stuff when the Föhn is blowing!"

The whole city suffers. Foreigners suffer because they don't know what to expect and old inhabitants suffer because they know all too well.

Meteorologically speaking, the Föhn is a wind which creeps up the Italian side of the Alps, cools off and deposits its load of rain. Then, after reaching the summit, it rushes down the north side as a dry downdraft. For every 300 feet (100 m) it descends, the air warms up by 1° centigrade. It also picks up a hefty charge of static electricity, and when it reaches Munich this has a thoroughly disturbing effect, not only on the weather but on your circulation and entire state of mind.

This usually lasts about three days, and all those who are rash enough to declare themselves immune to the Föhn head off into the mountains. On days like this the visibility up there can be as far as 60 miles (100 km).

People who work at the top of one of Munich's few high-rise buildings are greatly envied for their view, which turns Munich into another Innsbruck. In many

a beer garden on "Föhn days," even in winter, the bars are opened and the benches wiped down so that people can sit and enjoy their mug of beer like a gift from the Almighty.

The Föhn is Munich's special bonus; it gives the city an incomparable quality, something close to Nirvana. The entire population abdicates all responsibility for anything that goes wrong. The extrovert offers a sympathetic hand to the depressive. The Föhn can be blamed for whatever the day may bring. "The Föhn's blowing today," means much the same as: "What can I do about it?"

Everyone is supposedly a helpless victim of the weather. Not even the Chief Burgomaster is held accountable for decisions he makes when the Föhn is blowing. And when the evening sky over Munich turns to such a brilliant red that the whole city seems to be ablaze and the Alps glow like burning coals, then the Münchener snuggles into bed, breathes a sigh of relief and dreams of the next Föhn.

WITTELSBACHS AND FUGGERS

Excursions to the opulent castles, the clean lakes, and the "walkable" mountains in the environs of the city are part of a trip to Munich. As a starting point, the palaces of **Schleissheim** (7 miles/12 km from Munich) are highly recommended. Here you can see not one but three palaces belonging to the royal Wittelsbach family. The **Altes Schloss** (Old Palace) was originally built as a retirement home for Wilhelm V, in what was then a remote area of heathland; it was almost entirely destroyed in the Second World War. Behind its reconstructed façade you can now find sections of the Bavarian National Museum, including the **Crib Museum**. Facing it is the wide baroque frontage of the **Neues Schloss** (New Palace), built as a summer residence by Elector Maximilian II Emanuel and often referred to as the "Versailles of Munich." Every year the Schleissheim Summer Concerts are held here. The park stretches for three-quarters of a mile, ending at the little **Lustheim** palace, which houses a museum of porcelain.

Dachau

Unfortunately, the world knows the name of Dachau (10 miles/17 km north of Munich) only as a symbol of the Nazi reign of terror. Thousands of visitors come all year round to see the Concentration Camp Memorial outside the town, and remain unaware of the town's idyllic historical center, with its charmingly-restored old houses beneath the Schlossberg. The **Schloss** itself, a four-winged renaissance palace, was built by the Wittelsbach dukes Wilhelm IV and Albrecht V, and was expanded into a baroque extravaganza by Max Emanuel I in 1715. Little remains of it today, but it is worth looking at the handsome staircase leading

Preceding pages: Neuschwanstein Castle. Above: Schleissheim Palace. Right: Perlach Tower and the Town Hall in Augsburg.

to the banquet hall with its wooden coffered ceiling in the renaissance manner.

The **Concentration Camp Memorial** lies just beyond the town. Behind its high walls and watch towers even today, more than half a century later, the horrors of Nazism have an almost tangible presence. You can see the barracks and crematorium, and most important of all, the museum in the former working quarters, where shattering evidence of Nazi atrocities is displayed (Tue-Sun 9 a.m. to 5 p.m.; admission free; tel. 08131/1741).

Augsburg

Augsburg, once home of the merchant dynasty of the Fuggers, is the third largest city in Bavaria (city info: 0821/502070). The history of its foundation goes back to the Romans, who established a military camp here in 15 BC – making Augsburg one of the oldest cities in Germany. The physical evidence of the religious and secular power wielded by Augsburg during its long history can be seen in the buildings which line **Maximilianstrasse**. This runs from the Cathedral of St. Maria in the north, to Ulrichskirche at its southern end. The Romanesque **Cathedral**, a pillared basilica with three aisles, to which a Gothic choir was later added, has a particularly fine south door and an impressive Prophets' Window. The gravestones on the **Römermauer** (Roman Wall) recall the origins of the city.

The center of the old merchant city of Augsburg lies around the Romanesque **St. Peter's Church**, whose onion-domed **Perlach Tower** was designed by Elias Holl. This emblem of the city stands beside the mighty **Rathaus** (City Hall) with its two onion towers and the "Golden Hall" upstairs, considered the most important example of renaissance secular building north of the Alps (built 1615-20). The **Augustus-Brunnen** (fountain) in front of the Rathaus, and the fountains

of **Mercury** and **Hercules**, both on Maximilianstrasse, complete this impressive townscape.

Just a ten-minute walk from here is the **Fuggerei**, the world's first social housing project established for "industrious, innocent, poor citizens of the Catholic faith." The Fuggerei was established in 1516 by merchant and banker Jakob Fugger, and contains 67 small houses, a church and a fountain. People still live in the complex today. The annual rent is the equivalent of a Rhenish Gulden, i.e., one mark and 72 pfennigs. A historical apartment can be seen here in the Fuggerei Museum (March-Oct. daily from 9 a.m. to 6 p.m.).

Augsburg's Maximilianstrasse culminates in the Protestant-Catholic church complex of **St. Ulrich and St. Afra** and **Evangelical St. Ulrich's Church**. The evangelic church was built over the grave of the martyr Afra. The larger late-Gothic building has renaissance decoration and a 300-foot (93 m) tower, and conceals in its crypt the bones of Ulrich, the patron saint of Augsburg.

LAKE STARNBERG

LAND OF THE FIVE LAKES

Take a large-scale touring map and find the villages of Inning, Wessling and Starnberg to the north, Schondorf, Utting and Diessen to the west, Weilheim, Iffeldorf and Penzberg to the south, and Ambach, Ammerland and Berg to the east. In the middle you will see two kidney-shaped areas of blue and, scattered around them, three glinting cyclopean eyes: these are Munich's Five Lakes, nestling in the foothills of the Alps; Ammersee and Starnberger See, Pilsensee, Wörthsee and Wesslinger See (*See* is German for "lake"). Then, around the southern edge of Starnberger See, long ago hollowed out by glacial action, there is a galaxy of idyllic lakes and ponds. These are the *Osterseen*, 21 of them in all, and with the larger lakes they create an enchanting sub-Alpine landscape.

Above: On Lake Starnberg near Seeshaupt – the Föhn makes the Alps seem to be right up close. Right: On the way to Andechs.

The town of **Starnberg** itself is the classic excursion destination for Müncheners, the well-to-do of whom have settled into the villas and holiday homes around **Starnberger See**. Nowhere else in Germany are there so many millionaires per capita. Top businessmen and industrialists, as well as film, television and radio stars, are willing to pay any price for one of the rare lake-shore properties.

The town's most attractive feature is its well-kept lakeside promenade, which has a yacht marina which was recently enlarged. On a hill above the town, reached by a flight of steps, is the little parish church of St. Joseph, with a splendid high altar by Ignaz Günther. But apart from this, there is not much to see in Starnberg. Unless you are keen to look at the "beautiful people" in the fashionable Undosa swimming pool, the best thing to do is board an **excursion boat** from the jetty right beside the train station. You can briefly break your trip at various points and take a short walk ashore, for example, at nearby **Berg,** birthplace of

the writer Oskar Maria Graf, who created a literary monument to this landscape with his novel *Das Leben Meiner Mutter* (My Mother's Life).

Berg has, however, become much more celebrated through its connection with the mysterious death, unexplained to this day, of that tragic fairy tale monarch, Ludwig II. It was on June 13, 1886, that the bodies of the king and his doctor, Professor von Gudden, were recovered from the lake, and today the spot is marked by a large cross. Every year on the anniversary of his death, devotees of the king gather here for a memorial service in the nearby **Votive Chapel**.

From here you can take a pleasant walk along the shore through **Leoni** and past **Schloss Allmannshausen** as far as **Ammerland**, where the towers of the **Pocci-Schlössl** appear. This little castle was built by the same Count Pocci who created the popular Larifari the Clown.

For those who still have the energy, this walk can be extended as far as **Ambach**, where a beautiful old country inn, "Fischmeister" – whose menu has long since become like that of a big city restaurant – stands right at the edge of the lake. If the beer garden is too full, you can board the steamer again, which takes you to **Seeshaupt** at the southern end of the lake and then on to **Bernried** on the western shore, where, even from a distance, you can see the huge outline of the former Augustinian monastery and the picturesquely gnarled beeches and oaks in the park.

From here the boat continues to **Tutzing,** well known as the seat of the Evangelical Academy. Here you can make an excursion to the **Ilka-Höhe**, which at over 2,000 feet (728 m) is the highest point on the lake, and from where one gets a magnificent view of the lake and the nearby Alps. When you return to the promenade, you may be lucky enough to catch one of the amazing sunsets, when the mountains are reflected in the water like orange glowing embers.

If you do not have time to wait, it is best to board the boat again for **Feldaf-**

WESTERN UPPER BAVARIA

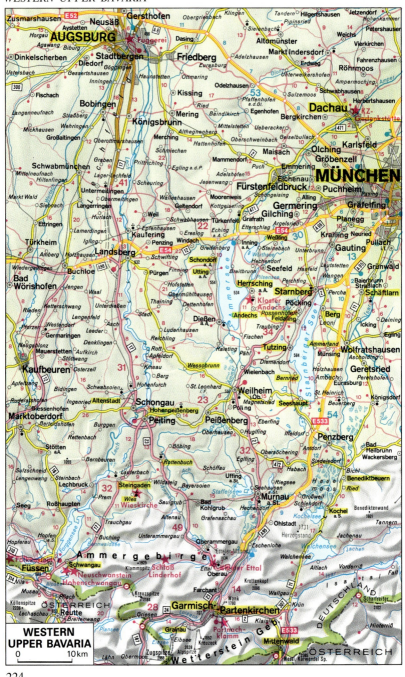

ing, with its **Roseninsel** (Rose Island) a little way offshore, where Max II, the father of the "Fairy Tale King," built himself a little castle and had 15,000 roses planted round it. No wonder that Ludwig and his beautiful cousin Sissi, later the empress of Austria, returned again and again to Feldafing and to nearby **Possenhofen** (now a popular sailing center). The castle of Possenhofen, built in 1536, is where Sissi spent her childhood. There was an inn on the road to Tutzing, now converted into a luxury hotel for the super-rich, where Sissi spent every summer holiday, and where she arranged secret meetings with Ludwig.

Ammersee

Lake Ammersee is quieter, more rural, less prettified and altogether more unspoilt than Starnberger See. In the villages around the lake, with the exception of Herrsching on the eastern shore, one still often sees tractors, farms and simple inns. The best way to reach it is by the S-Bahn line 5 to **Herrsching**, the "capital" of Ammersee, with its short but attractive promenade and its *Seeschlösschen*, as the aristocratic lakeside residences are called. In Herrsching you can take another excursion steamer across to Diessen on the opposite shore. The main street of the town leads directly up to the collegiate church of **St. Maria**, a true jewel of the rococo period.

Another boat takes you on to **Utting**, where it is worth having a look around. Its charming period architecture has been preserved almost intact. A beautiful path lined with trees and bushes leads along the western shore, from which there are frequent views of the lake. You pass by old, secluded country houses which give off a feeling of the tranquility and splendor of a bygone age.

In **Schondorf**, look at the Romanesque chapel of St. Jakob before returning to Herrsching, where you should not miss the climb to the "Holy Mountain" and a visit to the monastery of **Andechs**, Bavaria's oldest place of pilgrimage. The Benedictine monks have been offering prayers and brewing beer here since the beginning of the 15th century, as well as guarding a priceless horde of relics from the crusades. The **Mariä Verkündigung** church, originally late Gothic, was rebuilt in the baroque style by Johann Baptist Zimmermann and is one of the most-visited shrines in Germany. But the fame of the "Holy Mountain" is perhaps more attributable to the beer brewed there by the monks, and still served in generous measure in the monastery's **beer garden**. Being a pilgrim can be thirsty work!

The Smaller Lakes

On the S-Bahn line 5 from Munich to Herrsching, three lakes are worthy of a visit: the idyllic **Wesslinger See**, which is really not much more than a large pond, rich with fish, that is lined with tall trees. Delicious homemade cakes are served at the terrace café on the shore. The clear waters of **Wörthsee** (S-5 to Steinebach) shimmer like green velvet. Here you can wind surf or rent a row boat. If you prefer to stay on dry land, though, head for the big grassy sunbathing area on the western shore – but be prepared to share it with a lot of others on weekends. The quiet **Pilsensee** (S-5 to Seefeld) is rather overgrown with reeds in places.

Culinary delicacies in the Five Lakes region include fresh and smoked fish, such as trout and whitefish.

South of the Five Lakes, beyond Seehaupt, the **Ostersen** lakes are particularly beautiful. The whole area is a nature preserve and swimming is only permitted in a few places, so you can wander around the moorland lakes instead.

Still further to the south, already in the Alps at an altitude of 2,630 feet (802 m), **Walchensee** is a magnet for wind surfers.

LINDERHOF

MONASTERIES, CASTLES AND MOUNTAINS

In the Pfaffenwinkel Region

South of the Five Lakes rise the rolling contours of the western part of Bavaria's Alpine foothills. This region boasts a large number of architectural splendors – some known throughout the world – from the Wieskirche to Neuschwanstein Castle. It really needs a weekend excursion to appreciate the charm of the countryside and its numerous churches, monasteries and castles.

It is best to take the road through Starnberg and on to the pretty little town of **Weilheim**. You should explore the old quarter behind its almost intact walls and look at the **Mariensäule** pillars and the **Stadtbrunnen** (town fountain). The **Pfaffenwinkel Museum** is also worth visiting. *Pfaffenwinkel* is the local name

Left: The elegant palace of Linderhof.
Above: Ceiling fresco in the Wieskirche.

for the region that lies between the rivers Lech, Ammer and Loisach, and items from its history are on display here. So far – thank goodness – Pfaffenwinkel has been spared the onslaught of mass tourism. The Wieskirche may be world-famous, but it is only one of 21 churches and twelve monasteries in the area whose interiors are considered the finest examples of the rococo decorative style.

Pfaffen was the rather contemptuous name given by the local people in the 18th century to the priests who commissioned the church decorations and were responsible for the cohorts of chubby-cheeked cherubs and trumpet-blowing angels which adorn the fine stucco ceilings. In those days, the clergy were less concerned with saving the souls of their parishioners and rather more with sciences such as astronomy. They also saw themselves as patrons of the arts, a weakness which led to the financial ruin of so many monasteries. Pfaffenwinkel, and especially the abbey of Wessobrunn, was once the home of many celebrated

WESSOBRUNN / THE WIESKIRCHE

architects and stucco artists who were deluged with commissions from princes and prelates all over Europe.

Seven miles (11 km) north-west of Weilheim lies the abbey of **Wessobrunn**, founded in 753 AD and later one of the most powerful monasteries in Bavaria. During the guided tour, visitors are shown the grandiose guest wings of the former Benedictine abbey and the Tassilo Hall. Wessobrunn also became famous for the discovery here of the oldest text in the German language, the *Wessobrunner Gebet* (Wessobrunn Prayer), which tells the Creation story in the old Bavarian dialect. The text can be read, carved in rock outside the monastery.

An extravagant example of rococo ornamentation can be seen in the *Gnadenkapelle* (Chapel of Grace) on **Hohenpeissenberg,** a hill south-west of Weilheim, where the stucco artist Josef Schmuzer, the sculptor Franz-Xaver Schmädel and the painter Mathäus Günther together created a dizzying display of shapes and colors here, as in nearby **Rottenbuch** (southwest of Peissenberg). The Augustinian canons built an obervatory as early as 1781, on a 3,000-foot (1,000 m) peak. Today, the antennae of the German Meteorological Service point skywards from this spot, from where there is a superb view of the surrounding countryside with its eleven little lakes.

Only a few miles from Hohenpeissberg, in **Altenstadt**, is the only Romanesque vaulted church (13th century) in Upper Bavaria that wasn't given a baroque make-over. A monumental crucifix (around 1200 AD) in the main apse is of interest, depicting Christ with a golden circlet instead of a crown of thorns.

From the **Echelsbach Bridge** there is a fantastic view 400 feet (130 m) down into the gorge of the river Ammer. Just before the bridge there are signposts to the Wieskirche and to neighboring **Steingaden** with its Romanesque Premonstratensian abbey and monastery church of St. John the Baptist. This was built under the medieval Guelph monarchy, but its interior was remodelled in the rococo idiom by artists of the Wessobrunn school.

After many years of restoration, the Pilgrimage Church of the Savior Scourged, to give it its full name, can once more be seen without its scaffolding. If only for its beautiful setting the **Wieskirche**, as it is usually called, has become universally known, and on maps this miracle of German rococo art is marked with the single word *Wieskirche*. The building of this outwardly rather unassuming church was begun in 1745 by Dominikus Zimmermann, at the behest of the abbot of Steingaden.

Royal Castles and Palaces

From the *Wieskirche* it is only a short drive to **Füssen**, close to the border with

Above: Romanesque cloister in the monastery of Steingaden. Right: Panoramic view of Neuschwanstein and Hohenschwangau.

Austria, and the place where the *Romantische Strasse* (Romantic Road) reaches its end. Back in Roman times, *Foetibus*, as it was called then, was a small garrison town on the busy *Via Appia Claudia*. The town's skyline is today dominated by a medieval fortress, the **Hohes Schloss**. On the same hill stands the Benedictine church of St. Mang. Below, beside the river Lech, the Spitalkirche is worth visiting to see its façade covered in elaborate murals in the traditional Bavarian style known as *Lüftlmalerei*. For most tourists, however, Füssen is simply the starting-point for visiting the royal castles.

In the 13th century, during the Hohenstaufen dynasty, there were three fortresses in the country around **Bannwaldsee.** In 1832, Maximilian II had a summer residence built on one of these vantage-points. It was in the English Tudor style and its walls were decorated with figures from German mythology, painted by Moritz von Schwind. This is the castle of **Hohenschwangau.** Maximilian's son, the ill-fated Ludwig, spent most of his childhood in its rather gloomy atmosphere. When he came to the throne in 1869, as Ludwig II, he started planning a neo-romantic castle, complete with battlements and turrets, just like something from Grimm's Fairy Tales. Designed by Jank, a stage designer, the famous **Neuschwanstein Castle** took 17 years to complete. Nowadays, millions of sightseers arrive every year, driving or walking up the broad approach road. Daily, thousands jostle their way in groups through the magnificent throne-room and the Singers' Hall, as well as the private appartments of the king, who wanted the castle to be seen as a homage to his revered friend, the great composer Richard Wagner.

Ludwig had a second royal residence, the small, neo-rococo palace, **Linderhof,** in the idyllic Graswang valley. It was designed by Georg Dollmann and was built between 1870 and 1879. The melancholy monarch took refuge more and more often in its small, over-decorated rooms, whenever he wearied of the hurly-burly

OBERAMMERGAU / ETTAL / GARMISCH-PARTENKIRCHEN

of his capital. Here, as in Neuschwanstein, he would have his meals served to him alone at a "magic dining-table" which could be made to disappear into the floor. In the 124-acre (50 ha) park you can see the artificial Grotto of Venus, the Moorish Kiosk and the hunting lodge called *Hundinghaus*.

The Majesty of the Mountains

Mention the name **Oberammergau**, and most people immediately think of the Passion Plays, yet these only take place once every ten years (the next one will be in the year 2000). More than a village but not quite a town, Oberammergau's attractions include the parish church designed by J. Schmuzer of Wessobrunn, with stucco added by his son Franz Xaver, and wonderful frescos by M.

Above: Even in summer it is always busy on the Zugspitze, the highest mountain in Germany. Right: The most beautiful church tower in Upper Bavaria, at Mittenwald.

Günther, the collection of Nativity scenes in the Local History Museum and above all the splendid murals *(Lüftlmalereien)* to be seen along the streets, for example on the Pilatus House.

The eleven-sided Benedictine monastery church at **Ettal**, three miles (5 km) away, has been described as a kind of Bavarian temple of the Holy Grail. Situated near the great trading highway from Innsbruck to Augsburg, it attracted pilgrims who came to see a small statue of the Madonna, which the emperor Ludwig the Bavarian had brought back from Rome.

Until the Winter Olympics of 1936, **Garmisch-Partenkirchen** consisted of two separate villages which each had its own parish church. Since then, they have grown together to form one of the most important winter sport resorts in Germany. Three big ski-runs, the Wankbahn, the Alpspitzbahn and the Zugspitzbahn provide a paradise for downhill skiers, while on the valley floor there is a wide choice of cross country trails. In winter and summer alike, skiers and sightseers

WALCHENSEE / KOCHELSEE / BENEDIKTBEUREN

are attracted to the neighboring **Zugspitze**, at nearly 9,000 feet (2963 m) the highest peak in Germany (take the cog railway from Partenkirchen or the cablecar from Eibsee).

To enjoy the natural surroundings of Garmisch-Partenkirchen, you can walk through the **Partnachklamm** gorge (starting from the Olympic ski stadium in Partenkirchen), while more adventurous hikers can explore the **Höllentalklamm** gorge (starting-point: Grainau).

From Garmisch-Partenkirchen take the B2 road for Scharnitz and turn off to the village of **Mittenwald**, renowned for its violin-makers, for its late Gothic church of St. Peter and St. Paul – whose tower is said to be the finest in Upper Bavaria, and not least of all for the unique murals on the house-fronts in the Obermarkt.

An alternative way to get back to Munich is the itinerary over Krün and Wallgau to **Walchensee**, which is surrounded by mountains. Visitors like it for its cool waters and high altitude, divers for its depth (630 feet/192 m), and windsurfers for its strong winds. The **Herzogstand** mountain rises above it. Its 5,200 feet (1,731 m) can easily be climbed with the cable car that departs from the lake's shore. On top of this mountain is a panoramic restaurant with Bavarian cooking.

In 1786, Goethe's post coach bumped along the hairpin bends of **Kesselbergstrasse** towards Italy. Today, motorcyclists test their machines' response here. Kesselbergstrasse brings you 600 feet (200 m) down to **Kochelsee**.

Near the village of **Kochel** there is a small museum devoted to the artist Franz Marc, one of the founders of the *Blauer Reiter* (Blue Rider) group, who is buried in the local cemetery. The house where he once lived, still privately owned, is not far away in **Ried**, close to the great Benedictine monastery of **Benediktbeuren**.

Built in the shadow of the 5,500-foothigh (1,800 m) **Benediktenwand** rockface, this is the oldest Benedictine foun-

dation in Upper Bavaria. When it was being restored, remains of its original Romanesque walls were found, dating from the 8th century. When Charlemagne presented the relics of St. Benedict to the order, the monastery developed into one of the most important pilgrimage shrines north of the Alps. This is where the texts, put to music and made famous by Carl Orff in *Carmina Burana*, were composed in the 12th to 13th centuries. Hans Georg Asam, father of the Asam brothers, painted the ceiling frescos in the church.

The Anastasia chapel built by J. M. Fischer (1750-53) is an architectural gem. Its side altars were designed by Ignaz Günther, and the silver gilt reliquary of St. Anastasia is the work of Egid Quirin Asam.

To end of your weekend tour through western Upper Bavaria, and as a grand finale, an evening visit to the cozy beer garden of **Schäftlarn Monastery** should not be missed. There is stuccowork to be seen in the church by J. B. Zimmermann, and altars by J. B. Straub.

EASTERN UPPER BAVARIA

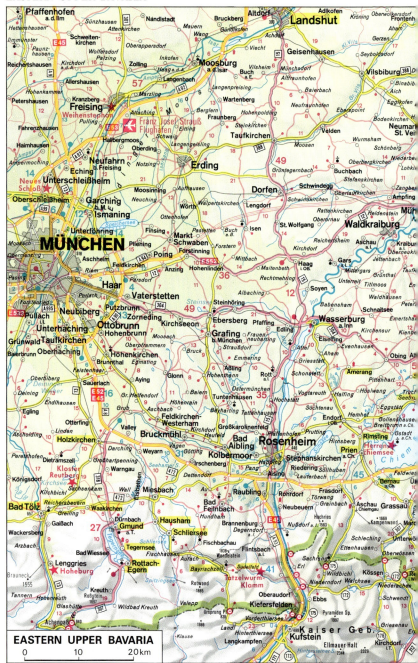

BAD TÖLZ

MOUNTAINS AND LAKES

The next excursion, to the eastern part of Upper Bavaria, takes in the famous beauty-spots of Tegernsee, Chiemsee and Königsee. You should allow yourself two days for a tour of the region, with an overnight stop along the way (there are plenty of places – pensions, *Gästehäuser* and hotels – to stay at around all of the lakes).

First, take the busy Munich to Salzburg *Autobahn* as far as the exit for **Holzkirchen**. From here, the B13 road takes you to Bad Tölz, a distance of 13 miles (22 km). About half way there it is worth making a stop just beyond Sachsenkam. There is a signpost to the Franciscan monastery of **Reutberg**, with its charming beer garden and cozy inn on the high ground above the little lake of Kirchsee (a flat moor lake in whose shallow waters you may swim). There is an absolutely fantastic view of the Alps from here as an added bonus.

A further short drive brings you to **Bad Tölz**. The Isar divides the town into two very different parts which are only linked by a single bridge. The old town of Tölz centers on the **Marktstrasse**, which climbs a steep hill and is lined on both sides by handsome town houses in the Upper Bavarian style. Their baroque and rococo façades, painted in pastel colors, stand shoulder to shoulder under the jutting eaves, and many of them are decorated with colorful murals.

At the top of the hill stands the twin-spired **Kreuzkirche**, with its Leonhard chapel. Every year, on November 6, this is the scene of the *Leonhardi-Ritt* (Leonhard Ride), an event which attracts thousands of sightseers. On the other side of the bridge lies the spa resort of Bad Tölz, whose iodine-rich springs have guaranteed a good livelihood for the inhabitants on both sides of the river.

Your route then passes **Reichersbeuren** with its Sigriz castle, which

TEGERNSEE / SCHLIERSEE / SPITZINGSEE

today houses an exclusive boarding-school, and continues to **Waakirchen** where, beyond the monument with the Bavarian lion, you see signposts to **Gmund** and **Kaltenbrunn** on Tegernsee lake. From Kaltenbrunn, where excursion steamers berth at the jetty, the view stretches away to the 5,170-foot-high (1,722 m) **Wallberg**. A cable-car takes you to the summit which offers another superb view of the lake.

Since the beginning of the century, this idyllic setting has become one of the favorite places for the rich and famous to build their second homes. The earliest to succumb to the charm of the area were writers and artists like Ludwig Thoma and Olaf Gulbransson. But long before Tegernsee became fashionable, the Benedictine monks had settled here – in the 8th century in fact. The monastery they built in the town that is also called **Tegernsee** became one of the greatest in Bavaria, and was a focus of intellectual and cultural life in the region, while its library was renowned far beyond the frontiers of Bavaria. The monks were also renowned for their artistic skills, especially in glass-painting and bronze-casting. The good beer in the *Herzogliches Bräustüberl* (Ducal Brewery Parlor) draws crowds of visitors to this day. The monastery church is also well worth a look. The interior of this Romanesque building was redecorated in the 18th century by Johann Georg Asam, among others. Up the hill from the health-spa building you will find the **Olaf Gulbransson Museum**, where the works of this Norwegian artist are on show. He lived from 1873 to 1958, and contributed cartoons to the famous Munich satire magazine, *Simplicissimus*.

Bad Wiessee, on the opposite shore, attracts many short-stay visitors with its casino. The parish church of St. Lawrence, in the twin villages of **Rottach-Egern** at the southern tip of the lake, is probably one of the most photographed buildings in Upper Bavaria.

Returning to Gmund, the starting point of our tour around Tegernsee, the road continues to **Hausham**, formerly a coal-mining community, as is evident from the disused winding-gear above the mine-shaft. You soon reach lake **Schliersee**, with its town of the same name. In contrast to Tegernsee, it is still possible to buy holiday homes quite cheaply here.

Barely six miles (10 km) south of Schliersee, it is worth making a little detour to **Spitzingsee**, a favorite spot for weekenders from Munich. In winter, thousands of skiers take the drag-lift up to the superb pistes on the Stümplfling and Taubenstein mountains.

On the German section of the *Alpenstrasse* (Alpine Highway), head for Bayrischzell and you get a good view of the 5,500-foot-high (1,838 m) **Wendelstein**. You can take a giant cable-car to the summit to enjoy the magnificent pano-

Above: What a magnificent moustache!
Right: Frog Fountain on Herrenchiemsee.

rama. From Bayrischzell, a series of hairpin bends leads to **Sudelfeld**, another week-end ski-resort for Müncheners. To reach lake Chiemsee from here, the shortest and most attractive route is the tollroad through a gorge called the **Tatzelwurm-Klamm**. In the Middle Ages, folk stayed away from this damp and gloomy defile, since they firmly believed that it was haunted by a *Tatzelwurm* – the Bavarian word for a dragon.

Chiemsee, the "Bavarian Sea"

Chiemsee is a 33-square-mile (85 sq km) stretch of water which the locals with some pride call the "Bavarian Sea." The Romans were early settlers on its shores, and some excavated evidence of their presence can be seen at the Roman Museum in **Seebruck** on the north shore. In the Middle Ages, the monasteries of Herrenchiemsee and Frauenchiemsee became important bases for the Christianization and settlement of the region. Tradition has it that in the 9th century the abbess of Frauenchiemsee was the Blessed Irmingard, daughter of Emperor Ludwig the German.

If you want to gain more than a fleeting impression of the lake and its delightful setting, you should break your journey here for at least one night. If you do, the town of **Prien** provides an ideal starting point. In the summer months, a narrow-gauge railway with a train called *Feuriger Elias* (Fiery Elias) runs between the main-line station and the lake harbor at **Stock**, 1.25 miles (2 km) away. An all-year-round steamer service takes you from there across to **Herrenchiemsee**. There is evidence that this island was inhabited in pre-Christian times. Later, the Benedictine order founded a monastery there, which was largely destroyed in the 10th century. However, walking from the jetty to the *Neues Schloss* (New Palace), you pass the former library of the monastery, as well as a small chapel and a refectory which is now a café. The island was bought by Ludwig II in 1873 from its former owner, a timber-merchant, and in

1878, the king laid the foundation-stone of his "Bavarian Versailles." The plans for it were drawn up by his architect, Georg Dollmann – the same man who dreamed up Neuschwanstein – and completion of the building was to have taken 16 years. But up to the king's untimely death in 1886, only the large and small state appartments, the Hall of Mirrors and adjoining rooms were finished, together with the main bedchamber and the grand south staircase. Two wings were planned, but only the shell of the northerly one had been constructed, and this was demolished in 1903.

An annex to the palace now houses the **King Ludwig Museum**, which has several rooms displaying photographs of the monarch and personal momentos such as his christening-robe and his death-mask, beside that of his friend Richard Wagner. There are also some interesting sketches of stage sets for Wagner's operas.

A short boat-trip takes you to the much smaller island of **Frauenchiemsee**, where the last of the lake fishermen make a living from tourism rather than from their catches. Only 300 people live in the village which clusters round the nunnery; its Romanesque church is almost dwarfed by the free-standing octagonal belltower, surmounted by an onion-dome. Inside the church, the Romanesque frescoes are well worth seeing. To the west of lake Chiemsee and north of the town of Rimsting lies the **Eggstätter Seenplatte** nature reserve, a wetland area of small lakes and ponds. Swimming is only allowed at designated points, but extensive walks can be enjoyed through this delightful landscape.

In the castle of **Amerang**, which has the largest renaissance courtyard north of the Alps, concerts are held every year during the summer. The village of **Pavolding** is notable for the over-lifesize bronze sculptures by Heinrich Kirchner

Above: The Hall of Mirrors at Herrenchiemsee. Right: The Watzmann rises steeply above St. Bartholomä on Königssee.

(1902-84), which stand in a meadow in front of his farmhouse studio. The road winds on to **Seeon**, a Romanesque monastery on a tiny island in lake **Klostersee**. Originally a Gothic building, it has breathtaking net-vaulted ceilings from this period. In the renaissance period it was decorated with fine paintings.

The Country around Berchtesgaden

The last stage of our weekend expedition takes us from lake Chiemsee into a district known as **Berchtesgadener Land**. From Bernau a stretch of the German Alpine Highway passes through landscape of exceptional beauty. It skirts the winter resort of **Reit im Winkl**, then **Ruhpolding**, from where a cable-car will take you to the top of the 5,000-foot-high (1,648 m) Rauschberg. The road then passes **Schneizlreuth** before reaching the *belle époque* resort town of **Bad Reichenhall** with its *Kurpark* and the former monastery church of St. Zeno.

In **Berchtesgaden**, 11 miles (18 km) away, the right to extract salt or "white gold" as it used to be called, was hotly disputed between Austria and Bavaria over many centuries, leading time and again to bloodshed. But today, only those guests seeking a cure for allergies or respiratory complaints visit the ancient underground tunnels. A visit to the salt mines is a unique experience: you descend 1,500 feet (500 m) in a "cage," dressed as a miner, to explore the subterranean galleries.

From the village of **Königssee**, motorboats take you for a trip across the lake of the same name. Over four miles (7 km) long and enclosed by the steeply rising walls of the surrounding mountains, this is probably the most beautiful of all the mountain lakes in Bavaria. In less than an hour – the famous "trumpet echo" is included in the price – you land at the little country church of **St. Bartholomä**. This is the starting point of the so-called *Sau-*

gasse (Sow's Lane), the notorious ascent to the **Steinernes Meer** (Sea of Stone). The east face of the **Watzmann**, a sheer cliff 5,400 feet (1,800 m) high, presents a tremendous challenge to alpinists. The **Watzmann Massif** (8,900 feet/ 2,713 m) is one of the most difficult and strenuous climbs in the eastern Alps, and has claimed nearly a hundred lives to date.

Inevitably, the name of Berchtesgaden will always be associated with Adolf Hitler. It is true that only the foundations remain of his country house at nearby **Obersalzberg**, since it was dynamited at the end of the war. But somehow the place still seems to exert a strange fascination on the visitor. Close by is the guest-house, which was taken over by the US Army in 1945 and converted into a hotel for GIs. From here you can go through a tunnel in the rock to Hitler's *Adlerhorst* (Eagle's Nest), today called the **Kehlsteinhaus**. It is built at an altitude of 5,500 feet (1,834 m), and in good weather commands a fantastic view over the Berchtesgaden mountain range.

FREISING

THE MIDDLE AGES BROUGHT TO LIFE

About 20 miles (33 km) north of Munich lies the old town and former episcopal seat of **Freising** (pop. 36,000). This one-time rival of Munich was founded much earlier than the Bavarian capital by the Agilolfing dynasty who, as early as 700 AD, established themselves on the Domberg, a hill which later became known also as the *mons doctus* because so many scholars lived and worked there. On its summit stands the Romanesque cathedral of **St. Maria and Korbinian**, with its two white towers. Built between 1160 and 1205, it is the oldest brick building north of the Alps and is the town's emblem. The cathedral is a sort of national shrine for Bavarians. Its interior was remodelled in 1724 by the Asam brothers in the late-baroque style to celebrate the 1,000th anniversary of the bishopric of Freising, for which Elector Max Emanuel donated the great **Korbinian Bell**. Weighing five tons, it was cast from the melted-down metal of 40 Turkish cannons. Beneath the cathedral is the oldest Romanesque crypt in Germany, with its famous **Bestiensäule** (Bestiary Pillar) with its dragons and demons.

Also of interest are **St. Benedict's Church** (circa 1340), with the Gothic Mary window, the early Gothic church of **St. Johannis** and the **Bischofsschloss** (Bishops' Palace). Built on Agilolfing castle's foundations, it has the oldest renaissance colonnades north of the Alps. High above the roofs of the **Old Town** rises the Gothic church of **St. Georg**.

The monastery of **Weihenstephan**, south of town, was founded as a Benedictine abbey in 1020 AD. The *Bräustüberl* inn of the Weihenstephan brewery offers fine Bavarian cuisine. In summer, you can enjoy a drink in the tranquil beer garden. You can also tour the brewery – the oldest in the world, founded in 1050 (by appointment only, tel. 08161/5360).

A Princely Wedding in Landshut

The old town of **Landshut** (pop. 55,000) was founded in 1204, and its two parallel main streets known as the *Altstadt* and the *Neustadt* (Old Town and New Town) have preserved their medieval appearance unchanged, making this one of the most attractive towns in Germany. **Martinskirche** in the Altstadt has a tower 430 feet (133 m) high and is the tallest brick-built structure in the world. Dating from the 14th and 15th centuries, the church contains one of the great masterpieces of German art; this is the **Rosenkranz-Madonna** (Madonna of the Rosary), carved by Hans Leinberger between 1516 and 1520.

The castle of the Wittelsbachs in Landshut, **Burg Trausnitz**, was partly destroyed by fire in 1960, but has been

Above: The fine vaulted roof of Freising Cathedral. Right: Procession of the citizenry at the Prince's Wedding in Landshut.

restored, and remains one of Germany's most important and best-preserved castle complexes. Until the 13th century it was only a timber-built fortification, but in 1204 Duke Ludwig I had it reconstructed in stone, in the Gothic style. In the following centuries it was enlarged and a double row of arches was constructed, and now the castle is considered one of the most important renaissance buildings in Germany. In the "Italian annex," look for the exceptionally well-preserved **Narrentreppe** (Fool's Staircase). Painted for Duke Wilhelm V by the Italian artist Scalzi, it depicts life-sized scenes and figures from the *Commedia dell'Arte*.

The **Stadtresidenz** in the Alstadt was built for Duke Ludwig X in 1537-43. Returning from a visit to Mantua, he felt so inspired that he wanted to have his own unique *palazzo* north of the Alps.

The **Rathaus** (Town Hall), also in the Altstadt, was built around 1380 and subsequently altered many times. In the ceremonial hall there is an elaborately-carved ceiling with decorations dating from 1882. The same street has many fine gabled houses from the 15th and 16th centuries, such as **Pappenbergerhaus** (No. 81) and **Grasbergerhaus** (No. 300).

However, the greatest attraction that Landshut can offer is the colorful re-enactment, every three years, of the **Landshuter Fürstenhochzeit** (Prince's Wedding), which first took place in 1475. This vast historical pageant, probably the greatest in Europe, will be staged again in the year 2000. It celebrates the wedding of Georg, son of Duke Ludwig the Rich, to Jadwiga, daughter of the King of Poland. On that occasion, the Duke entertained the entire population of the town for a week at his own expense. Nowadays, alas, you have to pay for everything yourself, but at least you can immerse yourself in medieval street-life for a few hours. There are games, jousting and court-ceremonials; and you can witness the procession through the town of the historic bridal couple, which is so authentic that no spectators are allowed to wear sun-glasses or wrist-watches.

PRACTICAL TIPS FROM A TO Z

Accommodation

Munich has about 300 hotels and pensions with a total of 36,000 beds. Reservations should be made as far ahead as possible, especially for the Oktoberfest and trade fairs.

Accommodation Office (*Zimmervermittlung*): Hauptbahnhof, south exit to Bayerstrasse, tel. 23330255/-58, 9 a.m. to 8 p.m., Sun 11 a.m. to 7 p.m.; airport, Tourist Information and Accommodation Bureau, tel. 2330300, 8:30 a.m. to 10 p.m., Sun 1 p.m. to 9 p.m.

LUXURY HOTELS (DM 500-2,500): **Bayrischer Hof**, Promenadepl. 2-6 (near Opera), tel. 21200; **Rafael**, Neuturmstr. 1 (near Opera), tel. 290980; **Vier Jahreszeiten Kempinski**, Maximilianstr. 17 (near Opera), tel. 230390.

HIGH-QUALITY HOTELS (DM 250-500): **Arabella Hotel**, Arabellastr. 5 (Bogenhausen), tel. 92320; **Arabella-Westpark**, Garmischer Str. 2 (West End), tel. 51960; **City Hilton**, Rosenheimer Str. 15 (Gasteig), tel. 484040; **Eden-Wolff**, Arnulfstr. 4 (Hauptbahnhof), tel. 551150; **Excelsior**, Schützenstr. 11 (Hauptbahnhof), tel. 551370; **Holiday Inn** (north), Leopoldstr. 194 (near Nuremberg Autobahn), tel. 38170; **InterCity Hotel**, Bayerstr. 10 (in Hauptbahnhof), tel. 545560; **Marriott**, Berliner Str. 93 (near Nuremberg Autobahn), tel. 360020; **Opera**, St. Annastr. 10 (Lehel), tel. 225533-36; **Preysing**, Preysing Str. 1 (Rosenheimer Platz), tel. 481011; **Sheraton**, Arabellastr. 6 (Bogenhausen), tel. 92640;

MID-PRICE HOTELS (DM 100-200): **Astoria**, Nikolaistr. 9 (Schwabing), tel.395091; **Bavaria**, Gollierstr. 9 (Theresienwiese), tel. 501078; **Bonifatiushof**, St-Bonifatius-Str. 4 (Ostbahnhof), tel. 6917105; **Europäischer Hof**, Bayerstr. 31 (Hauptbahnhof), tel. 551510; **Isartor**, Baaderstr. 2-4 (Isartor), tel. 292781; **Renata**, Lämmerstr. 6 (Hauptbahnhof), tel. 292781; **Stefanie**, Türkenstr. 35 (university), tel. 284031.

PENSIONS (DM 60-120): **Armin**, Augustenstr. 5 (Hauptbahnhof), tel. 593197; **Am Karlstor**, Neuhauser Str. 47 (center), tel. 593596; **Am Siegestor**, Akademiestr. 5 (university), tel. 399550/-51; **Diana**, Altheimer Eck 15 (center), tel. 2603107; **Englischer Garten**, Liebergesellstr. 8 (Englischer Garten), tel. 392-034; **Josefihof**, Trivastr. 11 (Neuhausen), tel. 151187; **Westfalia**, Mozartstr. 23 (university clinic), tel. 530377/-78.

INEXPENSIVE: **Bed & Breakfast Service** Carmen Grill, Schulstr. 36, tel. 1688781; **Münchener Mitwohn-Börse**, Georgenstr. 45, tel. 19445 (rooms and apartments for one-month minimum).

CAMPING: **Langwieder See**, Eschenrieder Str. 119, 81249 Munich (on the A8 road), tel. 8641566 (winter camping by reservation); **Obermenzing**, Lochhausener Str. 59, 81247 Munich, tel. 8112235; **Thalkirchen**, Zentralländstr. 49, 81379 Munich, tel. 7231707. All three sites open March 15 to Oct. 31.

YOUTH HOSTELS: **CVJM-Jugendgästehaus** (YMCA), Landwehrstr. 13 (near Hauptbahnhof), tel. 5521410; **Haus International**, Elisabethstr. 87 (Schwabing), tel. 120060; **Jugendhotel Marienherberge**, Goethestr. 9 (near Hauptbahnhof), tel. 555891; **Kolpinghaus St. Theresia**, Hanebergstr. 8 (Neuhausen), tel. 126050; **DJH München**, Wendl-Dietrich-Str. 20 (near Rotkreuzplatz), tel. 131156; **DJH Jugendgästehaus**, Miesingstr. 4 (Thalkirchen), tel. 7236550/-60; **4you münchen** youth hostel, Hirtenstr. 18 (at Hauptbahnhof), tel. 484407.

Arriving By Air

In May 1992, the new *Franz Josef Strauss Airport* near Erding, 24 miles (39 km) north of Munich, came into service. The city can be reached by the S-Bahn line 8 (travel time to Hauptbahnhof: 40 minutes). This runs at 20-minute intervals, from 3:55 a.m. to 12:55 a.m. (Fri-

Sat until 1:35 a.m.) between the airport and Pasing, via the Hauptbahnhof, Karlsplatz (Stachus) and Marienplatz stations. There is also a Lufthansa airport bus from Terminal A to the Hauptbahnhof (about a 45 minute trip) that runs every 20 minutes from 7:55 a.m. to 8:55 p.m. The S-8 train to the airport leaves from Pasing, and stops at the Hauptbahnhof every 20 minutes from 3:22 a.m. to 12:42 a.m. The airport bus also runs every 20 minutes, from 6:50 a.m. to 7:50 p.m., and leaves from the stop at the north entrance to the Hauptbahnhof.

Car Breakdown Service

ACE . . . . tel. 19216
ADAC . . . . tel. 19211
Lübben GmbH . . . . tel. 304569
DTC . . . . tel. 8111212

Car "Pilot" Service

If you are driving to Munich for the first time and are afraid of getting lost, there is a useful service you can make use of: approaching Munich, 2 km from the end of the Stuttgart and Salzburg Autobahns, you will find a *Lotsendienst*, where you can pick up a "pilot" who will guide you to your city destination. The fee is DM 29 for the first hour, DM 19 for each additional hour. English spoken.
Autobahn Salzburg . . . . . tel. 672755
Autobahn Stuttgart . . . . tel. 8112412

Car Rental

Autohansa, Schiessstätterstr. 12 (near Theresienwiese) tel. 504064; *Avis*, toll-free phone: 0130/7733, at Hauptbahnhof, tel. 5502251, at the airport, tel. 975-97600; *Buchbinder*, Dachauer Str. 248 (Moosach), tel. 1492510; *Europcar InterRent*, Arnulfstr. 1 (at Hauptbahnhof), tel. 557145, at the airport, tel. 97597001; *Hertz*, Bahnhofplatz 2 (at Hauptbahnhof), tel. 5502256, at the airport, tel. 978-860; *Sixt Budget*, in the Hauptbahnhof gallery, upstairs, tel. 5502448, at the airport, tel. 97596666, international reservations, tel. 089/666950; *Swing*, Schellingstr. 139 (Schwabing) tel. 5232005.

Changing Money

Exchange offices of the DVKB (*Deutsche Verkehrs- und Kreditbank*): at the Hauptbahnhof, open 6 a.m. to 11 p.m., tel. 5510837; at the airport, open from 6:15 a.m. to 10 p.m., tel. 9701721; *Schmidt's Wechselstube*, Bahnhofsplatz (entrance on Dachauerstr.), tel. 557870; *Wechselstube am Hauptbahnhof,* Schillerstr. 3a, tel. 598236. In addition, all banks, savings-banks *(Sparkassen)* and large post offices exchange currency.

Cinemas

Telephone for information: 11604. Addresses, programs and performance times of cinemas can be found in Munich's daily newspapers.

City Information

City information in the Rathaus (Town Hall), Marienplatz 8, tel. 222324, Mon.-Fri. 10 a.m. to 8 p.m., Sat. 10 a.m. to 4 p.m. *City information at Karlsplatz* (Stachus), underground level, tel. 2336666, Mon. 11 a.m. to 6 p.m., Tue.-Thu. 8:30 a.m. to 6 p.m., Fri. 8:30 a.m. to noon, closed weekends and holidays.
Youth Information Center, Paul-Heyse-Str. 22 (south of the Hauptbahnhof), tel. (after 10 a.m.) 51410660, Mon.-Fri. noon to 6 p.m., Thu. until 8 p.m. Closed weekends and holidays.

City Tours and Sightseeing

Guided tours of the city, with commentary in English and German, can be booked at the following address: *Panorama Tours, Stadtrundfahrten,* Arnulfstr. 8, 80335 Munich, tel. 55028995. The short tour lasts one hour and the long tour 2 1/2 hours. There is a separate tour of Olympia Park. The tours start out from Bahnhofsplatz in front of the Hertie department store, at 10 a.m. and 2:30 p.m. In the summer there is an additional tour,

GUIDELINES

"Munich By Night," including dinner in a Bavarian inn, a trip to a night club and to the Olympia Tower (4 1/2 hours).

Radius Touristik (Hauptbahnhof, platform 31, tel. 596113) provides city tours on foot, by streetcar or by bicycle. *City Hopper Touren*, c/o Stefanie Pokorny, Hohenzollernstr 95, tel. 2721131, specializes in bicycle tours of Munich, as does *Spurwechsel* (tel. 6924699). Walking, bike and streetcar tours that show you the more unusual aspects of Munich, with special activities for children, are offered by *Stadtreisen e.V.*, tel. 54404230.

The Upper Bavarian Tourist Office has information on sightseeing in the countryside around Munich, tel. 8292180.

Climate

Both maritime and continental climatic systems influence the changeable weather in Munich. Its most notable characteristic is the *Föhn*, a warm, dry southerly wind that comes down off the Alps. It is often associated with very clear visibility, which appears to bring the mountains quite close to the city.

Rainfall in Munich is slightly above average and inversion conditions can lead to some smog formation. Ozone values reach their highest levels in summer. The hottest months are June, July and August, and in winter it can be distinctly cold – down to -5°F (-20°C) and below – with heavy snowfalls. The best time to visit Munich is from April through October.

Consulates

Canada: Tal 29, 80331 Munich, tel. 2199570; *United Kingdom:* Bürkleinstr. 10, 80538 Munich, tel. 211090; *USA:* Königinstr. 5, 80539 Munich, tel. 28880. The nearest consulates of Australia and New Zealand are in Bonn.

Emergency Telephone Numbers
AIDS helpline 5446470
Alcoholics Anonymous 555685
Childrens' Helpline . . . 0800/1110333
Drugs: emergency line 7242003
Fire service/doctor 112
Homeopathic
emergency doctor 0172/961011
Medical emergencies 551771
Pharmacy, emergency 594475
Poisons, emergency 19240
Police, emergency 110
Women's helpline 763737
Rescue Service/doctor 777777
Spiritual comfort:
Catholic 0800/1110222
Evangelical 0800/11101
Suicide emergency line 334041
Veterinary emergency 294528

Festivals

In January and February, Munich celebrates *Fasching*, the pre-Lenten carnival. Every seven years the Guild of Barrel-makers perform their traditional *Schäffler* dance, dating back to a medieval plague (next performance in 2005). Starting on March 19 *(Josefitag)* there is the *Starkbierausschank* (strong beer festival) on Nockherberg Hill. April sees a spring fair, the *Auer Dult*, as well as the *Frühlingsfest* on Theresienwiese, which runs in to May, the time of the *Maibock ausschank* (May bock beer festival).

On alternate years, in June, there is the Munich *Biennale* of music and drama. Annually in June is the *Tollwood Festival* of handicrafts, culture and entertainment, followed in late June/early July by the week-long *Munich Film Festival*. In July there is the *Opera Festival*, the outdoor *Freiluftkonzerte* concerts in the fountain courtyard of the Residenz, the *Magdalenenfest* in Hirschgarten Park (Nymphenburg) and a medieval tournament, the *Ritterturnier*, in Kaltenberg (S-Bahn line 4 to Geltendorf). In late July comes the *Jakobi-Dult* fair in the Au district, a variation of the Auer Dult. August is the time for traditional festivals in the towns around Munich, like Freising, Erding and Dachau.

From mid-September to the first Sunday in October, Munich is taken over by the legendary *Oktoberfest*. October also sees yet another fair in the Au, this one called the *Kirchweihdult*. In December, the famous *Christkindlmarkt* on Marienplatz puts everyone in a Christmas mood, while on Rotkreuzplatz there is a small but charming Christmas Fair. December also sees the Winter Tollwood on the grounds of the former container station.

Further details about these events can be found in the official calendar of events in Munich *(Veranstaltungskalender)*, available at news stands.

Lost and Found

Items lost on main-line trains: *Fundbüro der Bundesbahn*, Hauptbahnhof, Bahnhofplatz 2, tel. 13086664. Items lost on S-Bahn (city and suburban) trains: *Fundbüro im Ostbahnhof,* tel. 13084409. Items lost on buses, streetcars, U-Bahn, or in the street: *Fundbüro in der Stadtverwaltung,* Arnulfstr. 31, tel. 124080. Items lost in Post Offices or telephone booths: *Fundbüro der Bundespost*, Arnulfstr. 195 (Room 103), 80634 Munich, tel. 12221552.

Media

The main Munich newspapers are the *Süddeutsche Zeitung*, *Münchner Merkur*, *Abendzeitung* and *Tageszeitung*. *Munich Found*, a monthly magazine in English, can keep you up to date on English-language films, plays and events in the city. It is available at news stands in the Hauptbahnhof, and others around town.

Voice of America radio broadcasts to Central Europe in English off and on throughout the day and night on the AM band at 1197, though sometimes they switch abruptly to broadcasts in Czech or Slovak. *BBC World Service* broadcasts can be picked up on AM sometimes at 648, and on the following short-wave bands, depending on the time of day: 6.195, 9.410 and 12.095. *Relax FM* (92.4 FM), a light jazz station, broadcasts a few minutes of *CNN Radio News* in English once an hour on the half hour.

Munich in Figures

The city of Munich covers a total area of 194 square miles (310 sq km). The distance from north to south is 16 miles (26 km) and from east to west 13 miles (21 km). During the city's last census, taken Dec. 31, 1994, the population of the 41 city districts was 1.3 million, of which some 21% were foreign citizens.

Opening Times / Business Hours

The larger stores in the city center are open Monday through Friday from 9 a.m. to 8 p.m., and on Saturday from 8:30 a.m. to 4 p.m. Some smaller shops open as early as 7:30 a.m. Since new business hours were introduced a few years ago, some of the smaller shops, which used to close at 6:30 p.m., now stay open as late as the bigger ones although, expecially outside the city center, many smaller shops still stick to the older opening times (i.e., Mon.-Fri. unil 6 or 6:30 p.m., Sat. until 2 p.m.)

Shops in the underground mall at the Hauptbahnhof are open every day from 8 a.m. (some open as early as 6 a.m.) to 11 p.m. (though some of them close as early as 9 p.m.).

Banks are normally open Mon.-Fri. from 8:30 a.m. to 12:30 p.m. and from 1:30 p.m. to 3:45 p.m. (Thu. until 5:30 p.m.). Branches of Citibank (e.g., on Sonnenstrasse near Sendlinger Tor) are open from 9 a.m. to 6 p.m.

Post offices throughout the city are open Mon.-Fri. 8 a.m. to noon and 3 p.m. to 6 p.m., Sat. 8 a.m. to noon. In the city center they are mostly open Mon.-Fri. continously from 8 a.m. to 6 p.m. The Post Office inside the Hauptbahnhof is open until 8 p.m.

Most museums in Munich are open Tue.-Sun. from 10 a.m. to 5 p.m., They are closed on Monday and public holidays (for precise opening hours see Guidepost "Museums" on p. 183).

Parking Lots, Multi-story
City Center: *Am Färbergraben 5*, 520 spaces, Mon.-Sat. 7 a.m. to midnight, closed Sun./hol., enter via Altheimer Eck, tel. 266177; *Am Stachus*, 450 spaces, Mon.-Sat. 7 a.m. to midnight, Sun./hol. 1 p.m. to midnight, enter via Goethestr./Bayerstr./Schillerstr., tel. 594-961; *beim Kaufhaus Karstadt-Oberpollinger*, Neuhauser Str. 44; *Garage am Deutschen Theater*, Schwanthalerstr. 10; underground garage at the *National Theater*. **Haidhausen**: *Motorama,* Hochstr. 3, 81669 Munich; underground garage at the *Gasteig*, Rosenheimer Str. 5. **Schwabing**: *Parkgarage Schwabing*, Occamstr. 18; near Hertie dep't store on Leopoldstrasse (Münchener Freiheit).

Public Transport
There is a unified fare-structure covering *S-Bahn* (suburban trains) *U-Bahn* (underground/subway), buses and *Strassenbahnen* (streetcars). It is operated by the *MVV*, Thierschstr. 2, 80538 Munich, tel. 210330. The city area is divided into two concentric fare-zones, and there are three further zones extending to the outer suburbs. The inner zones are marked in blue on the zone-maps in U-Bahn and S-Bahn stations. Before boarding a train, bus or streetcar, you must validate your ticket in the punching-machine *(Entwerter)*. If you have bought a strip of tickets *(Streifenkarte)* and are traveling outside the blue zone, find out how many strips you need to punch for any given destination. To travel within the central area, you need to use two strips (you only have to punch the second one) or a single-fare ticket. If you are going four stops or less (a maximum of two of which can be by S-Bahn or U-Bahn), you only have to punch one strip or use a *Kurzstrecke* (short trip) single-fare ticket, which is about half the price of a normal fare.

Children (and dogs) travel at reduced fares and, in the summer tourist season, the MVV makes special offers, e.g., a combined MVV and lake ticket (the *Kombikarte*, running from late May to mid-October), which in addition to train travel lets you take the excursion steamers on Starnberger See and Ammersee.

For short visits, a *Tageskarte* is recommended, either for the inner zone only, or for the whole MVV area. This gives you one day's unlimited travel Mondays to Fridays from 9 a.m. onward, and all day at weekends and public holidays. There is a *Single-Tageskarte* for one person and a *Partner-Tageskarte* for two adults and up to three children. Bicycles may be taken on S-Bahn and U-Bahn trains outside of peak commuting times (which are posted in the trains).

Single and multiple tickets and *Tageskarten* can be bought from automatic ticket-machines at S-Bahn and U-Bahn stations, at MVV sales points, e.g., in the underground concourse of the Hauptbahnhof, at Karlsplatz (Stachus), Marienplatz, or at newsstands.

When punching your ticket, be careful to note the area and time period for which the ticket is valid, and remember that once punched, a ticket (other than a *Tageskarte*) can only be used in one direction. For a return trip a new ticket must be punched.

Night owls are serviced hourly (half-hourly on weekends) from 1 a.m. to about 4 a.m. by special night buses and streetcars. The stops (in the center, for example, at the Hauptbahnhof, Karlsplatz and Sendlinger Tor) can be recognized by a sign with a large "N" on it.

Night streetcars: N17 from Amalienburgstr. to Effnerplatz; N19 from Pasing to St.-Veit-Str.; N20 from Moosach to Sendlinger Tor; N27 from Peeulring to Grosshesseloher Brücke.

Night buses: N33 from Keilberthstr. to Parkstadt Solln; N54 from Münchener Freiheit to Johanneskirchen; N68 from

Münchener Freiheit to Kemptener Str.; N81 from Münchener Freiheit to Dülferstr. via Peteulring; N95 from Ostbahnhof to Neuperlach.

Note: There are random ticket inspections, and traveling without a valid ticket can result in a heavy fine.

Ride Sharing *(Mitfahrzentralen)*

In Germany, people making long car journeys alone often register with a *Mitfahrzentrale*, so that others heading the same way can travel in the car and share the cost of gas and tolls. In Munich, you can apply to the following places, either as a driver or passenger: *McShare*, Lämmerstr. 4 (near the Hauptbahnhof), tel. 594561; *Känguruh*, Amalienstr. 87 (Schwabing, in Amalien Passage), tel. 19444.

Sport

The *Städtisches Sportamt* (City Sports Office), Neuhauser Str. 26, 80331 Munich, tel. 2336224 and 2338715, provides information on sports facilities and events in Munich.

Mountain climbers should apply to the *Deutscher Alpenverein*, Service Office at the Hauptbahnhof, Goethestr. 21, 80336 Munich, tel. 555051/-2.

Great fun for larger groups (up to about 50 people) is a **Raft trip down the Isar**, from Wolfratshausen to Thalkirchen; advance booking is essential (sometimes as much as six months in advance!). Bookings from *Flösserebetrieb Seitner*, tel. 08171/18320, from *bavaria euroraft*, Heubergstr. 6a, 82441 Ohlstadt, tel. 08841/7751, fax 79413, or through a travel agency, for example, *ABR*, Landshuter Allee 38, tel. 1204481.

Golfers should apply to: *Bayerischer Golf-Verband*, c/o Peter von Winkler, Moosacherstr. 80, 80809 Munich, tel. 3520642, or directly to individual golfclubs in Munich. Here is a selection: *Münchner Golf-Club e.V.*, Tölzer Str., 82064 Strasslach, tel. 08170-450; *Golf-Club Olching e.V.*, Feurstr. 89, 82140 Olching, tel. 08142-3240; Golf-Club Iffeldorf, Gut Rettenberg, 82393 Iffeldorf, tel. 08856-81809.

Horses play an important part in Munich life: an amusing afternoon can be spent at the trotting races at *Daglfing*, tel. 9300010, easily reached by the S-Bahn line 8 to Daglfing. For regular horseracing, contact the (former) Olympic riding course at Riem, tel. 907061.

For **bicyclists**, Munich offers enormous choice: not only can you take your bike on S-Bahn and U-Bahn trains outside peak hours, but there are many bicycle rental firms in Munich and the surounding area. General information can be obtained from the *ADFC* (German Cycle Club) in the Radlerhaus, Steinstr. 17, tel. 4801001. You can rent bikes from: *Radius Touristik*, Arnulfstr. 3 (Hauptbahnhof), tel. 596113; *Fahrradverleih* (bicycle rental) at the Englischen Garten entrance on Veterinärstr., tel. 282500 or 596113. You can also hire bikes at the following S-Bahn stations: Aying (S1), Freising (S1), Fürstenfeldbruck (S4), Geltendorf (S4), Herrsching (S5), Holzkirchen (S2), Starnberg (S6), Tutzing (S6). Information about bicycle tours in the area can be obtained from the Munich Tourist Office, in the Hauptbahnhof, and at branch offices (addresses p. 248). Bicyclist's guides to the area are available in many bookshops.

For **sailing** and **windsurfing**, the relevant body to contact is the *Deutscher Seglerverband*, Georg-Brauchle-Ring 93, 80992 Munich, tel. 1574672. The large lakes around Munich are wonderful for sailing and wind-surfing.

You can play **tennis** on courts of all kinds, all over Munich. The big sports stores like *Sport-Scheck* are happy to give information, or you can apply to tennis-schools, e.g., *Park Club Nymphenburg*, Stievestr. 15, 80638 Munich, tel. 782055, or *TSC Moosach*, Günzburger Str. 46, tel. 1492875.

GUIDELINES

Winter sports: Information on snow conditions can be obtained from the *ADAC-Schneetelefon*, tel. 76762556, or the *Deutscher Alpenverein* (Alpin-Auskunft) tel. 294940. From October to June, you can go skating at the *Olympia Ice Stadium* and the *Prinzregenten Stadium*.

Swimming – in Lakes

Deininger Weiher, near Strasslach, south of Munich, is a lake set in moorland where the water is usually warm. In winter you can skate there. *Ebersberger Klostersee* is another moorland lake, which can be reached by car or by the S-Bahn line 5 to Ebersberg. *Echinger See* is a former gravel-pit, with a large, grassy sunbathing area; car or S-Bahn line 1 to Eching. *Feldmochinger See* is a very attractive large lake north of Munich. It has a water play-area for children and barbecue facilities. Take the S-Bahn line 1 to Fasanerie of Feldmoching stations, from where it is a short walk. If you are driving, there are plenty of parking spaces. *Feringa-See* is the place to go if you want to swim or windsurf in the nude. A peninsula is reserved for this purpose. Take the S-Bahn line 8 to Unterföhring, then it is just over a mile's walk (2 km). Parking space is usually hard to find close to the lake. *Heimstettener See* is a gravel-pit lake east of Munich with a restaurant and sunbathing area; S-Bahn line 6 to Feldkirchen, or by car. *Karlsfelder See* is a large bathing lake between Dachau and Karlsfeld, only accessible by car or bicycle. *Kranzberger See* is a lake near Kranzberg, about 18 miles (30 km) from Munich, with leisure area, suitable for families. Can only be reached by car or bicycle. *Lerchenauer See* is Munich's "local lake," easily reached by No. 81 or No. 83 bus, to the "Lerchenauer See" stop. Snack-restaurant and sports facilities available. *Olchinger See* is a gravel-pit lake near Olching; S-Bahn line 3 to Olching, or by car or cycle. *Unterföhringer See* is a small lake in meadowland near the Isar, with a restaurant and children's play-area. S-Bahn line 8 to Unterföhring, then just over a one-mile (2 km) walk.

Swimming – Outdoor / Indoor Pools

The outdoor pools operated by the city of Munich are open weekdays from May to early September from 10 a.m. to 6 p.m., weekends and holidays from 9 a.m. to 6 p.m. When the weather is good, the

RAPID TRANSIT WITH THE MVV

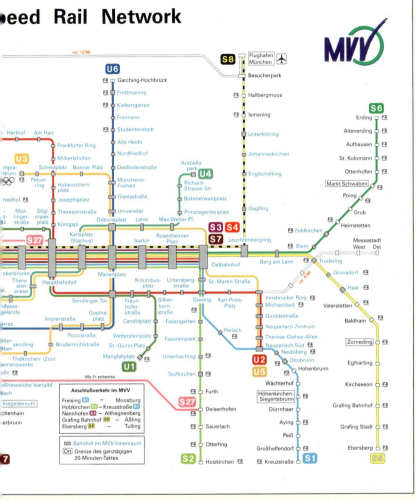

pools stay open from May to July until 8:30 p.m., and in August until 8 p.m. Entry until one hour before closing time.

Outdoor Pools: *Dantebad*, Dantestr. 6, (Neuhausen) tel. 23617981 (also heated – 85°F/30°C – in winter; entrance at Postillonstr. 17); *Georgenschwaige*, Belgradstr. 195 (Milbertshofen), tel. 309913; *Maria Einsiedel*, Zentralländstr. 28 (Thalkirchen), tel. 7231401; *Michaelibad*, Heinrich-Wieland-Str. 16 (Ramersdorf), tel. 407691; *Prinzregentenbad*, Prinzregentenstr. 80 (Bogenhausen), tel. 474808; *Schyrenbad*, Claude-Lorrain-Str. 24 (Au), tel. 653715; *Sommerbad Allach*, Eversbuschstr. 213 (Allach), tel. 8125427; *Sommerbad West*, Weinbergerstr. 11 (Pasing), tel. 885441; *Ungererbad*, Traubestr. 3 (Schwabing), tel. 369842.

Indoor Pools: *Cosima-Wellenbad*, Cosimastr. 5 (Bogenhausen), tel. 911790;

Hallenbad Forstenrieder Park, Stäblistr. 27b (Forstenried), tel. 756057; Hallenbad Giesing-Harlaching, Klausenerstr. 22 (Giesing), tel. 6925517; *Müller'sches Volksbad*, Rosenheimer Str. 1 (Lehel), tel. 23613434; *Nordbad*, Schleissheimer Str. 142 (Schwabing), tel. 23617941; *Olympia-Schwimmhalle*, Olympiapark, Spiridon-Louis-Ring 21 (Olympiapark), tel. 30672290; *Südbad*, Valleystr. 37 (Sendling), tel. 761569; *Westbad*, Weinbergerstr. 11 (Pasing), tel. 885441.

Taxis

To book a taxi, call the control center at 21610 or 19410; if you want a collection or delivery made, call 216157 or 264220. For large groups, mini-buses and station-wagon taxis are available on request. Taxis cost a base DM 3.60 plus DM 2.20 per kilometer; from the airport to the center costs about DM 90.

Telecommunications

The Post Office inside the Hauptbahnhof is open: Mon. to Fri. 7 a.m. to 8 p.m., Sat. 8 a.m. to 4 p.m. and Sun./hol. 9 a.m. to 5 p.m.. There are phone booths where you can make a call by leaving a deposit, from which the cost of the call is deducted afterwards. There are also 20 card phones, two coin phones and a credit-card phone (all major credit cards). There is also a fax machine, and check cashing and currency exchange.

Calls within the Munich area can be made from any street phone, most of which are now card phones. Phone cards for DM 12 or DM 50 can be bought at any post office, at many kiosks, and at the advance ticket outlet in the Marienplatz U-Bahn station. The number for international directory enquiries is 11834. For numbers within Germany, 11833.

Tourist Information

Tourist information is provided by the *Fremdenverkehrsamt der Stadt München* (Munich City Tourist Office) at its various branch offices: Sendlinger Str. 1, tel. 2330300; Hauptbahnhof, Bahnhofplatz (beside main entrance), tel. 23330256; at the airport, tel. 2330300. Regional tourist information is provided by the *Fremdenverkehrsverband Oberbayern*, tel. 8292180. For information about trade fairs, exhibitions and conferences, tel. 23330070. Public transport information is provided by the Munich transit authority, *MVV*, Thierschstr. 2, tel. 210330.

Trade Fairs

Messe München GmbH, Messegelände, 81823 Munich, tel. 94920720, fax. 94921419, provides information on the major trade fairs and exhibitions in Munich. They also have an Internet site at http://www.messe-muenchen.de – the new exhibition ground will be accessible by U-Bahn beginning in June 1999.

What to Wear

In summer you should wear light clothing, but always keep a raincoat or umbrella near at hand because of the frequent rain showers. In winter, a warm overcoat or anorak is essential, together with strong waterproof footwear. In spring and autumn you should be prepared for chilly or wet days.

As regards style, you can wear whatever you like in Munich. Only in a few high-class bars and restaurants is formal dress required.

AUTHORS

Andreas Ascher lives in Munich and works as a freelance writer. The articles "All About Beer," "The Oktoberfest," "Munich, City of Fairs" and "Munich's 'Silicon Valley'" were written by him.

Joachim Chwaszcza is a freelance writer and photographer. He wrote the chapter "Royal Splendor and Everyday Life" and, together with May Hoff, about dining in Munich.

AUTHORS / PHOTOGRAPHERS

Petra Englmeier composed the segments "Schlachthofviertel" and "Glockenbachviertel," and is co-author of "In the Au" and "Giesing."

Brigitte Henninges is a freelance travel journalist and photographer who lives in Munich. She has an intimate knowledge of the city, and provided us with the segments on cultural life and night-life in Munich.

Peter Herrmann, the project editor of this book, was born in Munich and is a freelance writer.

Gert Hirner, a freelance travel journalist, photographer and author of travel guides, wrote the "Schwabing" chapter.

May Hoff lives in Munich and works as a travel journalist and editor. She wrote the segments "Museums," "Shopping," "Wittelsbachs and Fuggers," "Monasteries, Castles and Lakes," "Mountains and Lakes" and, together with Joachim Chwaszcza, "Eating Out."

Hans and Inge Obermann work as freelance writers in Munich. They wrote the feature "The Middle Ages Brought to Life."

Andrea Russ works as a freelance writer and editor in Munich. She wrote the segments "Gärtnerplatz" and "Munich for Kids."

Dr. Sabine Tzschaschel received her doctorate in Social Geography in Munich. In this book she reports on the various sections of Munich's city center.

Rainer Vestner is a freelance writer and photographer. He wrote the segments "Munich Life," "Lehel," "Haidhausen," "Bogenhausen," "The Shimmering Isar," "On the Ski Slopes," "The Notorious 'Föhn'," "Land of Five Lakes," and was co-author of "In the Au" and "Giesing."

PHOTOGRAPHERS

Angermayer, Margot 192
Archiv für Kunst und Geschichte, Berlin 14, 17, 18, 19, 23L, 23R, 24L, 24R, 26, 28, 30, 174
Beck, Josef cover
Bugdoll, Eddie / Freelance Press 187
Chwaszcza, Joachim 12, 21, 27, 50, 84-85, 138, 160, 163, 164, 170-171, 178, 184, 226, 227, 234, 236, 238
Eising, Peter / LOOK 35, 81, 110, 125, 150, 151, 159, 162, 165, 165, 199
Gronau, Emanuel 22, 120-121, 129, 130, 131, 189, 218-219, 221, 222, 223, 228
Gross, Andreas M. 42-43, 92
Grosse, Heinz 68
Haake, Conny 173
Halliday, Anthony 155
Henninges, Heiner 194-195, back cover
Hinze, Peter 40-41, 71, 204
Janicke, Volkmar 235
Kantner, Claudia 136, 167
Kappelhoff, Marlis 237
Kiwitt, Eckhardt 235, back cover
Kunert, Rainer E. 34, 105, 108, 113, 116, 202, 207
Nicolaus, Gisela 166, 180
Priegnitz, Jürgen 216
Radkai, Marton 8-9, 48, 77, 79, 97, 103, 104, 107, 109, 111, 117, 142-143, 144, 177, 179
Reuther, Jörg 210, 231
Schiffl-Deiler, Marianne 76
Schneider, Günther 51, 114, 132, 190, 191, 230
Schwarz, Berthold 57, 69, 72, 90, 139, 148, 152, 157, 176, 182, 212
Seer, Ulli / LOOK 10-11, 15, 33, 205
Simon, Gerd 52, 106, 146, 198
Skupy-Pesek, Jitka 39, 60, 188
Srzentic, Robert 16, 36, 37, 80, 96, 112, 122, 158, 196, 200, 203
Stadler, Hubert 59, 65, 66, 73, 91, 94, 103, 185, 214, 215, 220
Stadtarchiv München 31
Thomas, Martin 44, 54, 56, 58, 86, 93, 128, 154, 172, 201
Vestner, Heinz 137
Vestner, Rainer 38, 55, 62, 63, 67, 78, 99, 101, 149, 156, 186, 229
Weissfuss, Heinz 211
Weithase, Gert 118, 217, 239.

INDEX

A

Ainmillerstrasse 110, 112
Akademie der Bildenden Künste 94
Albrecht III, Duke 17, 131
Albrecht IV, Duke 18, 80
Albrecht V, Duke 19, 68, 76
Allerheiligen-Kirche am Kreuz 73
Alpine Museum of the DAV 152, 183
Alte Pinakothek 24, 90, 97, 175
Alter Hof 14, 15, 75
Alter Nördlicher Friedhof 96
Alter Peter 58-59, 193
Alter Simpl 95
Alter Südlicher Friedhof 146
Altes Hackerhaus 70, 186, 211
Altes Rathaus 58
Altheimer Eck 54
Alt-Schwabing 106-111
Altstadtring 62, 78, 152, 181
Amalienpassage 94
Amalienstrasse 94
Ammersee, lake 222, 225
  Andechs Monastery 16, 225
  Collegiate Church of St. Maria 225
  Herrsching 225
  Schondorf 225
  Utting 225
Antiquities collection 175
Arabellapark 166
Arbeitsamt 145
Arcade 54
Arco auf Valley, Count 29
Arco-Zinneberg Palace 99
Asam, Cosmas Damian 64, 71-72, 81, 149, 238
Asam, Hans Georg 231
Asam, E. Q. 59, 71-72, 149, 238
Asamhof 72
Asam House 71
Asamkirche 71
Au 156-158
Auer Dult, fair 156, 157, 214
Auer, Erhard 29
Auer Mühlbach 156
Augsburg 13, 17, 221
  Augustus-Brunnen 221
  Evan. St. Ulrich's Church 221
  Fuggerei 221
  Hercules Fountain 221
  Maximilianstrasse 221
  Mercury Fountain 221
  Perlach Tower 221
  Rathaus 221
  St. Peter 221
  St. Ulrich and Afra 221
Augustiner-Bräu 53
Augustiner-Keller 140, 193

B

Baaderstrasse 155
Bad Reichenhall 237
Bad Tölz 233
  Kreuzkirche 233
  Marktstrasse 233
Bad Wiessee 234
Bamberger Haus 114
Barelli, Agostino 87, 123
Baroque, archictectural style 24, 55, 59, 87, 220, 233
Bavaria Monument 134
Bavarian Radio 30
Bavarian State Chancellery 90
Bavarian State Orchestra 199
Bavarian State Library 91
Bayerisches (Bavarian) National Museum 150, 181, 183, 193
Bayerischzell 234
Bavarian Beer-Purity Law 186
Beckenbauer, Franz 159
Behmishc, Günther 114
Beer gardens 187-189
Benedictines 13, 225, 231, 238
Benediktbeuren 231
Benediktenwand 231
Berchtesgadener Land 237
Bernauer, Agnes 17
Bernheimer House 50
Blauer Reiter (Blue Rider Group) 28, 98, 175
Blumenstrasse 66
Blutenburg, castle 131
BMW Headquarters Building 114
BMW Museum 114, 182, 193
Bögner (see Paulaner im Tal)
Bogenhausen 165-167
Bogenhausener Kirchplatz 167
Bordeaux Platz 163
Botanical Gardens 131
Bräuhausstrasse 62
Branca, Alexander von 177
Briennerstrasse 87, 98
Bürgersaal 53
Bürklein, Friedrich 151

C

Center for Unusual Museums (ZAM: Zentrum für Aussergewöhnliche Museen) 63, 178, 183, 193
Chamber Pot Museum 179
Chiemsee, lake **235-237**
Classicism 24, 77, 81, 87-88, 92-93, 98, 175
Concordia Garden 188
Coopers 16, 57
Corkscrew Museum 179
Cornelius Bridge 154
Cornelius, Peter 92
Council of Workers and Soldiers 29
Crailsham Palace 108
Cuvilliés, François, the Elder 77, 81, 87, 129, 197
Cuvilliés Theater 24, 39, 77, 197

D

Dachau 31, **220-221**
  Concentration camp 221
  Schloss 220
Dallmayr, delicatessen 165, 185
Delp, Father Alfred 31-32
Deutscher Alpenverein 152
Deutsches Jagd- und Fischerei Museum 53,177, 193
Deutsches Museum 27, 30, 154, 156, **179-180**, 192
  Flugwerft Schleissheim 180
Deutsches Theater 49, 200
Doll Museum 183
Donisl 186
Dorn, Dieter 198
Dreifaltigkeitskirche 81

E

Easter Bunny Museum 179
Effner, Joseph 80
Eggstätter Seenplatte 236
Einstein, Albert 146
Eisner, Kurt 29
Elisabethplatz 113, 185
Elisenhof 48
Englischer Garten 21-22, 102, **116-118**, 188
  Aumeister 118-119, 169, 188
  Carousel 118, 193
  Chinesischer Turm 22, 39, 117-118, 188, 193
  Eisbach 117
  Hirschau 118, 188
  Japanisches Teehaus 117
  Kleinhesseloher See 118, 193
  Monopteros 117
  Rumford Monument 117
  Rumford Schlössl 118
  Seehaus 118
Epp, Franz Xaver, knight 29
Ernst, Duke 17, 18
Ettstrasse 54
European Patent Office 155
Everding, August 198

F

Färbergraben 54
Fasching, carnival 65
Fassbinder, Rainer W. 167
Feierwerk 206

INDEX

Feilitzschstrasse 106
Feinkost-Käfer 48, 165, 185, 211
Feldherrnhalle 24-25, 30-31, 87
Ferdinand Maria, Elector 20, 128
Feuchtwanger, Lion 149
Fischbrunnen 57
Fischer, Johann Michael 231
Fischer, Karl von 23, 78, 93
Flaucher 156, 173
Föhn 217
Forum der Technik 180, 183
Franziskaner Poststüberl 78
Franz-Joseph-Strasse 110
Franz Marc Museum 231
Franz-Prüller-Strasse 12 157
Frauenchiemsee, monastery 236
Frauenkirche 17, 19, 55
Fraunhofer 147
Freibank 66
Freising 16, 238
  Bestiensäule 238
  Bishop's Palace 238
  Korbinian Bell 238
  St. Benedict's 238
  St. Johannis' 238
  St. Maria and Korbinian's 238
  Weihenstephan 213, 238
French Quarter 164
Friedensengel (Angel of Peace) 27, 166
Friedrichstrasse 112
Frundsberg 126
Führer Buildings 31
Fünf-Seen-Land 222-225
Füssen 228-229
Fugger 220-221

G

Gärtner, Friedrich von 24, 87, 91-93
Gärtnerplatz 155
Gärtnerplatzviertel 154-155
Gärtnerplatz Theater 39, 155, 198
Ganghofer, Jörg (see Halspach)
Garmisch-Partenkirchen 230
Gasteig Cultural Center 160, 162, 199, 209
  Aspekte Gallery 162
  Black Box 199, 209
  Carl Orff Hall 199
  Munich Philharmonic 199
  Philharmonie 160, 209
  Richard-Strauss-Konservatorium 160, 199
  Stadtbibliothek 160
Geiselgasteig 35, 193
Georg Maier's Gasthof Iberl 201
George, Stefan 34, 102
Geschwister-Scholl-Platz 92
Giesing 158-159

Gise Palace 80
Glockenbach 146-148
Glockenspiel (in Rathaus) 57
Glyptothek 24, 98, 175
Goebbels, Joseph 31, 181
Goetheplatz 145
Gollierplatz 136
Gothic, architectural style 55, 59, 69, 80, 131, 221, 237
Graf, Oskar Maria 167, 223
Graf Spreti Palace 80
Graggenauer-Viertel 61
Grasser, Erasmus 18, 58-59, 69
Günther, Ignaz 167, 222, 231
Gunetzrhainer, Johann 107
Gunetzrhainer House 81

H

Hackenstrasse 71
Hackenviertel 70-75
Hackerbrücke 125
HAI (theater) 203
Haidhausen 37, 61, **160-165**
Haimhauser Strasse 107
Halspach, Jörg von 17, 55, 73
Hans-Sachs-Strasse 147
Harras 139
Harry's Manhattan Bar 205
Hartlieb, Johann 17
Hauberisser, Georg von 133
Hauberisser House 134
Hauptbahnhof (Main Station) 45
Haus der Kunst 31, 117, 149, 181
Heiliggeist-Kirche 63
Heiliggeiststrasse 64
Heilig-Kreuz-Kirche 158
Henry the Lion 13, 102, 160
Hellabrunn, see Zoo
Heppel & Ettlich 202
Herbergsviertel 157
Herrenchiemsee, island 27, 235
Herzog Park 167
Herzogstand 231
Herzogstrasse 109
Hesse, Hermann 28
High Tech Industry 34, 215
Hildebrandt, Dieter 107, 202
Hinterhof Theater 202
Hirschau 188
Hirschgarten 127, 188, 193
Hitler, Adolf 29-32, 162, 237
Hitler Putsch 29-30
Hochschule für Musik 97
Höllentalklamm 231
Hofbräuhaus 30, 61, 186, 189
Hofgarten 88-90, 181
Hohenpeissenberg 228
Hohenschwangau, castle 229
Hohenzollernstrasse 111, 184
Holbeinstrasse 166
Holnstein Palace 80

Hotel Bayerischer Hof 81
Hotel Kempinski Vier Jahreszeiten 79
Huber, Kurt 32
Hugendubel, book stores 51, 185
Hundskugel 71, 186, 211
Hypobank Building 167

I

Ignaz Günther House 70, 178
IMAX, cinema 180, 183, 192
Isar, river 13, 36, 172-173
Isartor 62
Isarvorstadt 154

J

Jesuits 19, 53
Jews 14, 17
Johannis Café 163
Johannisplatz 163
Jonas, Bruno 202
Josephspitalstrasse 73
Jugendstil, architectural style 28, 79, 93, 98, 102, 109, 112, 124, 166, 175
Jungfernturmstrasse 81

K

Kabelsteg, bridge 152
Kästner, Erich 104, 167
Kaffee Giesing 159, 207
Kaiserstrasse 109
Kammerspiele 79, 198
Kandinsky, Wassily 28, 34, 102, 110, 112, 175
Kapuzinerplatz 145
Kardinal-Faulhaber-Strasse 80
Karl Albrecht, Elector 21
Karlsplatz, see Stachus
Karlstadt, Liesl 66, 167
Karlstor 23, 51-52
Karl Theodor, Elector 21-22, 49, 90, 116-117, 176
Karl Valentin Fountain 66
Karolinenplatz 98
Kaufinger Tor 56
Kaufingerstrasse 56
Kaulbach, August 27
Kazmair, Jörg 16
Kehlstein House 237
Kinder und Jugend Museum 183, 193
King Ludwig Museum 236
Klee, Paul 28, 95, 102, 106, 112
Kleine Komödie 200, 209
Klenze, Leo von 24, 77, 87-88, 90-91, 98-99, 117, 134, 175
Klenzestrasse 155
Klosterkirche St. Anna 149

251

INDEX

Kochelsee, lake 231
Königsplatz 31, 98, 175
Königssee, lake 237
Kolb, Annette 167
Komödie im Bayer. Hof 200
Kreuzviertel 79
Krone Circus 124, 193
Künstlerhaus a. Lenbachplatz 51
Kunstbau 175, 183
Kunsthalle der Hypo-Kulturstiftung 80, 181
Kunstpark Ost 163-164, 203, 206, 209
Kurfürstenplatz 112

L

Landauer, Gustav 29, 159
Landshut 238-239
 Burg Trausnitz 238
 Grasberger House 239
 Landshuter Fürstenhochzeit 239
 Martinskirche 238
 Narrentreppe 239
 Pappenberger House 239
 Rathaus 239
 Rosenkranz-Madonna 238
 Stadtresidenz 239
Lechner, Johann Baptist 118
Ledigenheim 137
Lehel 37, **149-154**
Lehmkuhl, book store 110
Leinberger, Hans 238
Lenbach, Franz von 27, 98, 150, 165, 175
Lenbachhaus 98
Lenbachplatz 50-51
Lenin, Vladimir 29, 34, 102, 110
Leopold Park 110
Leopoldstrasse 93, **103-104**, 184
Leuchtenberg Palace 90
Levien, Max 29
Leviné, Eugen 29, 159
Liesl Karlstadt Fountain 66
Linderhof Palace 27, 229
Lindwurmstrasse 139, 145
Literaturhaus 80
Littmann, Max 79, 165
Lock Museum 179
Löwenbräu-Keller 124, 186, 189
Löwenhof Passage 56
Löwenturm 59
Ludendorff, Erich, General 30
Ludwig the Rich 92
Ludwig the Stern 14
Ludwig I, King 23-25, 77, 80, 87, 91-93, 98, 117, 129, 175, 187, 190, 192
Ludwig II, King 26-27, 53, 197, 223, 229, 235
Ludwig III, King 29
Ludwig IV (Ludwig the Bavarian), Duke 14-15, 56, 63, 81
Ludwig X, Duke 239
Ludwig-Maximilian University 92, 93
Ludwigsbrücke 156
Ludwigskirche 92
Ludwigstrasse 87, **90-93**
Ludwig-Vorstadt 24
Lüftmalerei 230
Lueg-ins-Land 62
Luitpold, Prince Regent 27
Luitpold Park 114
Lukaskirche 152
Lustspielhaus 202

M

Macke, August 28, 175
Main Post Office 75
Mann, Thomas 28, 30, 34, 102, 106, 156, 167, 197
Marc, Franz 28, 95, 175
Maria-Hilf-Kirche 157
Maria-Hilf-Platz 157
Mariannenplatz 152
Maria-Trost-Kirche 127
Marienhof 58
Marienplatz 37, 51, **56-58**, 177-178
Mariensäule 57
Marionette Theater 192
Marktfrau Fountain 66
Marmorhaus 110
Marstall Theater 79, 198, 208
Matthäus-Kirche 73
Maxburg 81
Max-Emanuel-Brauerei 96, 201
Max Emanuel, Elector 19-20, 128, 176, 220, 238
Max I Joseph (Max IV Joseph), King 22-23, 75, 92-93, 117
Max II 26
Max III Joseph, Elector 21, 87
Maximilian I, Elector 21-22, 75, 117
Maximilian II, King 26, 66, 78, 151, 220, 229
Maximilianeum 26, 78, 151
Maximilianstrasse 78-79, 151
Max Joseph Bridge 167
Max-Joseph-Platz 75, 78
Maxvorstadt 24, **93-99**
Max-Weber-Platz 163
Max-Zwo-Monument 79, 151
Mayer, Rupert 31, 53
Maypole 139, 162
Menterschwaige 188
Messe, trade fair 214
Messegelände, old exhibition ground 136
Meyrink, Gustav 28

Michaelskirche 53
Michl, Willy 173
Middle Ring Road 125
Miller, Ferdinand von 87, 134
Miller, Oskar von 127, 179
Mineralogical Collection 97
Mittenwald 231
Modernes Theater 147, 201
Montez, Lola 25, 129
Montgelas Palace 81
Morris Dancers 18, 58, 69, 178
Moshammer, Rudolph 184
Moy Palace 88
Mozart, Wolfgang Amadeus 197
Mühsam, Erich 28-29, 102
Müllersches Volksbad 152, 162
Münchener Freiheit 102, 105
Münchner Isar-Brettl 201
Münchner Kunstverein 90
Münchner Lach- und Schiessgesellschaft 107, 202
Münchner Lustspielhaus 108
Münter, Gabriele 110, 112, 175
Munich Bach Choir 200
Munich Bach Orchestra 200
Munich Film Festival 203
Museum of Ethnology 151, 182
Museum Mensch und Natur 182, 193
Mustersiedlung Neuhausen 127

N

Napoleon I, Emperor 22
National Museum 27
National Theater 39, 78, 197
Nazi Architecture 97
Neue Pinakothek 97, 176
Neue Sammlung 181
New Town Hall 27, 57
Neues Residenz Theater 77
Neuhausen **123-127**
Neuhauser Strasse 37, 51-53
Neuschwanstein Castle 27, 229
Night-life 204-208
Nikolai and Loretto Chapel 162
Nikolaiplatz 108
Nockherberg 156, 158, 186
NT-Neues Theater 201
Nymphenburg Palace 20, 24, 123, **127-131**, 182
 Amalienburg 129
 Badenburg 129
 Chapel 129
 Chinesisches Lackkabinett 129
 Gobelin Zimmer 129
 Hubertus Fountain 127
 Magdalenenklause 129
 Marstall Museum 130
 Museum für Mensch und Natur 130
 North and South Avenues 127

252

INDEX

Nymphenburg Canal 127
Pagodenburg 129
Palace Gardens 129
Palmenhaus 129
Porcelain, manufacture 21, 130
Porzellan Museum 130
Schönheitsgalerie 129
Steinerner Saal 129
Steinernes Haus 129
Wappenzimmer 129
Nymphenburger Strasse 123-125

O

Oberammergau 36, 230
Oberpollinger House 53, 184
Obersalzberg 237
Occamstrasse 108
Odeonsplatz 79, 87, 181
Oktoberfest 25, 34, 136, **190-191**
Olaf Gulbransson Museum 234
Old Botanical Gardens 26, 49
Old Palace of Justice 49
Olympia Park 114-116, 193
 Olympiaberg 116
 Olympiahalle 115, 203
 Olympia Stadium 115, 203
 Olympic Pool 115, 248
 Russian Orthodox Chapel 116
 Television Tower 114, 193
 Theatron 116
Olympic Games 1972 32
Opera Festival 197
Orlandostrasse 61
Orleansplatz 163
Osterseen, lakes 225
Osterwald-Garten 188
Otto, Frei 114

P

Palace of Justice 27
Pariser Platz 164
Partnachklamm 231
Pasinger Fabrik 183, 202
Pedel-car Museum 179
Pedestrian Zone 51-56
Pathos Transport Theater 202
Paulaner Bräuhaus 145
Paulaner im Tal 61, 186, 211
Paulaner Keller 188
Peterhof 186, 211
Pettenkofer, Max 146, 172
Pfaffenwinkel 227-228
Pfistermühle 62
Pilsensee, lake 222, 225
Plague 15-16, 20, 57
Planetarium 192
Platz der Opfer des
 Nationalsozialismus 51, 99
Pocci, Count Franz von 203, 223
Polack, Jan 59, 131

Polling Jörg von 55
Porcia Palace 80
Postfranzl 137
Prähistorische Staatssammlung 181, 150
Praterinsel, river island 152, 173
Preysing Palace 80
Preysing-Neuhaus Palace 81
Prinz-Carl Palace 150
Prinzregentenbad 165
Prinzregentenplatz 165
Prinzregentenstrasse 27, 150, 181
Prinzregenten Theater 27, 39, 165, 198, 208
Promenadeplatz 81
Propyläen 24, 98

R

Radspielerhaus 71
Raft trips 173
Räterepublik 29
Rationaltheater 108, 202
Reichersbeuern 233
Reit im Winkl 237
Reithalle 209
Renaissance 53, 99, 220-221, 236, 239
Residenz 24, **75-78**
 Antiquarium 76
 Apothekenhof 76
 Brunnenhof 76
 Festsallbau 77
 Grottenhof 76
 Hofkapelle 77
 Kaiserhof 76
 Königsbau 77
 Neuer Herkulessaal 76, 88
 Nibelungen Rooms 77
 Prince's Appartments 76
 Residenz Museum 75
 Schatzkammer 77
 State Coin Collection 78
 State Collection of Egyptian Art 76, 88
 Wittelsbach Fountain 77
 Witwenstock 76
Residenzstrasse 79, 87
Residenz Theater 39, 197, 208
Reutberg Monastery 233
Reventlow, Franziska zu 28, 102
Revolution 15-17, 26, 29
Richard Strauss Fountain 53
Richter, Karl 200
Ried 231
Riemer Reitstadion 203
Riemerschmidtsche
 Schnapsfabrik 152
Rilke, Rainer Maria 28, 110
Rindermarkt 58
Rococo 21, 24, 59, 70, 77, 80, 87,

 129, 178, 227-228, 233
Römerstrasse 112
Romanplatz 127
Roncalliplatz 97
Rosenheimer Berg 156
Rosenheimer Platz 165
Rosenkavalierplatz 167
Rotkreuzplatz 125
Rottach-Egern 234
Rottenbuch 228
Royal Palaces 228-230
Ruffini House 59
Ruhmeshalle 134
Ruhpolding 237
Rumford-Schlössl 118

S

Salt Trade 13, 15, 81, 160
Salvator Church 80
Salvatorkeller 158
Sankt-Emmerams-Mühle 188
Schack, Count Adolf von 182
Schack Gallery 150, 182
Schäftlarn Monastery 13, 231
Scharnagel, Karl 32
Schauspielhaus 79
Schelling, Friedrich W. 96
Schellingstrasse 92, 96
Schillerstrasse 49
Schlachthofviertel 145-146
Schleissheim 128, 220
 Altes Schloss 220
 Crib Museum 220
 Lustheim 128, 220
 Neues Schloss 220
Schliersee, lake 234
Schmorell, Alexander 32
Schmied von Kochel Monument 21, 139
Scholl, Hans and Sophie 32, 92, 159
Schröder, Ruldolf Alexander 103
Schumann's 205
Schwabing 34, 37, 87, 93, 102, **207-208**, 211
Schwabinger Kunstmarkt 103
Schwabinger Streetcar Depot 111
Schwanthaler, Ludwig von 87, 98, 134
Schwanthaler Hoh' 133-134, 137
Schwind, Moritz von 150
Sckell, Friedrich Ludwig von 21, 23, 49, 93, 116, 129
Secession 27
Sedlmayr, Helene 129
Seebruck 235
Seeon Monastery 237
Seidl, Gabriel von 27, 51, 149-150, 179
Sendling 20, **138-139**

INDEX

Sendlinger Peasant Massacre 20
Sendlinger Blacksmith's Shop 139
Sendlinger Strasse 70
Sendlinger Tor 23
Siegestor 25, 93
Siegmund, Duke 17
Siemens Museum 80
Simplicissimus, magazine 28, 66, 95, 234
Singlspieler House 70
Sissi Museum 63, 179
Spielzeug Museum 58, 178, 183, 193
Spitzingsee, lake 234
Staatliche Antikensammlung 98, 175
Staatliche Graphische Sammlumg 98
Staatliche Sammlung Ägyptischer Kunst 181
Staatliches Museum für Völkerkunde 182
Staatsgalerie Moderner Kunst 150, 181
Staatssammlung für Paläontologie und Historische Geologie 98
Staatstheater am Gärnerplatz 155, 198
Stachus (Karlsplatz) **49-51**
Stadelheim 159
Stadt Museum 67-70, 178
  Brewery Museum 69, 178
  Everyday Life from 1650 to the Present 69, 178
  Film Museum 68, 178
  Historical Weapons Collection 69
  Morris Dancers 69, 178
  Musical Instrument Coll. 68, 178
  Photographic Museum 68, 178
  Puppet Theater Museum 69
  Santner's City Model 68, 178
Städtische Galerie im Lenbachhaus 98, 175
St.-Anna-Damenstiftkirche 72
St. Anna-Platz 149
Starnberger See 20, 27, 222-225
  Allmannshausen Castle 223
  Ambach 223
  Berg 222
  Bernried 223
  Feldafing 223
  Ilka-Höhe 223
  Leoni 223
  Possenhofen 225
  Roseninsel 225
  Seeshaupt 223
  Tutzing 223
  Votive Chapel 223
State Library 25
State Mint 75

Steiger, Ivan 58, 178
Steingaden 228
St. Georg, church 167
Stiglmaier, Johann B. 127, 134
Stiglmaierplatz 124
St. Jakobsplatz 67
St. Margaret, church 139
St. Paul, church 133
Strauss, Richard 197
St. Sylvester, church 107
Stuck, Franz von 27, 165, 182
St. Ursula-Kirche 112
Sudelfeld 235
Suresnes-Schlössl 106

T

Tal 37, **61-64**
Tatzelwurm-Klamm 235
Team Theater Comeday 201
Team Theater Tankstelle 201
Technische Universität 94, 97
Tegernsee, lake 234
Tierpark Hellabrunn, see Zoo
Television Tower 114
Theater 44 112, 201
Theater am Sozialamt (TAMS) 107, 201
Theater Blaue Maus 209
Theater der Jugend 113, 192
Theater für Kinder 192
Theater im Fraunhofer 203
Theater links der Isar 202, 209
Theatinerkirche 20, 87
Theatinerstrasse 79-80, 87
Theatron 203
Therese von Sachsen-Hildburghausen 25, 190
Theresienwiese 25, 136
Thiersch, August von 112
Thiersch, Friedrich von 27, 50
Thirty Years' War 20
Thoma, Ludwig 28, 234
Thompson, Benjamin (Count Rumford) 21, 116
Tilt 206
Toller, Ernst 29
Tollwood Festival 116, 203, 242
  Winter Tollwood 125, 203, 243
Tropical Greenhouse 131
Türkenstrasse 95

U

Üblacker House 163
Unterfahrt 207

V

Valentin, Karl 59, 65-66, 95, 104, 157
Valentin Museum 63, 179

Vater-Rhein-Brunnen 152
Viktualienmarkt 64-66, 185, 208
Villa Stuck 165, 182
Viscardi, Giovanni A. 53, 81, 128
Volks Theater 199
Vollmar, Georg von 29

W

Wagner, Richard 26, 165, 198
Walchensee 231
Walking Man 103
Wallberg 234
Wappenhaus 124
War of the Spanish Succession 20
Watzmann 237
Wedekind, Frank 28, 95, 106
Wedekind-Platz 106
Weilheim 222, 227
Weissenburger Platz 164
Weisses Bräuhaus 61, 186, 211
Weiss-Ferdl Brunnen 66
Wendelstein 234
Werkraum Theater 79, 199
Wesslinger See, lake 222
Wessobrunn Abbey 228
Wessobrunn Prayer 228
West End 37, **133-138**
Westermühlbach 147
West Park 137-138
White Rose, resistance group 32, 92
Wiener Platz 162
Wieskirche 227-228
Wies'n, see Oktoberfest
Wilhelm III, Duke 17
Wilhelm IV, Duke 17-18, 176, 186, 220
Wilhelm V, Duke 19, 57, 61, 220
Wilhelmstrasse 111
Wimmer, Thomas 32
Wirtshaus am Schlachthof 202
Wittelsbach, dynasty 13-14, 22, 53, 56, 75, 88, 175-176, 220, 238-239
Wittelsbach Fountain 51, 77
Wittelsbacher Palace 99
Wittelsbacherplatz 99
Wörthsee, lake 222, 225
Wolfskehl, Karl 28, 112
Wolpertinger 177

Z

Zerwirkgewölbe 185
Ziebland, Georg Friedrich 98
Ziegler, Clara 181
Zimmermann, Johann 225, 231
Zoo 193
Zuccalli, Enrico 87, 128
Zugspitze 230

Explore the World

AVAIBLABE TITLES

Afghanistan 1 : 1 500 000
Australia 1 : 4 000 000
Bangkok - *Greater Bangkok, Bangkok City* 1 : 75 000 / 1 : 15 000
Burma → *Myanmar*
Caribbean Islands 1 *Bermuda, Bahamas, Greater Antilles* 1 : 2 500 000
Caribbean Islands 2 *Lesser Antilles* 1 : 2 500 000
Central America 1 : 1 750 000
Colombia - Ecuador 1 : 2 500 000
Crete - Kreta 1 : 200 000
China 1 - *Northeastern* 1 : 1 500 000
China 2 - *Northern* 1 : 1 500 000
China 3 - *Central* 1 : 1 500 000
China 4 - *Southern* 1 : 1 500 000
Dominican Republic - Haiti 1 : 600 000
Egypt 1 : 2 500 000 / 1 : 750 000
Hawaiian Islands 1 : 330 000 / 1 : 125 000
Hawaiian Islands 1 *Kauai* 1 : 125 000
Hawaiian Islands 2 *Honolulu - Oahu* 1 : 125 000
Hawaiian Islands 3 *Maui - Molokai - Lanai* 1 : 125 000

Hawaiian Islands 4 *Hawaii, The Big Island* 1 : 330 000 / 1 : 125 000
Himalaya 1 : 1 500 000
Hong Kong 1 : 22 500
Indian Subcontinent 1 : 4 000 000
India 1 - *Northern* 1 : 1 500 000
India 2 - *Western* 1 : 1 500 000
India 3 - *Eastern* 1 : 1 500 000
India 4 - *Southern* 1 : 1 500 000
India 5 - *Northeastern - Bangladesh* 1 : 1 500 000
Indonesia 1 : 4 000 000
Indonesia 1 *Sumatra* 1 : 1 500 000
Indonesia 2 *Java + Nusa Tenggara* 1 : 1 500 000
Indonesia 3 *Bali* 1 : 180 000
Indonesia 4 *Kalimantan* 1 : 1 500 000
Indonesia 5 *Java + Bali* 1 : 650 000
Indonesia 6 *Sulawesi* 1 : 1 500 000
Indonesia 7 *Irian Jaya + Maluku* 1 : 1 500 000
Jakarta 1 : 22 500
Japan 1 : 1 500 000
Kenya 1 : 1 100 000
Korea 1 : 1 500 000
Malaysia 1 : 1 500 000
West Malaysia 1 : 650 000
Manila 1 : 17 500

Mexico 1 : 2 500 000
Myanmar (Burma) 1 : 1 500 000
Nepal 1 : 500 000 / 1 : 1 500 000
Trekking Map *Khumbu Himal / Solu Khumbu* 1 : 75 000
New Zealand 1 : 1 250 000
Pakistan 1 : 1 500 000
Peru - Ecuador 1 : 2 500 000
Philippines 1 : 1 500 000
Singapore 1 : 22 500
Southeast Asia 1 : 4 000 000
Sri Lanka 1 : 450 000
Tanzania - Rwanda, Burundi 1 : 1 500 000
Thailand 1 : 1 500 000
Taiwan 1 : 400 000
Uganda 1 : 700 000
Venezuela - Guyana, Suriname, French Guiana 1 : 2 500 000
Vietnam, Laos, Cambodia 1 : 1 500 000

FORTHCOMING

South Pacific Islands 1 : 13 000 000
Trekking Map *Kathmandu Valley / Helambu, Langtang* 1 : 75 000

Nelles Maps in european top quality!
Relief mapping, kilometer charts and tourist attractions.
Always up-to-date!

Explore the World

AVAILABLE TITLES

Australia
Bali / Lombok
Berlin and Potsdam
Brittany
California
 *Las Vegas, Reno,
 Baja California*
Cambodia / Laos
Canada
 *Ontario, Québec,
 Atlantic Provinces*
Canada
 *Pacific Coast, the Rockies,
 Prairie Provinces, and
 the Territories*
Caribbean
 *The Greater Antilles,
 Bermuda, Bahamas*
Caribbean
 The Lesser Antilles
China – Hong Kong
Corsica
Crete
Croatia – *Adriatic Coast*
Cyprus
Egypt
Florida
Greece – *The Mainland*
Hawai'i
Hungary
India
 *Northern, Northeastern
 and Central India*
India – *Southern India*
Indonesia
 *Sumatra, Java, Bali,
 Lombok, Sulawesi*
Ireland
Israel - *with Excursions
 to Jordan*
Kenya
London, England and
 Wales
Malaysia
Mexico
Morocco
Moscow / St Petersburg
Munich
 *Excursions to Castels,
 Lakes & Mountains*
Nepal
New York – *City and State*
New Zealand
Norway
Paris
Philippines
Portugal
Prague / Czech Republic
Provence
Rome
Scotland
South Africa
South Pacific Islands
Spain – *Pyrenees, Atlantic
 Coast, Central Spain*
Spain
 *Mediterranean Coast,
 Southern Spain,
 Balearic Islands*
Sri Lanka
Syria – Lebanon
Tanzania
Thailand
Turkey
Tuscany
U.S.A.
 *The East, Midwest and
 South*
U.S.A.
 *The West, Rockies and
 Texas*
Vietnam

FORTHCOMING

Brazil
Myanmar (Burma)

*Nelles Guides – authoritative, informed and informative.
Always up-to-date, extensivley illustrated, and with first-rate relief maps.
256 pages, appr. 150 color photos, appr. 25 maps*